THE WORLD OF THE CASTRATI

THE WORLD OF THE CASTRATI

The History of an Extraordinary Operatic Phenomenon

Patrick Barbier

Translated by Margaret Crosland

SOUVENIR PRESS

Copyright © Éditions Grasset & Fasquelle, 1989
English translation Copyright © 1996
by Souvenir Press and Margaret Crosland

The right of Patrick Barbier to be identified as author of this work
has been asserted by him in accordance with the Copyright, Designs
and Patents Act 1988.

First published in France by
Éditions Bernard Grasset
under the title *Histoire des Castrats*

This translation first published 1996 by
Souvenir Press Ltd.,
43 Great Russell Street, London WC1B 3PA

Reissued in paperback 1998

ISBN 0 285 63309 0 (casebound)
ISBN 0 285 63460 7 (paperback)

Typeset by Rowland Phototypesetting Ltd.,
Bury St Edmunds, Suffolk
Printed in Great Britain by
Biddles Ltd, Guildford and King's Lynn

The extract from Samuel Pepys' diary on p. 180 is reprinted from
The Diary of Samuel Pepys, ed. R. C. Latham and W. Matthews, by
permission of *Bell & Hyman,* an imprint of Harper-Collins *Publishers*
Limited.

To Dominique Fernandez

I should like to thank Andrew Benians, Gordon Rice and Geoffrey Simmonds for assistance with this translation, and Christopher Crofton-Sleigh for giving me valuable help with the word-processing of the text.

M.C.

Contents

List of Illustrations   xi
Preface   1

1 Castration   5
From time immemorial ... — 'Castration done here, clean and cheap' — Physiological disruption — The development of the voice

2 Origins and Recruitment   19
Geographical and social origins — The inevitability of castration — The road to the conservatoires

3 Training the Singers   35
The Neapolitan conservatoires — Internal organisation daily life — Classes and teachers — How the castrati studied — The otherItalian schools

4 The Theatre in Italy   62
The great theatres — The performances — Italian audiences

5 The Road to Fame   82
The choice of a name — Débuts in public — Vocal prowess — The castrati on stage — Escapades and temperaments — Fortune and honours

6 The Castrati and the Church   122
The Popes and castration — Music in church — The theatres in the Papal States

7   The Castrati in Society   136
    The castrati and women—Masculine rivalries and
    friendships—The castrati and their relatives—The
    patrons—Satires and pamphlets
8   European Journeys   174
    Perpetual travellers—Vienna and London—The French
    and the castrati—Farinelli in Spain
9   In the Evening of Life   209
    Farewell to the public and the return to roots—Old age
    and the voice—Last occupations
10 The Twilight of the Angels   223
    First signs of decline—The last two great castrati—The
    Vatican and the last castrati

    Epilogue   242
    Notes   243
    Bibliography   249
    Index   257

List of Illustrations

1 Portrait collection of the great eighteenth-century singers
2 Carlo Broschi, known as Farinelli
3 Theatre set by Burnacini for Draghi's *Il Fuoco eterno*
4 Antonio Bernacchi
5 Giovanni Carestini, known as Cusanino
6 George Frideric Handel
7 Hogarth's satirical engraving of Handel's *Flavio*
8 Francesco Bernardi, known as Senesino
9 Farinelli with Metastasio, Teresa Castellini and the painter Amigoni
10 Venanzio Rauzzini
11 Queen Christina of Sweden
12 Luigi Marchesi
13 Giovanni Battista Velluti

Preface

In 1773 the *Dictionnaire de l'Académie française* gave this definition of the word *castrato*: 'A man who has been castrated so that his voice may preserve a quality similar to that of women. *There are many castrati in Italy.*' This small addendum showed fairly clearly how France, as well as every other nation, saw Italy as the country *par excellence* of the eunuch singers. Angels for some, monsters for others, the castrati represented a musical, social and cultural phenomenon without precedent in Europe during the seventeenth and eighteenth centuries. They were protected by the Church but carried along most of all by the early opera which led to their blossoming followed by their disappearance from the musical stage with the dawn of romanticism, when the world of illusion, artifice, disguise and vocal ambiguity began to lose its meaning.

There is no point today in reopening the case so often brought in the past against castration and those who practised it or underwent it. How can we judge a medical procedure which influenced the whole of western music for more than two centuries, now that we are so far removed from the conditions prevailing in the baroque period? How can the 'modern' mind, moderately influenced by the nineteenth century, understand how a particular period dared to seek pure and 'gratuitous' Beauty through a mutilation so 'costly' to the individual who was subjected to it? Above all, how can we adopt an attitude towards emasculation when no great castrato has confided his deepest feelings to us? Was the operation inflicted on him felt as a tragedy? Was it not sometimes sanctified by a voice and a 'nature' which overturned the traditional plan of the masculine or feminine condition? We know, for example, that when people expressed pity for them the castrati Carestini and Salimbeni burst out laughing: were they exceptional or fairly normal?

For the historian only one thing matters: the presence and triumph of the castrati for nearly two hundred and thirty years on the stages of Europe, and still longer within the Roman Catholic Church. The Italians were of course the promoters and the greatest 'consumers' of these singers. It was the Italians too who most admired and honoured these unusual singers who suited so well their taste for artifice, their sense of the festive and their quest for sensual pleasures. The vocabulary used by the Italians certainly remains the most respectful towards them: while the French muttered about 'artificial men', 'eunuchs', 'cripples' or 'capons' the Italians preferred the terms *musico* or *virtuoso*, reserving the term 'eunuch' for the young castrati, the pupils in the conservatoires, without using it in this case in any pejorative sense. The descriptions *primo uomo* and 'sopranist', as opposed to *prima donna* or female 'soprano', were widespread, while the use of the term 'castrato' remained much more common in other countries than in Italy.

At this stage of our knowledge of the castrati we lack many pieces of the puzzle, beginning with the fascinating beauty of their voices—those, that is, of the greatest singers, which were in a way everything that we cannot hear today—a highly frustrating fact when we reread the enthusiastic praise of their contemporaries. We also lack the memoirs of these singers, which, if they could have been written down during their lifetimes, would have informed us about their origins, their childhood, the circumstances of their operation and their studies. True, we have archive documents and contemporary accounts, but they are often coloured by partiality and based on polemic. This was because the problem surrounding the castrati extended beyond the strictly musical domain and became also a social, moral or political problem, especially outside Italy. Lastly, the lack of information can also be explained by the fact that during the seventeenth and eighteenth centuries the castrati were so much a part of the musical scene that they were considered perfectly normal: they were 'natural voices' like the others, and certainly not 'circus animals', which might have provoked many long discussions. As a result it did not occur to anyone to make a separate study of them, other than what is done on women singers, tenors, composers, performances and theatre audiences, all topics on which people like to air their views.

The present-day revival of baroque music has to some extent driven the castrati out of reality instead of placing them at the front of the stage. This is the principal obstacle encountered by anyone attempting to revive the music of Cavalli or Alessandro Scarlatti in the absence of these singers for whom it was composed. This undeniable void and the different ways of filling it with other voices even provoke interminable polemics in the musical world today. Such arguments would have amused Gregorio Allegri who, as early as the seventeenth century, foresaw the death of *bel canto* (in the baroque sense of the term) when the castrati finally disappeared. Whatever the outcome of these discussions, the audiences of today, thanks to the new vogue for baroque music, at least have the advantage of fascinating intellectual discovery, the discovery of those singers who were 'almost' like others, whose voices and astonishing personalities have left their mark on nearly three centuries of theatrical and religious music.

1
Castration

Must we mutilate men in order to give them a perfection they did not possess at birth?

SARAH GOUDAR

A learned surgeon or a mere village barber—either might carry out the operation. Were these men aware, as they put aside their knives, that they were condemning a man, irrevocably, to fame or shame? Did they realise they were providing the history of music with one of its most legendary myths, while at the same time bringing humanity face to face with a moral dilemma that is still being discussed today? More simply, were they not influenced most of all by the considerable profits which this practice could earn for them, starting modestly in the seventeenth century and then increasing by leaps and bounds in the eighteenth? Did they not see themselves inheriting, in a modest, unruffled way, an age-old medical tradition that made castration one of the oldest professions in the world?

Unfortunately these questions remain unanswerable, since no one who practised castration, no doubt fearful of reprisals from the police or the Church, has left us a record of his private feelings about the act he performed.

From time immemorial . . .

The Papal States or the Kingdom of Naples were in no way innovators when, at the beginning of the seventeenth century, they allowed the practice of castration to spread freely, and made no attempt to put a stop to it.

The Bible and various writings from antiquity prove the very ancient origins of this act which was probably performed by various tribes or nations on enemy captives in order to prevent reproduction. This form of punishment seemed to have survived well down the centuries, since it is still practised today among certain Ethiopian ethnic groups. The Persians may well have been the first people to use emasculation, but it is difficult to establish a chronology among all the civilisations (Indian, Chinese or Arabic, for example) that have had recourse to it. The terms 'castrato' or 'castration' seem to have come from the Indian world, deriving more particularly from the Sanskrit word *sastram*, meaning a knife. It is known too that the Chinese used it in order to satisfy the widespread taste in their country for young boys with a feminine appearance.

The oldest reference to be found in the Bible occurs in Deuteronomy (Chapter XXIII, verse 1), 'He that is wounded in the stones, or hath his privy member cut off, shall not enter into the congregation of the Lord.' As for the Greeks and Romans, they operated a very widespread trade in eunuchs from Africa and Asia. It had been observed that castrated animals were usually more docile, easier to domesticate, and it was only a short step from there to the use of castrated and more 'manageable' slaves for unpleasant tasks.

Certain pagan cults adopted castration, especially the cult of Cybele which insisted on emasculation for its priests. From the start of the Christian era the Church severely condemned this attitude, not only among the pagans but among all those whose excessive zeal led them to interpret literally the words of Saint Matthew (Chapter XIX, verse 12): 'For there are some eunuchs, which were so born from their mother's womb: and there are some eunuchs, which were made eunuchs of men: and there be eunuchs, which have made themselves eunuchs for the kingdom of heaven's sake.' It is clear that the celibacy and chastity demanded by Matthew had no connection with authentic castration, which explains why, from the early centuries, the Church openly attacked figures such as Origen or Leonce of Antioch who had both chosen to castrate themselves. That did not prevent the presence of eunuchs in the army and administration of the Eastern Roman Empire. The case of the eunuch Narses, who became a general of the Byzantine Empire, has remained famous.*

Much more is known about the widespread castration in the Muslim world, through the eunuchs of the harem, those 'guardians of the bed', in the literal sense of the word, who were responsible for the chastity of the sultan's wives. This role, regarded a priori as humiliating, did not prevent many of them from gaining posts of very high responsibility, and it is known that the Turkish court absorbed a vast number of them, particularly in the Constantinople harem. Shortly before the capture of this city the Byzantine Empire had been the first to make public use of eunuch singers in the churches, as the canonist Theodore Balsamon recounts in his *Commentary* on the *Nomocanon* in the twelfth century. There is nothing surprising about that, since the profound oriental influence on the Byzantine ceremonies is well known, and so too is the considerable

---

* Narses (c. AD 478–573), was born in Armenia and rose to the rank of general in the army of the Byzantine Empire. He is best remembered for his reconquest of Italy from the Ostrogoths, at the age of 74.

importance of music and singing. Another well-known case, occurring closer to home geographically, is that of the Greek castrato Manuel who had gone to Russia and founded a song school in Smolensk.

Although it is not possible to establish a clear link with music and dance, it can be said that the whole of medieval Europe was concerned to a greater or lesser degree with the phenomenon of castration. It was still used in various places to torture prisoners and also to punish men who had committed crimes and rape. The medical profession, too, did not hesitate to use it, mistakenly as a rule, to cure or prevent certain illnesses such as leprosy, madness, epilepsy, hydrocele, gout and various inflammatory conditions. For a long time also it was claimed as a cure for hernia. This was one of the many pretexts put forward by Italian families in order to justify the operation during the golden age of castrato singers. In France castration remained very common, although it was not used for the same musical purpose. Statistics drawn up in 1676 by the Société Royale de Médecine mentioned more than five hundred cases of boys castrated because of hernia in the single diocese of Saint-Papoul near Carcassonne.

It was actually through Spain that everything was to be played out on the musical level. A group of eunuchs who had been introduced into the Mozarabic civilisation shortly before the twelfth century gradually, thanks to their amazing voices, won a considerable place in the catholic liturgy, obtaining their greatest successes during the sixteenth century. A papal bull issued by Sixtus V (1545–1590), addressed to the apostolic nuncio in Spain, proves quite clearly that castrati had been admitted for a long time into the principal churches of the Iberian peninsula. But were they true castrati or, as in many cases, simply falsettos (comparable to the voices of counter-tenors, better known to us now) who cultivated the high notes in their head register? It is difficult to be certain about this today. There is the same uncertainty about the group of Spanish singers in the Papal Chapel in Rome who, ever since the sixth century, had been the only ones authorised to interpret soprano parts. Although the Vatican archives of the sixteenth century do not mention them it is highly probable that some of these singers, especially the two as famous as Francesco Soto and Giacomo Spagnoletto, were true castrati and not falsettos. This theory seems all the more plausible since Loreto Vittori, the first great castrato of the seventeenth century, was Father Soto's student. One fact remains certain: the end of the sixteenth century was a decisive turning point which indicates the first use of castrati in the music of Rome, itself the centre of the religious musical world of the period.

The first two Italian castrati were officially admitted into the Papal Choir in 1599. The registers mention the entry of Pietro Paolo Folignati (Petrus Paulus Folignatus Eunuchus) and Girolamo Rosini of Perugia (Hieronymus Rosinus Perusinus Eunuchus). In fact Rosini was only formally accepted in 1601, since his first 'entry' provoked such a stir. The Spanish priests, whether they were falsettos or castrati, caused a real outcry, aimed at preventing him from taking up a post which for centuries had been reserved for Spanish singers alone. At first Rosini had to withdraw in the face of such pressure. Fortunately for him Pope Clement VIII, who had been present when he competed for entry, had been deeply impressed by his voice. Rosini had already left and become a Capuchin friar but the Pope, annoyed by the Spanish cabal, recalled the native of Perugia and released him from the solemn vows he had just taken, 'in order that he might serve in the Papal Chapel.'

Who would have believed that the long history of the Italian castrati, which began at the start of the sixteenth century beneath the frescoes of the Sistine Chapel, would end in precisely the same place on the eve of the First World War?

Once Rosini and Folignati were firmly established in his choir the Pope realised there could be no return to the voices of the contemporary falsettos which were often strident and forced. Within a few years he got rid of all the remaining falsettos and replaced them with soprano castrati, although for a long time the alto parts were still entrusted to falsettos. The first two Italian castrati were followed by a French singer with an italianised name, Giovanni Grisando, then came one of the greatest castrati of all time, the Spoletan Loreto Vittori, who was admitted in 1622. The early years of the century saw the adoption of an ambiguous policy by the Church which condemned castration and yet welcomed the best castrati into the Holy of Holies.

'Castration done here, clean and cheap'

Some travellers reported seeing signs of this type—but did they really exist? Were they not the result of jokes bandied about in Italian cities ever since the seventeenth century? Can one really believe that in the eighteenth century someone who knew he would be excommunicated by the Church if he operated on a boy would advertise his skills in broad daylight as a form of publicity? It seems doubtful. Some shops specialised in the castration of dogs and cats and it is known that various travellers, confused by what they had been told, mistook them for places for human castration. The writer Jean de La Lande himself admitted his mistake and if Silvagni claimed that a barber in Rome wrote over his door 'Singers for the papal chapels castrated here', Dr Burney stated that he had looked everywhere for such signs but had never found them.

Such casual investigations apart, the fact remains that

castration was practised more or less everywhere, both officially in the hospitals of certain large cities, for medical reasons which were more or less valid, and secretly in countryside dispensaries known to everyone, although that did not make them respectable. It is well known that many barbers had extended their medical or dental activities by carrying out orchidectomy (castration) with less than primitive instruments and a degree of hygiene best left to the imagination.

In these places, as in the hospitals, the first problem was anaesthesia. At best this might consist of drinks containing opium which could deaden the boy's reactions as far as possible. More often it was considered adequate to compress the carotid arteries in order to interrupt circulation briefly; this sent the boy into a comatose state. He was then plunged into a bath of milk in order to soften the genital organs, or into a bath of icy water which also had a slight anaesthetic effect and prevented too much bleeding. This practice was still widely used for amputations during the Napoleonic campaigns.

Castration itself was both simple and complex. Simple in principle, as summed up briefly by Charles d'Ancillon in his *Treatise on Eunuchs*: 'A eunuch [...] is a person whose genital organs have been removed.'[1] It was complex, however, in its application and above all very dangerous, for the operation might be carried out unsatisfactorily and cause haemorrhaging or infection, which were often lethal. Figures put forward by some doctors estimate mortality at between 10 and 80 per cent, depending on who was performing the operations. These statistics, which are perfectly plausible, take into account both the unreliable medical practices of the period and the considerable differences between surgeons as famous as those of Bologna and the primitive methods of abortionists living in the most remote villages.

The operation was never performed before the age of seven and rarely after twelve. It was essential for it to be carried out before the glandular function of the testicles had begun, so most boys were castrated between the ages of eight and ten. The act itself had to be carried out very swiftly. It began with an incision in the groin through which the surgeon removed the spermatic cord and the testicles. Total removal was then carried out with a knife, while the ducts were tied. This was a very different operation from that performed on the harem eunuchs whose entire external sexual organs were removed, generally after puberty; a child-like voice could then no longer be preserved. In the case of the castrati singers it was essential for both testicles to be removed in order to achieve the planned result. Some castrati maintained that the operation they had undergone had not been successful and that they had not been totally castrated, but this allegation was meaningless. Either the operation had been complete and the man possessed the voice of a castrato, or else it had been incomplete with the removal of only one testicle, or there had been a third testicle which had remained hidden. In the case of incomplete castration the subject retained all masculine characteristics, along with the singing voice of a light tenor or a falsetto. This is the reason too why the story about the castrato Balani, told by Archenholz, does not seem genuine. This singer, who had been born with an empty scrotum, was apparently considered throughout his youth as a 'natural castrato', and received a musical education leading to a future as a 'sopranist'. He embarked on a brilliant career, but one day, when he was on stage, certain vocalisations demanded that he exert a considerable physical effort, with the result that his testicles, which so far had remained invisible, descended to their rightful place. Consequently Balani immediately lost his voice and had to give up his singing career. Apart from the comic aspect of this incident it is obvious that the man could not have been a true castrato. He had probably succeeded in creating the illusion, thanks to a fine high-pitched voice which had not broken.

Physiological disruption

Apart from the transformation of the voice, which was the purpose of the operation, the morphological and psychological changes were many and exerted a decisive influence on the subject's entire life.

Some characteristics were common to all castrati, such as the absence of the Adam's apple or the near-absence of body hair, except perhaps in the pubic area since the secretion from the suprarenal glands still produced certain masculine characteristics. In any case, imaginary descriptions of castrati with beards or moustaches are meaningless.

Another trait shared by the castrati was the relatively small size of the sexual organ which did not develop as in other men. Although a late operation was likely to have little influence in this respect, precocious castration, at the age of seven or so, often led to the opposite effect.

In fact most castrati could experience virtually normal sexual relations: castration did not prevent either erection or the emission of sperm and prostatic liquid, although of course it contained no spermatozoa. Obviously the strength and regularity of the sexual act was noticeably less than in other men. Colourful Latin phrases used at the time by doctors and the Church recognised that castrati experienced *impotentia generandi* but not *impotentia coeundi*. It is also a fact that their exploits with women, which could go as far as marriage, would not have been so numerous if they had been mere pleasant dalliances, even during the century of libertine behaviour. On the other hand one can never generalise in this area, and it seems obvious that sexual appetite among the castrati varied greatly from one man to the next and could be 'voracious' in one case and virtually non-existent in another. This depended in particular on the operation itself, on which organs had been affected, on the circumstances in which it had been performed and at what age.

Other characteristics did not necessarily occur in all cases, particularly the 'feminisation' which might be obvious to a greater or lesser degree. The female hormones were overactivated by the absence of testosterone, which might lead, for example, to a greater or lesser development of the breasts. In the same way the castrato acquired a muscular mass closer to that of a woman, as well as fatty deposits on the hips, thighs or neck, producing a tendency to obesity which was often ridiculed by contemporary observers, although it was not general. Some travellers went into raptures before the angelic and disturbing beauty of Ferri, Matteuccio, Farinelli, Rauzzini or Marchesi, but when Charles de Brosses, President of the Dijon Parliament, travelled through Italy he wrote as follows: 'Most sopranists become big and fat like capons, their mouths, their rumps, arms, breasts and neck rounded and chubby as in women. When you meet them in a gathering you are completely taken aback on hearing these colossal men speak with a tiny childlike voice.'[2]

Another surprising aspect often observed was the abnormal height of the castrati, a somewhat awkward phenomenon for men who often took women's roles and stood a head taller than their partners. Président de Brosses was astonished to see the sopranist Marianini singing the part of a princess although he was six feet tall. Even if this abnormal height was not general it was due to the fact that the action of the pituitary gland was not counterbalanced by testosterone and could lead to overactivity of the growth hormone. The fact that the men's voices had not

broken meant that the cartilage links did not knit together
after puberty, as in other men. These growth cartilages
continued to function and the bones could still lengthen.

As for the longevity of the castrati, which some people
tried to attribute to emasculation, there is no medical
foundation for this. The operation itself did nothing to
prolong the life of these singers, it was only their age, often
advanced for the period, that could have caused the illusion.

One final observation of a psychological nature often
appeared in the musical treatises of the eighteenth and nineteenth centuries: it was alleged that castration caused neurasthenia which might develop into what would today be
called mental depression. It must be said at once that such
an operation could not, clinically speaking, lead to a result
of this type. It is clear, however, that secondary factors
linked to the social situation of the castrati could easily
bring about this type of manifestation. The loneliness of
the artiste, even the most admired among them, is a well-
known phenomenon. Many divas, many film stars have
experienced this 'down' that follows moments of great success. The castrati could sometimes feel remorse at not
having known an emotional life comparable to that of
everyone else; life ended for some of them in an isolated
retreat with no children who could have consoled them
for the miseries of old age. This could be the reason for
that sullen attitude which the nineteenth century soon
transformed into a hatred of human kind, a panic fear of
death, into egoism and despotism, all completely irrelevant.

The development of the voice

Once a boy had been castrated his voice did not break,
that is to say it did not deepen by an octave, as with all other
boys. It remained 'high', to use a general term, half-way
between that of a child and that of a woman, whose

tessitura, soprano or alto, it could adopt. Sometimes this voice changed as the years went by and passed from soprano to alto, or the reverse. In this way Pistocchi and Nicolino became contraltos at twenty and twenty-seven respectively, while Guadagni moved from contralto to soprano at about forty-five.

The great originality of the castrato was due to the form and position of the larynx. After a boy's voice has broken his larynx moves down. Even a girl experiences a minor change in her voice with a very slight downward movement of her larynx which affects her timbre. The castrato did not experience this descent of the larynx, with the result that his vocal cords remained closer to the cavities of resonance; this reinforced clarity and brilliance and affected the selection of harmonics. True, this larynx was similar to a woman's through its bone structure, its dimensions and the absence of angulation due to the Adam's apple. The pitch of the castrato was the same as the true female pitch, which meant that some roles could be sung either by a 'sopranist' or a female soprano; the role of Handel's Rinaldo was sung just as well by the castrati Nicolino or Bernacchi as by the women sopranos Barbier or Vico. But the castrato's larynx also retained the same position, form and plasticity as that of a boy. The combined advantages of this 'hybrid' larynx came into their own thanks to a remarkable muscular system of the vocal cords, acquired patiently through working four to six hours every day over the years.

In addition, castration led to a major development of the rib-cage which tended to expand slightly into a rounder shape. It then became a real sounding box in the service of small-sized vocal cords, which gave many castrati a ... not possessed by the falsettos. On the other hand ... ten been assumed, wrongly, that the castrati, ... their nature, enjoyed a greater lung capacity, a

totally exceptional 'reserve of air'. This argument was justified by the prowess shown by some of them, such as Farinelli, who exhibited an astounding capacity for inhaling
and exhaling and, while singing, could dispense with
breathing for nearly an entire minute. In fact only the vast
amount of work on breathing technique carried out by the
most gifted of the castrati could allow them to achieve such
exploits.

The castrato voice differed from that of the normal male
singer through its lightness, flexibility and high notes, and
from the female voice through its brilliance, limpidity and
power. At the same time it was superior to a boy's voice
through the adult nature of its musculature, its technique
and expressivity.

In this way the castrato embodied the trinity—man,
woman and child—distilled from an asexual personality
and a voice often judged sublime and sensual by contemporary observers who were certainly more kindly disposed
towards artifice than the general public of today. Since this
voice continually bridged the gap between masculine and
feminine it was very easy to use the descriptions 'angelic'
or 'celestial' which were constantly applied to it.

In popular imagery everything brought the castrati close
to angels. Did not the Neapolitan conservatoires dress the
young eunuchs as little angels when they kept vigil over
the bodies of children who had died? The same process
occurred in the aesthetic ideal of the period: objects of
contemplation, even veneration, they merged with the traditional figures of angel musicians and were the simul-
taneous incarnation (through their voices much more than
through their behaviour!) of purity and virginity. In
churches, thanks to voices that seemed to defy earthly laws,
they constituted a privileged and unique link between God,
music and mankind. Who, on listening to Allegri's *Miserere*, a work composed by a castrato for castrati, has not

thought of the word 'angelic'? Lastly, were not the castrati the clearest expression of that baroque art which, in sculpture, painting and music, made the representation of angels one of its most symbolic figures?

2
Origins and Recruitment

In Italy there are barbarous fathers who sacrifice nature for financial gain and hand over their children for this operation.
                                        JEAN-JACQUES ROUSSEAU

The practice of castration was still little known in sixteenth-century Italy, except for precise medical reasons, but it began to spread through the different states of the country during the first half of the seventeenth century and reached its peak during the eighteenth, like a bush fire that spreads so rapidly that it can no longer be kept under control.

Nobody was truly responsible for this, since nobody demanded it or promulgated it as a doctrine. It corresponded to a fashion, which was launched in one way by the Papal Chapel, spreading then throughout the Italian cathedrals and churches by means of the choir schools. Clement VIII, as we have seen, was immediately captivated by the 'sopranists' and authorised castration 'solely' *ad honorem Dei*, for the glory of God. The Church took refuge behind the famous words of Saint Paul in the First Epistle to the Corinthians, Chapter XVI, verse 34: 'Let women be silent in the assemblies, for it is not permitted to them to speak.' It goes without saying that the apostle did not demand the presence of eunuchs in Church singing: until then children and men had been sufficient to comply with this rule.

Once the first castrati were heard in Rome and the principal cities, the public's enthusiasm was enormous and the kingdom of Naples, following suit, allowed any peasant with at least four sons to have one of them castrated in order to serve the Church.

Another, if indirect, encouragement for the use of castrati was the edict introduced by Innocent XI and continued by several of his successors, forbidding women to appear on the stage in theatres within the Papal States. Since women's roles had to be taken by men the impresarios quickly understood the enormous advantages, vocal and scenic, presented by the use of castrati compared to the falsettos employed until then, or to children, who were too young to convey the expression of feelings or passions, both essential in baroque music.

Lastly, the amazing vogue for the first outstanding castrati, quite apart from the later one for Farinelli or Caffarelli, could only encourage a father somewhat more to sacrifice one of his sons 'for his own good'. How could a father fail to be influenced when he saw the excited public literally assail the doors of the church where Loreto Vittori, one of the earliest sacred monsters, was singing? How could one not start to day-dream on reading the impassioned lines written by Angelini Bontempi about Baldassare Ferri, in which he stated that the castrato 'was a treasure of harmony and the delight of kings; that his music was incomparable and angelic; [...] that his singing, because it was a gift from heaven, was totally perfect; [...] that his lips could calm the spirits; [...] that he held within his breast the harmony of heaven [...] that death had claimed him in the end because, being deaf, it had not been able to hear his singing'?[1] Beyond the poetic flights and stylistic effects in this much shortened quotation, we are touched by the emotion of one spectator among others whose writings seem to glow with the memory left behind by the singer.

Geographical and social origins

The behaviour of the parents was easy to understand: influenced as they were by the triumph of the great castrati and virtually absolved by religious authority, they saw castration as a means of removing their son from their modest way of life, especially from the daily poverty in which they lived. It would ensure that he would have a brilliant career, leading to honours and riches. No doubt they also hoped that they themselves would benefit from the success that their son would not fail to achieve a few years later. This was an obvious bait, confirmed by the more than distrustful attitude of the adult castrati towards their parents. It is revealing moreover that nearly all the castrati came from very modest families who had been impressed by the glittering prospects described to them, and they were aware that one child in the conservatoire meant one mouth less to feed, especially in the poverty-stricken countryside of the Italian south. This kind of problem did not affect aristocratic families who were more concerned to see their son perpetuate the line or rise to high ecclesiastical office.

As a rule, therefore, castrati came from very humble origins: Farinelli alone belonged to a minor, recently ennobled but poor family in Apulia. His father, Salvatore, had been a governor of Maratea and Cisternino between 1706 and 1709, and died soon after the operation on his son Carlo. A few castrati came from families already well versed in music: Pistocchi's father was a violinist in Bologna cathedral, Marchesi's was a trumpeter, while Aprile's father sang in the church in addition to his work as a notary. In the seventeenth century the Melani family provided a case somewhat unique in the history of music, for the father, a bell-ringer in Pistoia cathedral, had seven sons, all musicians: the eldest succeeded to his post, two others became composers and the four others were castrati; in addition their cousins Domenico and Nicolo were also castrati, which increased to six the number of castrati in one generation of Melanis! A strange distinction, truly revealing of the socio-musical context of the period. All the other singers came from country families, although we have no documents about their early life.

The geographical origins seem to have been much more widespread than previously admitted and were not limited especially to Apulia, nor even to the south in general. Statistics established for forty great castrati of the seventeenth and eighteenth centuries show that seventeen of them, that is 42 per cent, came from the Papal States, six of them from the Marche, five from Latium, three from Umbria and three from Emilia. Of the remaining twenty-two, nine came originally from the Kingdom of Naples and Sicily (22 per cent), seven from Tuscany (18 per cent) and seven from Lombardy (18 per cent). It is clear that the majority came from the Papal States, which were of course very extensive, but they were the first to be affected by the vogue for the castrati in the religious field during the seventeenth century. As for the Kingdom of Naples, Apulia produced many more than Naples and Palermo. Apulia could also claim the honour of having produced not only the singer Aprile but the two greatest celebrities of the eighteenth century: Farinelli and Caffarelli. If a 'Book of Records' had existed at this period it would probably have mentioned Arpino, a little village in Latium near Forsinone, which had produced the castrati Gizziello, Filippo Sedoti, Giuseppe Sedoti, Cossa and Quadrini, as well as the woman singer Angelina Sperduti, who received the name of La Celestina. The common origin of so many singers could be explained, as was usually the case in Italian villages, by the presence of a particularly efficient *maestro di musica*, who knew how to select from among the boys he knew or trained those who seemed best suited for a career in music and singing.

The inevitability of castration

Nearly all the singers, then, had been along the same road to initiation: a choir master or an organist found them to possess surprising musical capacities and, with the agreement of the parents, would begin a course of training, sometimes very rudimentary, unless the boy's father could provide it at his own expense.

This was the turning point in the boy's life. Evidence of a few gifts for singing was enough to lead to the immediate possibility of early castration, while music and the boy's future were more important than any other consideration of a moral kind. It was then only necessary to convince the parents, which would be either a mere formality or an insurmountable obstacle. The case of the young Caffarelli illustrates a situation that was quite usual. Gaetano Majorano, to use his real name, was born into a peasant family in Bitonto, near Bari. His precocious passion for music, including religious chants, was at variance with the wishes of his father, who saw no future for him beyond working on the land. Gaetano had been noticed by the musician Caffaro who had soon discovered that he possessed a more than promising voice. The *maestro* then tried to convince the parents of the advantages that would accrue to their family. After the parental veto had been lifted and the castration carried out at Norcia, in Umbria, Gaetano returned to Bari to study with his teacher Caffaro who worked in much greater depth to train this boy's voice which in future would be unaffected by the passing of the years. The boy's progress and the incomparable gifts he possessed led the honourable and modest Caffaro to entrust him to the *maestro* who surpassed all others, Porpora of Naples, who was a genius. Like many of his fellow singers, the young man later showed much more gratitude towards his first teacher than to his parents and for this reason chose to call himself Caffarelli.

This story, which was quite commonplace, calls for comment. It was possible to win over the most obdurate parents by dazzling them with something more than possible hopes of fame and fortune. A real market had gradually become organised which consisted in guaranteeing the families a certain income deducted from future profits. Archive documents show that the Teatro Valle in Rome guaranteed these transactions with parents whose only aim was to exploit the talent of their offspring. But they were not all so avid for gain and some were satisfied with a different and more attractive future for their sons than the one destined for them by their birth.

Castration was not supposed to take place before the age of seven and through convenient hypocrisy could only take place if the boy himself asked for it. 'The police imposed this condition,' Charles de Brosses tells us, 'in order to render its tolerance slightly less intolerable.'[2] It can be imagined how far the request of a seven- or eight-year-old boy counted, when he was urged by his parents to accept a medical operation whose physical or psychological consequences he could not measure. On the other hand, a boy who had been well 'prepared' might be attracted by the dazzling artiste's life led by those 'demigods' whose exploits he was told about. The young Antonio Bannieri, who was brought up at the French court when Louis XIV was young, demanded castration in order to preserve his superb voice and prepared for it himself with the connivance of a relative who was a surgeon. One day the King learned his secret; he summoned his singer in a fury, in order to learn who had dared to perpetrate such a deed. Bannieri begged him not to force him to reveal the name, to which Louis XIV replied, 'You are right, for I would have him hanged, and that is how I shall treat the first man who carries out such an operation.'[3] It is also known that Luigi Marchesi, who had developed a passion for the musical studies he had begun, and on the advice of his teacher, obstinately demanded castration against his parents' wishes. His persistence was worthwhile, for he became one of the greatest castrati of the late eighteenth century.

An official request from the boy, and an unofficial one from the parents, still did not satisfy everyone. Families who admitted they had had the operation performed on their child to make him into a singer were very rare. As a rule they had to find a subterfuge for carrying out castration without feeling too guilty towards themselves, towards local society and towards the boy later, when he became adult. This was a further form of hypocrisy in a world that sought and lived with castration without wishing to take total responsibility for it. Further, a medical excuse exonerated in some way the person who carried out the operation, for he knew that if there was no valid reason for it he would be excommunicated.

This is why everything might be used as a pretext in support of castration: malformation from birth, a bad riding accident, a bite from some animal or a kick in the wrong place by a young friend. Certain remarks by adult castrati, who were already deeply resentful towards their parents, show that they did not know precisely why the operation had been performed on them and restricted themselves to believing the explanations about accidents or health problems that had always been given to them. In addition, many of them no longer had any contact with their families who were geographically far away and lost sight of for many years. The case of Domenico Mustafà, a castrato in the Papal Chapel in the nineteenth century, is revealing. He too had never known the precise reason for his operation. Officially he had been told that when he was very young he had been left alone in a field where a pig had bitten his genitalia very badly. Other people, possibly members of his family, had assured him that the operation had been legal, due to a congenital malformation. Quite apart from these two plausible explanations, we are moved today when we learn that Mustafà suffered all his life from this doubt that assailed him from time to time. It was something he shared with many other men in his situation: had his father deliberately arranged the operation in an attempt to guarantee his own fortune? Thoughts of this kind surfaced regularly and drove him into a fury. One day, while he was at table with friends, a tactless guest alluded once more to his physical 'imperfection'. Mustafà seized a knife. 'If by chance,' he exclaimed, 'I learnt at this moment that it was my father who reduced me in this way, I would kill him with this knife.'

The search throughout Italy for young castrati led to amazing and unusual incidents, like the one involving the page employed by the French poet, composer and lute-player Charles d'Assoucy. While travelling in the north of the country he was received by Duke Carlo III of Mantua, a patron of the arts and a great music-lover. His page Pierre-Valentin, who accompanied him, captivated the Duke by the beauty of his voice. D'Assoucy himself admitted what this boy was like: 'He is a drunkard, a liar and a debauchee, but he has an incomparable voice.'

Three months later Charles III ordered his henchmen to remove him from his master and send him to Venice for castration under the supervision of the Abbé Grimani-Calergi, who with his two brothers was co-director of the

Teatro SS Giovanni e Paolo. D'Assoucy did all he possibly could to recover his page, but in vain. The two men did not meet again until six years later in Naples, after the death of the Duke of Mantua. Pierre-Valentin, who had been renamed Valentino, had become a famous castrato on the Italian stage, but success had gone to his head: ungrateful and capricious, he ruined his former master, relieved him of the little money he still possessed and fled, taking care not to reappear in France.

The places where castration was carried out were the object of polemics and errors. It must be made clear first of all that Naples, which was rightly regarded as the capital of the castrati, was not the capital of castration, as certain travellers alleged. The Parthenopean city gave the illusion of it in the sense that it possessed the four largest 'reservoirs' of castrati, the conservatoires. It is known that the boys came there from other provinces when fairly young and were not necessarily castrated on the spot. On the other hand, it was very usual to take promising children into the Neapolitan or any other Italian schools for them to be heard by the leading choir masters of the time. These latter restricted themselves to pronouncing unfavourable or enthusiastic verdicts on each boy's capacities but took good care not to suggest the operation. The parents or tutors then returned to their home town.

Castration was probably carried out more or less everywhere throughout Italy, and particularly in Milan, Venice, Bologna, Florence, Lucca, Norcia, Rome, Naples and Lecce. All these centres were well known, although the work was carried out in semi-clandestine conditions, without any need to advertise it. Dr Charles Burney alludes to it in a much-quoted paragraph: 'While travelling across Italy I made enquiries in order to know to which town one could attribute especially the operation of castration for singing, but I could not obtain precise and satisfactory replies. In Milan they told me: in Venice. In Venice they referred me to Bologna, in Bologna they denied the fact and blamed Florence. Florence attributed it to Rome and Rome to Naples ... The Italians are so ashamed of this practice that each province blames another for it.'[4] This is also why it seems so unlikely that certain shops were able to display signs announcing proudly 'cheap castration done here' or 'boys fixed here'.

Dr Burney does not mention Norcia, a little town in Umbria less than sixty miles from Assisi, which was certainly a centre for castration, even if many poets and observers have exaggerated its importance. Norcia had acquired fame in the sixteenth century for the castration of pigs and the manufacture of an early form of sticking plaster. This was enough for the town to be regarded as a kind of castration capital, although it was no more than one centre among many others. In fact the adjective *norcino* remained in the Italian language with the meaning 'castrator of animals'. However, surgeons certainly operated on boys there since Caffarelli was one of them. Were those Umbrian doctors more competent than others? Calzabigi, when he writes in his *Lulliade* of the French dislike of castration, does not seem to think so, and he adds in conclusion, 'In France they do not carry out castration, even if their excellent surgeons would do so better and more safely than those Italian butchers in Norcia.'[5]

The most famous centre was definitely Bologna. It was there that the most skilful surgeons were to be found, so much so that during the eighteenth century they were 'exported' when requested by foreign courts. Two of them went to the court of the Duke of Württemberg in 1752 in order to operate on fifteen or so boys, nearly all German. Twenty years later two other Bolognese were observed at the same court while other doctors carried out similar functions for the Elector of Saxony. The archives of the

Santa Maria Nova Hospital in Florence also mention castrations carried out there in about 1715 by a doctor named Antonio Santarelli. The records state the fees current at the period: the operation and the stay in hospital cost 24 écus when the leading surgeon officiated himself, while his assistants charged 18, sums relatively high for the period. The document even states that a room with eight beds was specially reserved for the boys who had just undergone the operation.

The road to the conservatoires

Once the operation had been carried out, the convalescence and the threat of danger past, the next step was to begin serious work on the lengthy studies which were to transform a still unsophisticated boy into a singer beyond compare. This at least was the hope of any parent and protector, aware that at this irreversible stage in the boy's life nothing had been truly gained. Castration was like a lottery from which very few emerged victorious, for while the fortunate winners would be received and admired by the great ones of this world, the others, for whom the operation had brought no success, would have no future beyond taking their place sadly in the depths of some obscure parish church choir. Some castrati in fact had horrible voices, shrill and strident: the composer Paisiello used to say of them that they had been castrated 'in bad weather'.

Various solutions were now available to parents and tutors. One possibility was to hand the boy over to recruitment agents who went through the villages on behalf of princes and sovereigns, Italian or foreign. Naples and Rome were not the only two centres of musical excellence in the country. Every court was on the lookout for young castrati in order to train them and turn them into the finest treasures of their bedchamber or their chapel: Turin, Milan,

Parma, Modena, Mantua and Florence competed with each
other for supremacy in the arts. At this period foreign
courts combed the country in order to recruit singers
whom they could not find at home. The German Nemeiz
compared Italy to a 'storehouse' from which everyone
drew musicians and *virtuosi* according to their needs. The
Electors of the Palatinate, Bavaria and Saxony, the King of
Prussia or the Duke of Württemberg lived amid sumptuous
courts where music occupied an important place. Even the
Tsar had his eye on Italy. On one occasion he sent Count
Peter Galitzine as a 'scout' for the purpose of locating and
recruiting young Italian singers. Alas, the enterprise was a
fiasco: nobody really wanted to leave the gentle hills of
Tuscany for the frosty banks of the Neva. Just at the time
of his failure Galitzine received the support of Cosimo III
de' Medici, who introduced to him, among others, the
young Filippo Balatri who was 'already of mixed sex, that
is to say soprano'. The Duke of Tuscany admitted that
the young castrato's voice did not yet send anyone into
ecstasies, but after a few years of study the Tsar would be
delighted with him. Cosimo III did all he could to obtain
the permission of Filippo's father and received it. Like
many other parents he had no doubt been persuaded by
means of a considerable sum of money.

There was another possibility for the families: they could
come to an agreement with 'intermediaries' who undertook
to place the boys in music schools with leading teachers
or in the houses of illustrious protectors. In this way
Cardinal Gonzaga, in the mid-seventeenth century,
obtained young singers who in Italian were called *puttini
castrati*, little castrated angels, through the machinations
of a more experienced castrato.

As he crossed Tuscany the Swedish traveller Grosley
became aware of the clandestine trade which had been
organised throughout Italy. 'In Florence,' he write, 'we

discovered a strange object of commerce but could not grasp the details of how the operation worked. The owner of our inn had gone to Rome with a young man whom he had trained since childhood for a musical career and for whom he had arranged all the teaching needed for this end, after causing him to undergo the operation usual in such a case. Had he taken the boy from the Foundling Hospital, observing the formalities required in these establishments for the placing of the bastards and orphans for whom they are responsible? Had he bought him from his parents? Was he going to sell him in Rome, or simply find a place for him, stipulating a payment to his own advantage, including the expenses he had incurred in advance, and a profit in proportion to the risks involved? This is what we could not find out, but we learnt enough to feel very surprised that such a trade took place in a Christian country.'[6]

In the Kingdom of Naples a barber-castrator in a little town or village would frequently form an association with a colleague in the capital in order to facilitate the boys' entry into the famous conservatoires. In this way the provincial found an 'outlet' for his enterprise while the sponsor took his commission on the way: there was something in it for everyone.

Like so many others the great castrato Matteo Sassano (Matteuccio) had passed through this skilfully organised network which linked the Neapolitan Figaros to those of Apulia, the Abruzzi or even the Papal States. In the case of Matteo his local barber, who came from Foggia, had teamed up with a certain Alessandro di Liguoro, a native of Basilicate, who plied his trade behind the Nuncio's palazzo, near the Via Toledo, the great thoroughfare of Naples. The latter worked on behalf of the Conservatorio dei Poveri di Gesù Cristo and obtained the necessary permits from the ecclesiastical authorities as well as the money for expenses. He later made the journey to Apulia himself in search of boys who had already been castrated or were delivered more or less 'free on board'. By good fortune the Neapolitan barber represented something more than a mere 'go-between' attracted by profit: during the whole period of the young man's study he remained the equivalent of a tutor, a guarantor, a kind of father, always ready to help both materially and morally first the child, then the adolescent whose entry to the conservatoire he had encouraged. Matteo Sassano remained friendly with his protector for a long time and was even to ask him one day for an unusual service which will be mentioned again later.

The last solution, in theory the simplest, consisted in petitioning by letter the governors of the conservatoires. However, if it was easy to write, it seemed difficult to gain admission, for priority was given to orphans or very poor children. Only the boys who were best off could gain entry more easily as *convittori*, paying boarders.

The internal regulations of these schools required the petitioner to explain 'humbly' his desire to enter them. But that was not enough: he had also to present himself in as pitiable a light as possible and prove great poverty in order to sway the governors. In fact the little castrati were some way ahead of the other children: they represented a form of much sought-after 'merchandise' which the conservatoires did not want to be without. The *conclusioni* or minutes of Santa Maria di Loreto, dated 15.1.1771, stipulate, for example, 'in view of the lack of soprani in this conservatoire X ... will be admitted with the obligation to serve for six years.'[7] In the seventeenth century the Neapolitan schools could not always satisfy the increasing demands for castrati caused by the public's infatuation, and brought in little *sopranisti* from Rome, Lucca or Foggia, even undertaking to pay the travel expenses.

Before children could be admitted they had to satisfy a few requirements: they had to be at least seven years old, undertake to stay for at least six months, not suffer from any infectious diseases and to have been baptised. This age limit for entry was raised in the eighteenth century in order to limit the number of students: in 1730, for example, Santa Maria di Loreto fixed it at twelve.

The Naples Conservatoire archives contain handwritten letters from little castrati asking for admission, and it is moving to read them today. One of them mentions: 'Giovanni Francesco Pellegrini, who has been castrated and sings contralto, a very humble servant of Your Most Illustrious Lordship, sets out humbly how, having come from Lucca in order to perfect himself in music, he wishes to enter the Royal Conservatoire of La Pietà dei Turchini...'[8] Another writes: 'Giuseppe Giuliano de la Terra de la Castelluccia kneels humbly at the feet of Their Most Illustrious Lordships and begs them to be kind enough to admit him a student of the Royal Conservatoire of Santa Maria di Loreto, being a eunuch, with a soprano voice, and undertakes to remain in the Conservatoire for ten years...'[9]

Even more touching is the letter from a young castrato of eleven in 1751, who seems to care little about music but explains that he 'finds himself to be a eunuch' and cannot really see what other profession he can follow apart from that of singer. The document does not state whether he was accepted or not.

Each manuscript letter usually carries below a few lines from one of the governors asking the choir master to hear and examine the petitioner's voice and make a report. Lower down still there is a third handwritten note from the teacher in question, giving the final response. On the letter from the young Giuseppe Giuliano, mentioned above, the maestro Gallo noted: 'Carrying out the orders from Your Most Illustrious Lordships, I have examined the above mentioned petitioner and found he has an excellent soprano voice, proving that he has talent and the wish, I hope, to sing well.'[10]

Many letters mention a 'poor orphan', aged ten or eleven, or describe the penury of his family: the father's death, the existence of many brothers and sisters, the mother's poverty. Sometimes the father himself writes to the King asking him to intervene on behalf of his son. The following lines do not state whether the boy has been castrated or not, but they are entirely typical of letters written at this period. The father described his son: 'Carlo di Leo, aged about twelve, a child of rare talent as evidenced by all the teachers in the town with whom he is studying literature; he is naturally inclined towards music, so much so that in applying himself to it he could in time be one of the best subjects of this capital and a good teacher; but since the poor petitioner who writes this finds himself burdened with a family, he cannot support his son in his studies and the practice of music; for this reason he sees no other possible course except to ask for the innate clemency of Your Majesty . . .'[11]

On receiving a positive reply from the conservatoire an important stage had been passed. It remained then for the student to prove himself and above all to 'hold out' for long years, faced with high-level teaching combined with iron discipline.

3
Training the Singers

Naples too has produced several singers equally famous for the
beauty of their voices and the supreme perfection of their art.
                                             Abbé de Saint-Non

Spaccanapoli, piazza dei Gerolomini, opposite the church
of the same name. The visitor who is fond of Naples, or
the musicologist searching for traces of the baroque period
remaining in the former capital, cannot escape some emotion as they go through the doorway to the left of the
chapel, surmounted by a coat of arms and a religious
inscription. It leads, down a corridor, to the centre of the
former Conservatoire of the Poveri di Gesù Cristo, a
square courtyard with a single palm tree in the centre,
while round the sides are two or three storeys which were
once the dormitories and classrooms of the young students.
Today they provide a hospice for the very poor. All visitors
to these places steeped in history are free to imagine the
smooth and limpid voices of the little castrati floating out
of the second-storey windows and mingling with the
cacophony of the many instruments being played close to
each other on the lower floor, while the teachers Gaetano
Greco or Francesco Durante crossed the courtyard on their
way to join their students. Fleeting images of a prestigious

past, restored to us by Naples in the way the city handles so well.

The Neapolitan conservatoires

Their history is bound up with the wretchedness of the Neapolitan poor at the end of the sixteenth century. The tragic conditions of life for part of the population demanded the largest establishment of charitable good works, but music played no part in them yet. The oldest documents date from 1537 and concern the foundation of the Conservatorio di Santa Maria di Loreto, while the three other institutions followed: the Pietà dei Turchini in 1584, the Poveri di Gesù Cristo in 1589 and lastly Sant'Onofrio in Capuana in about 1600. All four were originally, first and foremost, schools which aimed to house and educate orphans as well as the children of the poorest families.

The second half of the sixteenth century was a catastrophic period for the population; the demands of the Spanish government, the extortionate taxation and the monopoly of a few profiteers, plus several years of bad harvests, epidemics of plague, volcanic eruptions and wars brought starvation to thousands of families. The creation of the four charitable institutions, which corresponded to the greatest period of religious propaganda by the Counter-Reformation, brought some relief to these people. The starting point was always private initiative. The founder of the Santa Maria di Loreto was a simple craftsman shoemaker who saw it as a school with a professional aim, while a humble Franciscan struggled to obtain recognition from the ecclesiastical authorities for the Poveri di Gesù Cristo. That is why this institution passed into the control of the Church, while the three others were dependent on the secular administration of the Spanish viceroys, then the Austrian viceroys and finally the King of Naples.

These schools were united by their common aim: they would receive children who were very poor, abandoned or orphaned, at least if they had no father, in order to guarantee them, in addition to food and shelter, a high standard of education in literature and religion. The teachers, still few in number, were all churchmen.

The first half of the seventeenth century formed a precise turning point. The extraordinary blossoming of musical life over more or less the whole of Italy, and the need for extremely good composers and singers for church music, led Naples to rival the musical hierarchies in other cities and in this way to escape their influence. The four orphanages from the preceding decades were soon to set themselves up as schools of music which would become the most prestigious of their time. Their new ambition was to preserve, transmit and perfect musical tradition, and the verb *conservare*, to keep, led for the first time in Europe to this word 'conservatoire' which has never left us since then.

The first organisations appeared very quickly: the numbers of students and teachers increased, lay members joined the teaching staff, and the young castrati, responding to a fashion which remained irreversible for a long time, formed a special group within each of these four establishments, these 'seminaries for children who were destined never to produce any', as Madame du Boccage described them.

On the financial level the conservatoires expanded very well until the beginning of the eighteenth century, then came a slow decline during that period until the closure, in 1743, of the foremost among them, the Poveri di Gesù Cristo. At first the institutions lived on charity and the students, known as *figlioli* (little children) were ordered to beg in the streets of Naples, holding out baskets to the passers-by. Other baskets were placed permanently in the churches in order to collect the offerings of the faithful. At every period these were augmented by the income from the external services carried out by the children: they would sing at masses, in processions, at funerals, at ceremonies for those entering the priesthood. The records even distinguished between 'regular concerts' (*musici certi*), given each week and 'occasional concerts' (*musici incerti*) which were only given from time to time.

The Conservatorio di San Pietro at Majella, in Naples, as it is today, possesses the entire collection of the *Libri maggiori* from the former conservatoires, with the exception of those from the Poveri di Gesù Cristo which are at the bishop's residence. These documents give us a mass of information about the income and outgoings (*introiti* and *esiti*). The first includes five invariable categories: *musiche, figlioli angiolini, figlioli d'assistenza, esequie* and *introiti diversi*, that is to say little concerts, cherub children, attendance at concerts, funerals and miscellaneous receipts. The second category may seem surprising: it corresponds to a tradition maintained for nearly two centuries by which young students, usually castrati, were sent to keep vigil beside the bodies of children who had died and to take part in their funerals. The students were dressed as cherubs and in this way constituted an important source of revenue during times of high infant mortality.

Throughout the seventeenth century income began to pour in from all sides. Individual people, for example, signed contracts with one of the conservatoires by which children were sent twice a week to a chapel adjoining their house in order to sing the litanies of the Madonna. Some records noted all the requests for masses which were to be celebrated and paid for in the conservatoire church and even stated whether they were to be said at the high altar or in side chapels. Lastly, other books, described as 'inheritance books', listed the bequests from rich Neapoli-

tans to the conservatoires, and there were many legacies
from houses which were later to be managed by the
schools. In compensation the deceased had requested in
his will that the conservatoires should take responsibility
for his funeral and arrange for a certain number of masses
to be said in his memory.

Unfortunately, despite so much obvious revenue, the
conservatoires always experienced, and especially during
the eighteenth century, considerable financial difficulties.
True, they had to support between 100 and 300 children
each year, depending on the size of the school, they had
to pay the teachers and the staff and maintain the buildings,
even in a small way. But we should not forget either inef-
ficiency and bad management by the governors who, on
several occasions, made the boarders suffer living conditions and diet that verged on poverty. It was financial
loss, combined with the rebellious atmosphere that lasted
all through the eighteenth century, which led to the progressive disappearance of the conservatoires.

Internal organisation and daily life

The four schools were subject to a somewhat rigid pyra-
mid-style administration. Those at the top of the pyramid
surveyed from a distance the day-to-day life of the establishment, which was mostly left to the judgement of the
rector. Santa Maria di Loreto is a case in point. A president,
an honorary post near to the royal power, was supported
by six governors who shared among themselves the different sectors of the conservatoire: wardrobe and sacristy,
buildings and tenancies, music and classes, income and
musical performances, legal action and, lastly, food and
privileges. Whenever one of the governors left he put forward a list of three names from which his successor would
be chosen, with the approval of the King.

These six governors, all laymen, apparently, supervised an essentially ecclesiastical group of directors who resided permanently within the conservatoire. At their head was the rector, then came a vice-rector, a manager (*maestro di casa*), several prefects, a steward responsible for meals, several chaplains and a sacristan, all supported by a certain number of servants. This team of men looked after a group consisting of boys only. The Conservatoire of Sant'Onofrio alone included a building for girl students, since the other Neapolitan establishments for women did not teach music. Close to the directors were a great number of *maestri*, ecclesiastical or lay, who were not obliged to live on the premises. The 'academic teachers' taught the humanities, grammar, rhetoric, religion and philosophy; others, only at the end of the eighteenth century, taught the sciences and geometry. Lastly came the music teachers who taught an instrument and were subject to the *maestro di cappella*, the key person responsible for music teaching, specialising in composition, singing and harmony. Sometimes he had an assistant or a vice-chapel master.

Santa Maria di Loreto was very proud of having engaged in 1663 the teacher Francesco Provenzale and in 1739 the illustrious Nicolo Porpora. In the conservatoire minutes of 11 June can be read the official deed of appointment for Porpora, 'one of the leading *maestri* of this city, who through his high renown has become known not only here but in other cities, even abroad.'[1] On 25 April 1742 came the turn of Francesco Durante, the other great teacher of the Neapolitan school.

The late twentieth-century reader will find nothing cheerful in the statutes which regulated the slightest actions of the students and their directors, although they recall to some extent the austere discipline of some religious schools during the time of our parents or grandparents. Let us now follow one of our little castrati through the complex 'Rules and Statutes' of the Conservatorio della Pietà dei Turchini, just after his acceptance as a student.

His official entry followed an unchanging ritual. After confessing and receiving communion he had to kneel before the altar where the rector was standing, while carrying over his arm the cassock and surplice which he would wear later. A short prayer and the blessing of his clothes preceded a fervent *Veni Creator Spiritus* intoned, standing, by all the other *figlioli*; two assistants then helped him to dress before the recital by everyone present of the prayer to the Virgin and the psalm of David *Ecce quam bonum* ('How good and how pleasant it is for brethren to dwell together in unity'); the rector's blessing concluded this solemn ceremony.

In fact, from the time of his official reception the student entered the conservatoire as one entered the religious life: the music he was going to study would be a vocation entirely dedicated to the glory of God. His future career would indeed be his own, but nobody would be surprised if he decided to embrace ecclesiastical life rather than follow an artistic career. His entire education would be interspersed in this way by religious exercises skilfully perfected by the governors and directors. Confession would form one of the sacred duties of each student and would be obligatory every week until the age of twelve, every fortnight after that. From the time he got up, which would be at 6.30 in the depths of winter and 4.45 at the height of summer, the young castrato would have to leap out of bed and intone the *Laudate Pueri Dominum* ('Children, praise the Lord') along with all those in his dormitory, alternating with those in the neighbouring dormitory; while singing he would have to dress and make his bed, wash his hands and face. At the sound of the bell everyone went to the chapel for a half-hour of prayer followed by a mass celebrated by one of the prefects. Other prayers, individual or collective, would follow throughout the day until the evening examination of conscience, in the chapel. The young boy could then go to bed at about 10 pm in winter and at the latest 11.30 in summer. In this way chapters 4, 5 and 6 of the 'Rules and Statutes', 25 pages in all, were given over to the children's spiritual training!

The secular training was no less severely regulated. Dress, in the first place, must not give any cause for criticism. Each conservatoire possessed a uniform of its own which allowed the Neapolitans to distinguish the children in the street: a red cassock and blue surplice for the Poveri di Gesù Cristo, a white cassock and a beige surplice for Sant'Onofrio, a white cassock and surplice for Loreto and lastly a cassock and surplice in the 'turchino' colour, a kind of luminous and intense blue which gave its name to the Conservatorio della Pietà dei Turchini. This sacrosanct uniform could have no trimmings or additions such as bows, ribbons, heels, lace or other colours and there could be no long hair. Behaviour had to be dignified and composed all day long, and there was to be total silence during meals which took place exactly at noon throughout the year and at 9.30 or 10.30 pm according to the season. They were followed by half an hour of recreation during which boys could only converse with others from the same dormitory and not those who were younger or older. A siesta was allowed only in summer and conduct at night demanded silence and decency: chemise and drawers were the minimum clothing to be worn during the hottest night of summer and the rules made it quite clear that getting up naked was not only indecent but also 'caused the greatest displeasure in the eyes of God'.

Two kinds of students always rubbed shoulders in the Neapolitan conservatoires. One group consisted of the poor orphans for whom the establishments had been created in the sixteenth century, but this social situation did not lead to automatic admission. Preferably a boy had to be Neapolitan and, if possible, 'well born', meaning here an orphan born to legally married parents. It seems likely that certain musical gifts were demanded at different periods, but not in any systematic way. Children belonging to this category paid nothing, the charity took responsibility for everything. In return the boys signed a contract for four, six, eight, ten or even twelve years, which bound them physically and morally to the conservatoire; this ensured continuous and in-depth work. It goes without saying that entry into these schools represented for the most deprived a much-envied guarantee of security and relative material comfort. Many poor children who were not orphans also hoped for free admission but did not succeed in obtaining it.

The other group included paying scholars who, for this reason, could be neither poor, orphaned nor even Neapolitan. They were called *convittori* or *educandi*. Porpora had been one of them in 1697, among the Poveri di Gesù Cristo. These boarders paid by the term an annual fee varying, according to the period, between 25 and 45 ducats, a large sum which was not however enough to cover the expenses of their keep at the end of the eighteenth century. This paying guest status obviously conferred on them certain privileges, including the possibility of being slightly better fed and also the permission to go out when they wished. Some orphans could enter as *convittori* on condition that they were protected or kept by some rich family in the city or the kingdom. Less is known about the relationships existing between boys who were brought up free of charge and the *educandi*, but it is very probable that in the highly departmentalised life of the conservatoires the links between the two groups were strained, due to the divisions caused by money and the social milieu.

* * *

All the eighteenth-century travellers have confirmed what is clearly obvious from the minutes and statutes of the former conservatoires, that is the special place occupied by the young castrati, who were invariably called 'eunuchs'. They almost always received special mentions which placed them firmly in a fourth group in addition to the three traditional ones of young, intermediate and senior. There are references everywhere, such as 'including the eunuchs', 'and even the eunuchs'. If certain rules seem harsher on them than on the other students, such as the total ban on taking meals or spending the night outside the conservatoire, even with their parents, this was principally because the little castrati constituted a valuable 'commodity', sufficiently rare to be surrounded by precautions. On this point Dr Burney left us these few lines about his visit to Sant'Onofrio: 'There are in this college sixteen castrati, and they lye by themselves in an apartment upstairs, warmer than those of the other boys for fear of colds, which might endanger or injure the voice.'[2]

Many archive documents show that the castrati, even the senior ones, enjoyed privileges given normally to the youngest students in respect of comfort and dress as well as food. Two articles from 1763, at Santa Maria di Loreto, demand that 'the young students, including the eunuchs', be a little better nourished in the morning. On 15 August it was decided to give each of them a brown biscuit and, two weeks later, after possible complaints, the biscuit was replaced by a portion of bread. Much earlier, in 1699, an article of 4 November states that 'it has been observed that due to the dampness of the place the voices of the eunuch students are somewhat lacking in strength'. In future thick, warm underskirts were to be made for them to wear in winter.

It is well known, for example, that at Sant'Onofrio, at certain periods, richer food was served to the young castrati, especially broths, eggs and chicken. This was a kind of luxury compared to the severely rationed staple diet of the other students. The account books of the Poveri di Gesù Cristo mention special purchases made on behalf of the castrati. The steward notes, for example: 'I have bought seventeen rolls of *provolone* (a firm and fairly strong cheese) for the eunuchs, costing 1 ducat 4 carlins . . .' At Loreto a few feasts and special meals were offered to the little castrati, and must have been greatly appreciated when one compares them with the daily menus prepared for most of the students: on three evenings each week the boys had only salad, cheese and fruit to eat, on two other evenings they were fed on pasta, cheese and fruit while on the two remaining evenings they had only a single helping of meat followed by fruit. It was surely not enough to satisfy young adolescents who were growing fast.

All the seventeenth- and eighteenth-century observers denounced the material living conditions of these children, who were badly dressed, badly fed and subject to the draconian disciplines we have described. 'As a rule,' states Sarah Goudar, 'these schoolboys have thin faces, as pale as death. Only the administrators have full faces and florid complexions. Most of the latter are on the verge of death from overeating while their students lack nourishment.'[3]

The life of the conservatoires was interrupted by violent rebellions, signs of a seething ferment brought to boiling point through the laziness or dishonesty of certain directors. The *Diario Napoletano* of 1705, for example, describes a real mutiny at the Conservatorio della Pietà which was situated a few feet away from the Castel Nuovo, the Naples military fortress. During the night of 17 September, at 2 o'clock in the morning, the *figlioli*, driven to desperation by hunger, went into action and threw the rector and the vice-rector, in their nightshirts, out into the street. The Castel Nuovo was alerted, the drawbridge was lowered and a cannon loaded. The slightest incident of this kind, even in a conservatoire, was enough to alarm the viceroy's administration.

In the early morning officers of the judiciary and their guards were sent to fire blank cartridges in order to frighten the boys. In the end, during the morning, came the inevitable surrender: eight students were banished from the kingdom, some went to prison while the men who had filled their pockets with the money destined for the boys' food were not disturbed. There is no doubt whatever that in this case, as with others, the early missionary work of the sixteenth-century orphanages had already lost much of its meaning by the eighteenth.

Classes and teachers

Beyond the material problems and internal quarrels there remained, fortunately, music which, after the first half of the seventeenth century, formed the truly favourite subject of study within the conservatoires. Music alone, along with the study of literature, could dispel from the mind 'the dark shadows of ignorance', as set out in the statutes of the Pietà dei Turchini. Within a few decades the four schools, through the policies of their choir masters, were to acquire considerable fame which made composers and singers hasten to Naples from all over Italy as well as from abroad. Everyone, from mere students to famous composers, such as Handel, Haydn, Mozart, Gluck or Meyerbeer, set their hearts on taking advantage, at a particular point in their lives, of the musical skill of the Neapolitan school.

The record of the teachers was impressive: Greco, Durante and Feo at the Poveri; Provenzale, Fago and Leo at the Pietà; Gizzi, Porpora, Feo, Leo, Angelo Durante and his nephew Francesco at Sant'Onofrio; Provenzale, Veneziano, Alessandro Scarlatti, Porpora and Durante at

Loreto. Some of them spent some time in one conservatoire and then continued their teaching in another, and in this way Francesco Durante, for example, was on the lists of three schools. Several of them had themselves been students in these conservatoires: Provenzale had studied at the Pietà, Porpora at Loreto and Durante had entered Sant'Onofrio at the age of seven.

The lessons given by the greatest teachers took place only three or four times a week and lasted two to three hours. This was the moment the students awaited most eagerly, these were the masterclasses *par excellence* during which each boy showed the teacher the exercises in counterpoint he had written on his *cartella*, a kind of slate made of varnished goatskin. The teacher then corrected the mistakes and the definitive version was copied out again afterwards on paper and kept, while the *cartella* was wiped clean.

The middle of the eighteenth century saw the introduction of the *mastricelli* system, a kind of 'mutual teaching' given by the older students to the younger ones, which earned the admiration of foreign visitors. It was an excellent idea for it prevented the majority of the children being left too often to work on their own. The system allowed them to be better supervised by the older students, who were naturally chosen for their musical competence and in this way promoted to being assistants to the *maestri*: they could repeat explanations which had not been properly understood, guide the weakest students, encourage the others and do all this in the choir master's absence. Sometimes the *maestri* initiated a small intermediate group which then passed on this teaching to the youngest boys. This 'chain' system, which apparently worked very well, was even introduced into the new organisation of the Conservatorio di San Sebastiano during the nineteenth century.

The day was divided up for everyone into periods of

two hours, each taken up with literature or music lessons, periods of individual work in either music or literature. Included also were recreation, meals, siesta time (depending on the season) and walks. While musical theory was usually studied by everyone, other subjects were studied in separate classes: singing, composition, the playing of stringed instruments, woodwind and brass. The teaching of singing was itself divided into four classes: two for the castrati (sopranists and contraltists), one for the tenors and one for the basses. The Abbé Raguenet admired these schools 'where they go to learn how to sing as in France they learn how to read; they go when they are very young and spend nine or ten years there; as a result the children sing there as they read here when they have learned to read well, that is to say steadily, confidently, and without even thinking about it.'[4]

This high quality teaching was not always matched by ideal conditions of work. All the visitors passing through Naples, led by Burney, Michael Kelly and Espinchal, were astounded by the discomfort and cramped nature of the places where the *figlioli* studied. 'I had expected', said the Comte d'Espinchal, 'to find these establishments better organised and maintained in a country where the art of music appears to have reached the greatest state of perfection. I have however seen there young people singing with great taste but at the cost of part of their life.'[5] As for Burney, he criticises the crowding which the boys had to suffer, all working together in a large shared room in Sant'Onofrio: seven or eight harpsichords competed with many stringed instruments, and out of thirty or forty who were practising he saw only two who were playing the same piece: 'several voices all performing different things, and in different keys ... other boys were writing in the same room.' Burney criticised this continual dissonance for preventing each musician from perfecting the sound he was making. 'Hence,' he adds, 'the slovenly coarseness so remarkable in their public exhibitions, and the total want of taste, neatness and expression in all these young musicians, till they have acquired them elsewhere.'[6] But Espinchal, like several others, saw in this, on the contrary, an excellent exercise for educating the ear, and making it more reliable in spite of the surrounding cacophony. 'I was greatly astonished,' he wrote, 'by seeing many students in a long gallery, each one carrying out a totally different lesson with his voice or an instrument, and I was assured that this perfects the ear. It is from these conservatoires that nearly all the singers for the theatres or the churches emerge.'[7]

The lack of space remained a constant problem for the conservatoires. The archives abound with projects and decrees aiming to improve, if only partially, the working and living conditions for the students. It was only in 1758 that Santa Maria di Loreto succeeded in dividing the dormitories in order to separate the students, *convittori* and castrati in the same age group. In 1746 the 'Rules and Statutes of the Pietà' assigned with difficulty a work space for each group of instruments: 'The eunuch class will perform their singing exercises all together in their own dormitory, the tenors in the hall, the basses in the upper cloakroom; the violins in the lower corner of the senior dormitory; the *mastricelli* in the upper corner of the senior dormitory; the oboes in the reception hall; the cellos and double basses in the small passage to the upper cloakroom and the trombones and trumpets in the lower cloakrooms.'[8] As a general rule the students had no desks on which to stand their scores and had to be content with a chair, a table or even their own bed.

There was one appreciable compensation for these internal problems: the appearances of the students outside the conservatoires, both in the capital of the kingdom and in the neighbouring towns. Apart from the presence of many students at masses, funerals and in processions, fulfilling official requests from the inhabitants of Naples, many were asked to take part in private secular concerts, given for family celebrations or at Christmas time. Other students were asked to perform in 'sacred plays', which were acted in the convents, at Nola, Avellino, Monte Cassino, Amalfi or on the island of Ischia. Since the Conservatorio dei Poveri di Gesù Cristo was the only one administered by the Church, its students did not have the right to take part in secular shows and public concerts. They were required instead to participate in one of the principal Neapolitan processions, the *battaglini*. These were totally baroque and also typically Neapolitan in their religious and popular theatricality: many floats, representing the 'mysteries' of the Virgin and Christ, richly decorated and adorned with flowers, passed through the city streets. The last one of all, surrounded by a vast number of lights, represented the Immaculate Virgin accompanied by a choir of about forty young castrati dressed as angels and accompanied in their turn by instruments which, in the words of Padre Teofilo Testa, 'echoed the angelic choirs, praising the glory of the Queen of Heaven.' As in Spanish Holy Week processions today, all the floats were carried by sixty or so men who, at the sound of a whistle, raised or lowered their burden.

In all circumstances the castrati formed an excellent 'export product', well paid by the sponsors. In each case the records state the sum of money paid out in this way to the conservatoires, sometimes to the student himself: 'In the *battaglini* procession, for 4 groups of musicians and 36 angels: 28 ducats'; 'for the soprano Nicolino, sent to Aversa on San Biagio's day for three services ...'; 'paid to the soprano Biasello sent twice to sing, due for three services on each occasion ...'

The composition of sacred plays, or the instrumental or vocal participation in such works, usually constituted the '*passaggio* examination' undergone by the older students as they completed their studies. These performances often took place in summer in the cloister of I Gerolomini or Sant'Agnello, before an invited audience and some illustrious benefactors. They could also take place in the conservatoire or, more rarely, in the royal palace. The Loreto students performed, for example, *Il Martirio di San Gennaro* by Provenzale, also *Santa Teresa, la Fenice d'Avila*, or *La Vita di Santa Rosa*; Sant'Onofrio earned fame in 1671 with *Il Ritorno d'Onofrio in patria*, and the conservatoire della Pietà gave *Santa Clara o l'infedeltà abattuta* by Leonardo Leo and *Il Martirio di Santa Caterina* by Francesco Feo.

Another much sought-after outing was the participation of the young singers in the choirs of the royal Teatro di San Carlo, as from 1737. The students were often called in to augment the professional choirs which provided for them, whether they were castrati or not, an excellent initiation to theatrical music in which some of them were to make their careers. Unfortunately many of the rectors tended to hold back because of the 'moral danger' represented by a den of vice such as the San Carlo. In 1759 a long petition from the governors of the Pietà dei Turchini set out clearly the endless dangers which lay in wait for the young singers: the opera forced them to return late to the conservatoire which upset their routine and caused 'irreparable harm'. They had to make up for lost sleep by getting up late which meant that they missed essential activities such as private prayer, mass and grammar lessons, quite apart from the morning services in the convents for enclosed nuns. The friendships that sprang up at the opera house between the students and 'those women who sing and dance there' were the cause of moral laxity that was particularly dangerous. Night-time outings also led some young men to wander about the streets and play draughts or cards. Since the conservatoire doors could not be closed until they had returned the other students were likely to take advantage of this and go out unseen by anyone. Lastly, a night life so restless, if not depraved, had serious effects on the health and voices of the singers, forcing the conservatoires to engage replacements from outside in order to satisfy their needs, and that was much more expensive. For all these reasons the governors begged the King to prevent San Carlo from taking recruits from among the conservatoire students; through a member of his administrative staff the King let it be known quickly that he granted this request, except for the contracts already arranged for the month of November 1759. This document reveals how, through a careful administrative move, the conservatoires constantly tried to preserve the moral and physical health of their 'flocks' and prevent them from making any excessive contact with the outside world.

How the castrati studied

The conservatoires made all possible efforts to recruit a sufficient number of castrati and hold good classes. This search became even more obvious in the seventeenth century, at a period when there was no surplus and so many empty places waiting to be filled at the opera or within the Church. Many people received rewards for having 'handed over' a little eunuch to the school, and sometimes slightly older castrati were attracted by the award of a small salary. The records of the Poveri contain the following note: 'I gave 2 ducats to Maestro Natale for having brought me a eunuch for the Conservatoire,'[9] or again, 'Today, 10 December 1677, I took into the Conservatoire a soprano eunuch, Francesco Pacciarella, to sing in the concerts, I promised him 12 ducats per year and paid him for 6 months in advance, namely 6 ducats.'[10]

As already mentioned, the castrati received some favourable treatment: they could work alone in their dormitory, away from the general hubbub, and were allowed into the young students' dormitory, which was probably better heated in winter. The work with the choir master was the high point of their study and was certainly one of the most outstanding forms of teaching emanating from the Neapolitan school. The classes of Porpora and Gizzi produced some of the greatest Italian soprano and contralto castrati, as well as some tenors, while several famous women singers emerged from the girls' annexe of Santa Maria di Loreto. Porpora, between his individual courses and those he gave at the Conservatoire, created Farinelli, Caffarelli, Porporino and Salimbeni, as well as La Regina and La Gabrielli; Gizzi taught Giuseppe and Filippo Sedoti, Quadrini and in particular Gioacchino Conti who paid him homage by adopting the name of 'Gizziello'.

For six years, sometimes ten, the young castrati worked through a heavy programme of daily study which concentrated on breathing, in order to provide the maximum development of the muscles controlling inhalation and exhalation, which guaranteed a vocal technique capable of overcoming all problems. Thanks to these exercises the young castrati gradually abandoned the essentially abdominal breathing of childhood and acquired perfectly the deep costal-abdominal breathing which ensured regularity and flexibility.[11]

This work on breathing formed the basis of the astonishing baroque ornamentation technique which the castrato had to acquire and master to perfection: *passaggi*, repeated trills, *messa di voce*, *martellato* agility, *gorgheggi*, mordents, appoggiaturas, that is to say the endless refinements of flexible, nimble vocalisation. We should like to believe the fine story about Porpora who is said to have made his students sing every day, for six years, without flagging, all the way through one single sheet of exercises which included all possible difficulties in the art of vocalising. It seems likely that if all the castrati had been trained this way nine out of ten would have given way to exasperation, distaste and failure, which was not the *maestro*'s aim. Moreover, Porpora and his colleagues did not lack material for making their students work through an infinite variety of exercises. That said, the story cannot be too far from the truth because many students, at all periods, had to practise for months the *messa di voce* before singing the slightest melody. What is more, the story about Porpora focuses our attention on the unremitting and repetitive work which, with all this practice, enabled the singer to develop a technique that we cannot imagine today. Years of study ensured that the castrati, or the best of them, acquired a voice that never failed, capable of dealing with the worst vocal problems as well as the most tender feelings. Was this not the real explanation for that vocal longevity which earned the admiration of their contemporaries? Was it not this basic training, as patient as it was complete, that explained the absolute beauty of their voices at a very advanced age? And it is not surprising, when we consider the careers of the male and female singers of the early nineteenth century, who were often trained too quickly, to find that after six, eight or ten years these careers ended in catastrophe?

There is no point either in overestimating the feats accomplished by the castrati during their training. It is very probable that the most brilliant among them had to sublimate the operation they had undergone through the emotional and aesthetic power of their voices, the supernatural sounds which emerged from their throats. Is it not conceivable that they could have experienced a real sensation of pleasure through the warmth, fullness and angelic flexibility of a voice unlike any other, which united for ever the world of child and adult? How sad that none of these great singers have left us their intimate thoughts about the emotions, joys and sorrows which assailed them during their studies!

Unfortunately there were others, those whose studies seemed to distance them, year by year, from perfection. Lack of concentration on work was not necessarily the cause of it, but it became clear that castration had no positive effect on their voices. How then could one fail to understand the mixture of rancour and despair which must have increased the feeling of failure—the failure of an existence lived out with one purpose only: success as a singer. Many students found themselves in this situation and the deliberations of the governors concerning failed castrati remain poignant documents. For instance, in September 1763 they wrote: 'It has also been observed that certain eunuchs, although possessing good voices when admitted, later become, through adolescence or illness, incapable of singing. Since they are already in the Conservatoire, charity demands that they should not be abandoned; for this reason we charge the choir masters in the Conservatoire to do everything they can to guide them as singers, directing them to sing with a contralto voice if they do not succeed as sopranos. In case they could not sing as contraltos either, the choir masters should do all they can to ensure that they be taught to play some instrument at which they can succeed and thus supply their own needs.'[12]

This musical and psychological failure was made worse by the occasionally hostile attitude of the other non-castrated students. The general good feeling among the boys, which was much sought after and vaunted by the directors, was no more than a façade. The conflicts between the students remained latent at all periods, ready to break out into the open when fired by the slightest spark. The students formed two groups, with horrible names, the *integri* and the *non integri*, that is to say those who were 'whole' and those who were not. This schoolboy rivalry was caused by the stupidity and cruelty shown by the strongest towards the weakest, by the promiscuity of this communal life and the jealousy of some boys at the favourable treatment given to the eunuchs: it tended to come to a head at the end of the eighteenth century during the decline of the three remaining conservatoires.

At the Pietà the rector informed the students one day that, as from 1 January 1782, the castrati, acting on an equal footing with the others, would perform certain functions to which they had not had access before. The speech gave rise to a general outcry; at the next meal the *integri* utterly refused to accept the bread that was served to them by the little eunuchs. As a sign of protest several rose from the table and went out. One morning after this many students refused to enter the refectory and occupied the approach to the concierge's lodge, as if about to go on strike. The castrati, who were on their own, cut off from everyone else, the object of ridicule but at the same time unassailable, sat down at the tables and ate the meal before the eyes of the other students. As always, the incident ended with intervention from the royal administration which sent some 'conspirators' straight to prison and inflicted serious punishment on others.

In fact, apart from the very good students who received distinctions or honours and saw a promising career opening before them, many had difficulty in adapting to life within these schools and retained unhappy memories of it for a long time. While these four conservatoires had specialised in musical studies, they took in poor or orphaned children who lacked any particular enthusiasm or gifts and found music something they had to endure rather than something they had chosen. At the same time they were up against rigid discipline that was little concerned with individual states of mind and psychological problems. Only the conservatoire doctor allowed boys in distress to confide in him a little.

Judging from the number of reprimands and punishments given out to the students, it looks as though cases of disobedience and insubordination were frequent, even if they applied more to the *integri* than to the castrati. The most serious offences were punished by expulsion, including in particular any scandals that damaged the reputation of the conservatoire, disrespect towards superiors, stealing or misuse of weapons.

In the course of two centuries many students ran away, thus forfeiting any possibility of ever being allowed to return or redeem themselves. The Sant'Onofrio records contain the following entries: 'Francesco Paolo Agresto, eunuch. Admitted 27 April 1762. Ran away, being a rogue and badly behaved.' 'Angelo Bucci, from Rome, eunuch, admitted 22 March 1762 as contralto. Ran away March 1768.' 'Pietro Apa. Admitted 11 November 1754 to serve this place for twelve years. Ran away in July 1764. Left his bed, two tables, two chairs and two mattresses.' 'Francesco Juppariello. Admitted 28 March 1760. Ran away in April 1768 when he had one month to go before the end of his contract. But he was a student who behaved well.'[13]

The other Italian schools

If Naples was the nursery for castrati, thanks to the excellence of the conservatoires, the city never had a monopoly in training them. Rome and Bologna also had music schools with high standards, directed by eminent teachers, and in addition there were the schools of Francesco Peli in Modena, Giovanni Paita in Genoa, Francesco Brivio in

Milan and Francesco Redi in Florence. Their students did not consist solely of castrati, they also included women and tenors, while basses, who were much less sought after at the time, were rarer.

The Most Serene Republic of Venice was always a case apart, since its teaching was essentially reserved for young girls, through the intermediary of its charitable organisations, called *Ospedali*. It is surprising that, despite the quality of teaching supplied, these places of study involved only women, although the latter had very little chance of making a career in Italy during the seventeenth and eighteenth centuries. They were destined for marriage or convent life, and many talents revealed in the *Ospedali* disappeared in this way into the private life of the salons or the obscurity of the cloisters. Instrumental music constituted the essential training in the Venetian schools, and many travellers reacted with ecstasy to the perfection of the instrumental concerts played by these girls who were concealed from the public gaze by grilles. How many were astonished at the prowess achieved by such frail beauties blowing so bravely into horns and bassoons!

Singing completed their education and they were then grouped in vocal ensembles, either within their schools or outside, for religious ceremonies. Madame Vigée-Lebrun, Marie-Antoinette's personal painter, heard the young girls from Venice singing at the end of the eighteenth century. '[The] performers were young girls and these simple, harmonious songs rendered by such beautiful fresh voices, seemed truly celestial. These young girls stood on raised platforms with grilles in front of them. You could not see them, which meant that this music seemed to come from heaven, as though sung by angels.'[14]

Rome and Bologna were closely interested in the training of castrati. Two obvious reasons conferred eminence on Rome. The first was the presence within its walls of the

Pontifical Chapel, the high place of religious music and cradle of castrati singing since the sixteenth century, which necessitated a constant supply of excellent singers. The second reason was that for more than a century the ban against women in the theatre had favoured the development of castrato voices at the opera. This ban also extended to Bologna, which belonged to the Papal States. The high-level studies accorded to musical and social life in these States were guaranteed by the schools of Fedi and Amadori, in addition to the famous school of Virgilio Mazzochi.

A much quoted page by Angelini Bontempi allows us a glimpse of the discipline and rhythm imposed on the students. The morning included three hours of classes, one hour of singing practice and more especially difficult *passaggio* work in order to gain indispensable experience. Another hour was given over to the study of literature and a final one to the rehearsing of vocal exercises in the presence of the *maestro* and in front of a mirror, which would accustom the students to the avoidance of unsuitable movements of their body, forehead, eyebrows or mouth.

After midday dinner came a half-hour of theory, a half-hour of counterpoint, an hour of individual counterpoint, practice on the *cartella* and finally came another hour of literary study. The end of the day allowed each student to practise the harpsichord or any other instrument, compose a psalm or a motet. In the absence of any modern recording system, the young castrati went outside the walls of Rome to Mount Mario in order to hear their own voices sent back to them by an echo, which made them listen carefully to themselves, and correct their faults. On other days they were free to take part in all kinds of religious ceremonies in the churches of Rome in order to put into practice what they had learnt.

The school run by Tosi and Pistocchi in Bologna was equally famous. They were both castrati and decided to dedicate part of their careers to training the voices of the younger castrati as well as other types of voice. Francesco Antonio Pistocchi, who was born in 1659, decided to teach when his very fine contralto voice began to deteriorate after he reached forty-five. Strangely, he had already lost his soprano voice at the age of twenty, but had recreated a technique and a reputation in a lower register. It was as a contralto that he had won over the public in northern Italy, as well as at the courts of Vienna and Brandenburg. Through his training of future great names in opera, including the castrato Bernacchi, he remained a key figure in the evolution of voice training during the eighteenth century. Bernacchi himself, following in the steps of his master, founded a school of song in Bologna which produced the castrato Guarducci and the great Mozartian tenor Raaff.

Pier Francesco Tosi, thirteen years Bernacchi's senior, proved to be a remarkable teacher and theorist, if not a great singer. His treatise on the teaching of ornamented song (*Observations on Florid Song*), published in 1723, became a standard work of reference, was translated into English and German and received long commentaries up to the nineteenth century. It is true that it betrayed Tosi's rigid conservatism, acknowledging only the work of the classical composers and seeing no salvation beyond the precepts of the master himself; however, the book remains a mine of information about the training of singers, as it was understood at the time. It forms an essential link between the different treatises of theorists who, from Maffei in the sixteenth century down to Mancini at the end of the eighteenth, tried to maintain great vocal virtuosity by studying in detail the structure of the trill, the appoggiatura, *passaggi*, detached notes (*spiccate*), recitative and so on. Tosi also advised teachers to see that vowels were clearly articulated and to make the student stand in front of the mirror as he sang, assuming a noble and dignified pose;

this would help to correct facial contortions and at the same time ensure that the mouth assumed a gracious smile and not an expression of severe gravity.

Tosi advised singers to abstain from all disorderly behaviour and violent conduct, to perfect their study of Latin grammar in order to understand what they were singing in church, and lastly to learn how to read and pronounce perfectly, 'not having been born in Tuscany being no excuse for ignorance.'[15] The treatise constantly urged the tenor or the young castrato towards greater efforts, self-discipline and concentration. Some of Tosi's most famous maxims seem to apply to students of all eras. 'Study, study still more and never be satisfied with little,'[16] or 'He who does not aspire to occupy the first rank is very close to occupying the second, and gradually he will come to be satisfied with the lowest.'[17]

Apart from his moralising pronouncements, Tosi was essentially concerned with inculcating into his pupils the fundamental technique of combining the registers, little practised by singers up to that time. He insisted that the singer should succeed in uniting the upper and lower registers, proof of perfect virtuosity. The aim was to hear in the lower register the resonance of the head voice and in the higher one the resonance of the chest voice, with total ease in passing from one to the other. Tosi made his students work ceaselessly on this intermediate zone that was so difficult to cross, eliminating any sign of effort, any roughness, any change in timbre or intensity. In this way he enabled many singers, castrati in particular, to excel in this indispensable 'blending' of the registers. Farinelli, although not one of his students, was to become an absolute master of this art, moving up and down over three octaves with perfectly even colour and strength, and without the slightest perceptible change in his voice.

4
The Theatre in Italy

Any spectacle delights Italian eyes.
MONTESQUIEU

The first castrati had been trained principally to serve the Church and make their careers with the cathedral choir schools. This had not prevented some of them from taking part in the new Italian music dramas, starting with Peri's *Euridice* in 1600, then Monteverdi's *Orfeo* (1607) and Vitali's *Aretusa* (1620). Very soon it was the ambition of any student with even a little talent to follow the example of his elders, persuading himself that fame and fortune would come more easily from the theatre than from the churches. The growing popularity of operatic music, the rapid growth of theatres, the enthusiasm of the public and the impresarios for the voices of the castrati naturally attracted students who had been confined for a long time in the straitjacket of study and were impatient to conquer the musical scene that had been described to them.

The great theatres

'Opera is the great spectacle of Italy, almost the whole of Europe has adopted its language and music.'[1] The Abbé Coyer was quite right. In the area of musical performance

Europe owed almost everything to Italy: the word 'opera' itself and the musical genre it represented, the vocabulary connected with it, the first public performances, the theatres in the so-called 'Italian style', and finally the castrati who were to be the wonder of European courts and theatres for two centuries.

It comes as no surprise, then, that virtually all foreign travellers passing through Italy during the seventeenth and eighteenth centuries rushed to the principal theatres they found on their route and praised the astonishing beauties or the amazing performances they saw there. These accounts mention only a handful of famous theatres, to the detriment of countless others which were scattered throughout all the Italian states. About one hundred and fifty towns, and that obviously included some very small ones, possessed at least one opera house, and there were no less than fifty in the Papal States alone.

Some of the towns experienced a hectic musical activity, due to the vitality of the theatres and the number of musical productions. Rome and Venice were in the lead, with eight theatres each, half of them devoted to grand opera. Between five and eight different performances were offered to the public on the same evening during the particularly crowded carnival period.

Naples and Florence came next, with three or four theatres, followed by towns which had only one or two, although their prestige was immense: Milan, Turin, Bologna, Padua, Parma, Vicenza ... If there was one theatre that earned the admiration of travellers more than any other, it was the Teatro San Carlo in Naples; its inauguration in 1737 made it the world's leading theatre, through its size as well as its beauty, forty-one years before La Scala, fifty-five before La Fenice in Venice. Charles III of Bourbon had been the prime mover, so the new theatre would bear his name, and from then on the musical season would always open on 4 November, Saint Charles's day. The King and his wife, Maria-Carolina of Saxony, formed without any doubt the ugliest royal couple ever seen in Naples; he was small, looked clumsy and had a huge nose which took up his entire face; she, as Charles de Brosses described her, had 'a nose like a marble, a face like a lobster and the voice of a shrike.'[2] And yet this couple were probably the best loved of all those whose role was to govern the Kingdom of Naples.

In any case their theatre was something of a masterpiece: seven tiers made up of nearly a hundred and eighty boxes with ten or twelve seats each, a superb royal box, a real salon filled with fifteen seats surmounted by a gigantic crown, and a wide, deep stage that made possible magnificent settings. Since the front of each box was equipped with a mirror surrounded with candles, thousands of luminous and wavering reflections flickered against the rose-beige and gold tints of the auditorium. The Abbé Coyer could not conceal his stupefaction: 'The palace Theatre is a building of a terrifying size, height and magnificence.'[3] When de Brosses saw it, as well as the Aliberti and Argentina theatres in Rome, he could not help making comparisons: 'In truth we should be ashamed that in the whole of France there is no real auditorium, apart from the one in the Tuileries which is hardly ever used.'[4] La Lande described San Carlo as 'of all the modern theatres in Italy, the most remarkable for its size', even if the French writer, like Dr Burney, preferred the Teatro Regio in Turin, 'the most carefully planned, the best assembled, the most complete to be seen in Italy.'[5]

Many other theatres astonished passing foreigners. During the seventeenth century there was particular admiration for the Teatro Regio in Milan, before La Scala was built, the Pergola in Florence, the San Giovanni Crisostomo and the San Samuele in Venice, the Tor di Nona, the

Aliberti, the Argentina and the Capranica in Rome and the San Bartolomeo in Naples, in addition to the Palladian theatre in Vicenza, built in 1580, where there was a permanent décor on the stage representing streets bordered with palazzi which ran in foreshortened perspective from the front of the stage. In the eighteenth century the very fine Teatro Comunale in Bologna was added to the three 'greats' which were never surpassed: San Carlo, La Scala, La Fenice.*

The music-lover of today is fortunate: he can see, in these superb, unchanged places, the same works as those given there two centuries ago, with the difference that the roles of Farinelli or Pacchiarotti are replaced now by tenors or women contraltos. This immersion in the musical past by means of the old theatres is unfortunately impossible in Paris, so Italy remains one of the rare countries able to allow us this pleasure. The reason there are so many splendid theatres is due not only to the frenzied passion for opera in the past but also to the fact that almost every Italian city served as the capital of a fairly large state: no expense was spared in order to adorn it, reinforcing and spreading the influence of the ruling family. San Carlo remained so important throughout the eighteenth century because Naples could pride itself on being both the capital of a kingdom and at the same time the third most important city in Europe after London and Paris.

The performances

In the Italy of the seventeenth and eighteenth centuries individual initiative probably expressed itself more strongly through opera than in any other way. The fact

---

* Sadly, La Fenice was gutted by fire on 29 January, 1996, shortly after the completion of a massive refurbishment.

that finance capital and private investors took over this type of entertainment as soon as it came into being supplies a further proof of its immediate and endless popularity. The Italians realised from the beginning of the seventeenth century that in order to satisfy their passion it was better to expect nothing from the authorities; they must organise the building and running of the theatres themselves. Venice was certainly the leading city from this point of view, for within a few decades, with the help of its most prominent families, theatres opened more or less everywhere along the Grand Canal. Venice also had the privilege, in 1637, of opening to the public, for the first time in Europe, and thanks to the Tron family, one of its principal theatres, San Cassiano.

The building of the other Venetian theatres followed the same pattern, which was taken up by all the Italian cities: an aristocratic or princely family had a theatre built, opened it to the public, entrusted the management to one or several impresarios and was repaid from the profits. This private system offered great advantages, for it worked quickly, guaranteed independence from control and allowed freedom of initiative. But there was a major drawback which occurred many times during the baroque period: the system could lead to a possible failure through the incompetence of an impresario, lack of support from the public or losses due to a badly planned season with works or singers earning no money.

Venice preserved for a long time this privileged organisation and sureness of judgement in the field of opera. Its musical fame, deservedly acquired during the seventeenth century, lasted until the end of the eighteenth and earned the admiration of many foreigners. 'After Naples,' La Lande was to say, 'Venice is the Italian city with the best music performed in the best way.'[6]

Many cities were to follow its example. In Turin the

opera functioned thanks to a group of forty entrepreneurs who organised a musical season, advanced the necessary money and reimbursed themselves from the takings, while sincerely hoping they would make some profit. The King of Piedmont took part in the arrangements all the same, by granting usually 18,000 livres each season and supplying carriages and horses according to the needs of the organisers. The public had to rent the boxes by the year, unless they were content with the pit, where they merely paid on entry.

In Brescia the fate of the opera lay in the hands of an impresario who paid himself out of the profits but could count on help if necessary from the local learned society. The Teatro Regio in Milan, the predecessor of La Scala, belonged to a group of thirty entrepreneurs who kept it going for the entire season. One box was granted to each of them while all the others were rented out. Whenever it was decided to build a new theatre a group of individuals contributed money to the project, knowing that they would be repaid through the sale of the boxes: this was how La Scala was built in only two years. In fact only the rich Milanese families could acquire one of the boxes, for they had to pay 14,000 livres when they bought it, plus 200 livres per year as a kind of subscription as well as a small sum for each person who entered their family box. La Lande noticed the comfort of these boxes, which were real properties that were bequeathed to heirs, and justified it by the fact that the owners passed 'one quarter of their lives there'.

At the San Carlo the boxes in the first three tiers were sold to the Neapolitan and Spanish aristocracy, but their owners also had to pay an annual tribute to the impresario. The boxes in the upper tiers were merely rented. The more modest members of the audience had to be satisfied, as in all Italian theatres, with the pit or the *piccionaio*, the pigeon-loft, and they merely paid on entry.

As can be imagined, the impresarios had to work hard in order to succeed in their enterprise. They could not make any mistakes, they had to work out good programmes, recruit excellent singers, at least for the leading roles, take on vast expenses for machinery and settings and maintain privileged contact with their aristocratic subscribers. The money available to them was usually fairly limited, and they often had to cut back on many expenses in order to preserve what was essential: a famous castrato and a *prima donna* in the title roles. Since they hardly ever had a permanent troupe they had to recruit singers for a season which eight times out of ten lasted from Christmas to Shrove Tuesday. Naples was the exception, opening on St Charles's day (as from 1737), and in Venice the season ran for at least four months, from the end of October to Shrove Tuesday.

In order to avoid unnecessary expense the impresario could not indulge in the luxury of engaging understudies in case any of the leading singers let him down. As a result he lived permanently on tenterhooks, torn between his wish to save money and the fear of seeing the production cancelled by the illness of some singer. This is why Sarah Goudar wrote that when a performer was ill he coughed as he sang and if the leading singer coughed the whole opera suffered from a cold.

The impresario's torments were not caused only by the economic problems of his undertaking but also by his relationships with the artistes. In France he was usually in command but in Italy he was a mere pawn in their hands and had to suffer constantly from their insults and tantrums as well as their jealousy of each other. It was rare to find an impresario who did not endure the tyranny of performers whose fabulous popularity and fiery temperament made them overbearing and impossible to live with. So much diplomacy was required to make the *prima donna* accept that she was singing one aria less than the castrato, or to explain to the *seconda donna* that she was to receive 600 ducats less than her rival! These constant worries were described with humour by Carlo Goldoni in his play *L'Impresario di Smyrne*.

As well as winning these daily power struggles the impresario had to perform further feats in coordinating and financing every aspect of the production; there was no question of skimping on the number of extras or the indispensable quadrupeds of all kinds which enhanced the splendour of the performance. In *Alessandro nelle Indie* Caffarelli shared the star role with an elephant. In *Orfeo* in Turin a little monkey played endless tricks on the stage, while in *L'Innocenza giustificata* two real camels appeared on stage beside Farinelli, La Tesi and the tenor Amorevoli. A vast number of horses appeared in performances in Turin, Milan, Rome or Naples: they played an integral part in the magnificent stage effects offered to audiences constantly more avid for spectacular thrills. At the beginning of the seventeenth century opera was an interminable court performance which we would find hard to accept today: sixty-seven different scenes in Cesti's *Il Pomo d'oro*, seventy-eight arias in Sartorio's *Massenzio*, thirteen scene changes in Rovetta's *Ercole in Lidia* ... In the eighteenth century, after the reforms by Zeno and Metastasio, subjects were slightly simpler, the comic and tragic parts were separated and the proportions of the opera became more reasonable. But the productions now included more sensational 'effects', more fights, more crowd scenes and it was not unusual to see three or four hundred extras on stage at the San Carlo or La Scala.

Naples was surely the place for the most astounding productions. 'The performance,' said Coyer, 'is interspersed with marches, battles and triumphs, all carried out on a grand scale. Reality is even mingled with it, for in the

battles and triumphs they use the king's horses.'[7] Nothing
was spared in order to portray with heightened realism the
confrontation between Aeneas, his Trojans and his fleet,
and Iarbas, his Africans and his elephants. When Sarah
Goudar, who was usually so critical, saw Piccini's *Alessandro* she could not conceal her admiration: 'In this opera
there is something better than songs and dances. The men
fight as though at war. Troops take part in organised battles
and you witness a siege carried out according to the rules.
These are not wretched men picked up on street corners,
as happens in Paris and London, but real soldiers trained
in military skill. All the combatants are masters of arms.
The scenery is superb and in keeping with the rest of the
performance.'[8] Grosley also confirms the sensational effect
produced by the marches and triumphs, by the clash of
arms mingled with the sounds from the orchestra and by
the impressive cavalry charges by horses from the royal
stables. Much earlier these equestrian demonstrations were
one of the specialities of Florence: when the first *opera
seria*, *Ipermnestra*, was performed at La Pergola it included
ninety-four mounted soldiers directed by the Marchese
Salviati. During one particularly colourful scene the spectators could admire three troops of fourteen horses each,
the first with trappings of white and scarlet, the second in
green and gold, the third in yellow and gold. For *Ercole
in Tebe* (Hercules in Thebes), in the same theatre, three
hundred and fifty costumes had been made, for, apart from
the eleven principal characters, the seventeen divinities and
five different choirs, a crowd of extras had been engaged
for the roles of pages, attendants, guards and nymphs.

On the other hand, the scenic credibility of the costumes
did not concern the organisers. There are endless eye-
witness accounts about the lack of realism to be found
in baroque productions. When Caesar fell to the ground,
assassinated, during a performance at the Teatro Argentina

in Rome, he sported elegant court shoes with blood-red heels and buckles set with brilliants; he was wearing silk stockings with flowers embroidered up the sides, green knee-breeches with emerald buttons, and his hair was dressed in beautiful curls which framed his face in charming fashion. Naturally it was the castrato himself who had imposed such an outfit on the impresario, and all protests from anyone had been in vain. In the same way the castrato who played the female role of Dido demanded a hairpiece built up into a pyramid, decorated with feathers, flowers and birds. As for scenes involving sacrifice or madness, they formed the perfect *bravura* piece for all the castrati: they wore fancy costumes, they were powdered and made up, wearing tall wigs and high heels, they demanded to appear in chains, even if the action did not warrant it, and they enjoyed rattling these chains in all directions in order to make the situation more pathetic and overwhelm the audience with emotion. The scholar Laurisio Tragiense, in an important work of 1753, railed against such abuses and attacked the 'insolence of the castrati and the female singers who will not tolerate any costumes apart from those in which they hope to appear handsome and dashing.' That is why, he added, 'the Roman heroes and their soldiers have themselves dressed in the fashion of our time; they wear a knee-length jerkin open in front beneath the belt to allow a glimpse of tight-fitting breeches.'[9]

The magic of the performance was often due to the scenery and the stage effects. For two centuries Italy possessed a remarkable series of scene-designer architects, the most important among them being Bernini in Rome, the Bibiena family in Bologna or the Galliari brothers in Turin. Perhaps it was the Most Serene Republic that surpassed all the stage presentations of Europe by the matchless splendour of its productions, especially at San Giovanni Crisostomo at the turn of the century. In 1695 the audience watching *Il Pas-*

tore d'Anfriso saw the palaces of Apollo descend on to the stage. They were a superb piece of architecture, consisting entirely of crystals in different colours which rotated constantly; lights placed inside them emitted thousands of luminous rays which almost dazzled the audience. Six years later, in *Catone in Utica*, the audience saw high up over the stage a globe representing the world which moved forward through the air and opened out in three sections, indicating the three continents known in Caesar's time. The interior was resplendent with gold, precious stones, multicoloured decorations and even a small orchestra.

The special effects required by the action were the object of unending inventions by the scene designers. At the start of the seventeenth century Sabbatini collected them in a most interesting treatise, a real mine of information about the ideas of the period on stage design, from the most basic devices to the most ingenious techniques. For example, a reproduction of a rock, excellently made out of cardboard, was raised from under the stage and behind it an actor gradually disappeared down a ladder: thus a character was turned into stone, a frequent phenomenon in baroque opera. In order to represent the sea a series of cylinders was covered in black or blue canvas, with silvery highlights; the cylinders were pierced lengthwise by an iron bar connected to a handle which was operated by scene-shifters in the wings, producing the impression of a sea in motion. Hell was represented simply by a trapdoor through which the scene-shifters, hidden beneath the stage, brandished cauldrons pierced with holes: burning pitch, 'Greek fire', escaped from it in flames and in this way evoked the 'bowels of the earth'. Sabbatini took care to indicate that such operations should not be carried out by clumsy or stupid people.

From the beginning of the seventeenth century the art of stage machinery and its perfecting became the obsession of the theatrical producers. In Rome Cardinal Barberini, a nephew of Pope Urbino VIII, wanted each carnival to surpass the splendours of the previous one. He therefore locked himself in for days on end with his scene-designer architect in order to invent new effects and received no visitors, however important they might be. Gradually, everywhere in Italy, the same consuming passion united the impresarios in their desire to improve visual effects and to perfect the rapidity of the scene changes which, in a few seconds, whisked the spectator from a seaport to a bank of clouds or a royal palace. 'Are you languishing in a fearful desert?' asks Dufresny ... 'The sound of a whistle transports you to the gardens of Idalia: another takes you from hell to the land of the Gods; one more and you are among the Fairies.'[10] What did it matter if certain winches or pulleys creaked and jammed, if the trapdoors closed heavily and if the gods remained marooned half-way up on their way to Olympus! The audiences of the baroque era enjoyed illusion: nothing, from their point of view, could detract from the physical pleasure procured by a few moments of enchantment.

Italian audiences

Unless you have attended a big religious ceremony in southern Italy, you cannot today understand the atmosphere of a theatrical evening performance in the eighteenth century. In the midst of the service you can see people coming and going, greeting each other with a wave of the hand, turning round, admonishing a child while saying the Lord's Prayer at the same time, or chatting with neighbours as if they were in a drawing-room. They lose nothing of the sacred character of the service and yet do endless other things at the same time, an art which illustrates fairly well the behaviour of an Italian theatre audience in centuries past. Music-lovers of today, especially in the shrines of *bel canto* (with the exception of outdoor performances as in the Verona amphitheatre or the baths of Caracalla in Rome) have become accustomed to more seriousness and dignified conduct in the theatre. Thanks to a near-international purism which, ever since Wagner, has wanted opera to be a kind of sanctuary where all excessive behaviour is frowned upon, Italian audiences have become a little more disciplined, although they have not given up displays of enthusiasm or anger at which they excel.

What a difference, in less than two centuries, between the behaviour of the Neapolitan spectator who went to hear Caffarelli and that of the spectator of today who rushes to acclaim 'his' diva. Although an evening at the opera in Italy is still something of a celebration, it is no longer the whirl of multiple pleasure, the social, musical, gastronomic and gambling delights which drew the crowds during the golden age of *opera seria*. Apart from Turin, where people could think of nothing to do after leaving the theatre at 10 pm and merely went to bed, all the Italian cities saw the opera as the basis of their evening. The operas formed the sole entertainment for a population that was quite ready to spend an interminable evening there until 11 pm, midnight, even one o'clock in the morning. For all these cities, the largest, the smallest and the dullest, the opera was the one centre of entertainment which often brought all the social classes together. Music certainly played a large part in this, but it was only one part of the whole: playing cards, eating, drinking, visiting one box after another, discussing politics, moving in and out of amorous intrigues, were at least as important as the performances on stage.

Let us imagine ourselves in that period when everything combined to foster this wonderful ferment of activity: the auditoriums were spacious, more like huge, luxurious salons; the boxes formed intimate hideouts where gossip and badinage rivalled the stage performance. In Venice some boxes could even be closed off with shutters on the side facing the auditorium, in order to preserve the privacy of the occupants without inconveniencing anyone with oversensitive ears. There or elsewhere the boxes formed a kind of second home for the aristocratic families. You entertained in whatever way you preferred, you played cards or chess, and during the recitatives or the minor arias you could be served with sorbets, refreshments and any other kind of food. In Naples, on evenings when there was a ball, a complete supper was taken into the royal box or those that surrounded it. In Milan, you could do anything you liked with your box, you could decorate it, add carpets and furniture to suit your taste. The corridors leading to the boxes were constantly filled with servants coming and going: buffet tables were set up and covered with food, little kitchens were available to reheat refined dishes. All this left the corridors and staircases crowded and dirty. Espinchal found those in the Teatro Argentina 'unimaginably filthy'.[11] A few steps farther on you could see a spectator whose slight boredom during the recitatives had taken him to the gaming rooms which functioned not only during the entr'actes but even during the whole performance: you could go there freely to play a game of faro before returning to your box when the *primo uomo* was about to sing a bravura solo.

As a rule the pit was reserved for the working people or, in Rome, for the abbés, that category of person, lay or ecclesiastical, who clustered round the papal administration and reigned over the auditorium where they had taken their places. 'The pit in Rome is dreadful,' wrote Carlo Goldoni, 'the abbés reign over it with much rigour and noise; there are no police; whistling, shouting, laughter and invective can be heard on all sides.'[12] Amid a fairground atmosphere the abbés openly provoked the cardinals and the personalities in the boxes, they shouted their anger at bad singers, hurled sonnets and 'Evvivas' at the best performers, dictated the atmosphere of the auditorium as they did in cafés and salons. Neither the Curia nor the nobility could deal with them.

The seats in the pit were always the cheapest and could be acquired at the last moment. As for the mingling of the various social groups, Venice certainly remained the most democratic city of all; workmen, craftsmen and above all the well-represented corporation of the gondoliers invaded the pit, where the price of a ticket was cheaper than anywhere else. Saint-Didier, in about 1680, was surprised by the high standing of these men and admitted that 'there are no pleasures in Venice which they do not share with the nobility.'[13] The gondoliers formed a separate group to which everything seemed permitted, they were the more plebian counterpart of the Roman abbés. Their enthusiasm, their exclamations and insults often verged on indecency, but this lack of discipline, which was barely more shocking than that of the rest of the audience, was tolerated. There was a tradition in fact, borne out by all travellers, which held that in Venice the spectators in the boxes vied with each other in spitting on the ordinary people in the pit; the latter, who were used to it, responded not with fury but with humour, even with some heartfelt cutting remarks. In 1738 Luigi Riccoboni warned his readers about it: 'The men and women who intend to occupy the seats in the pit take great care not to wear fine clothes for the occasion. The habit of spitting from the boxes down into the pit and throwing the remains of food down there makes these seats very unpleasant.'[14] Forty years later Giuseppe Baretti, an Italian immigrant to England, confirmed this strange behaviour: 'Venice is the only city where public order seems to be totally disregarded. The nobles are pretty well accustomed to spitting down from the boxes into the pit. This disgusting and unspeakable habit can only arise from the scorn felt by the great nobles for the common people; however, the people suffer this insult very patiently, and what is even more surprising is that they like those who treat them so outrageously. If anyone feels the impact of these indignities on his hands or face, he does not get angry, he only takes his revenge by pulling very funny faces.'[15] Pamphlets and satires of the time never fail to mention the unique behaviour of the Venetian public and often make it their principal point of attack. The contrast in the behaviour of these inhabitants who were rude in the theatre and respectful in daily life made Baron Pöllnitz say 'that they spend half their time committing sins and the other half beseeching God to forgive them.'[16]

William Beckford left us a splendid description of Italian society at the end of the eighteenth century: 'In the fashionable world, the morning is spent in a slovenly deshabille, that prevents their going out, or receiving frequent visits at home. Reading, or work takes up a very small portion of this part of the day, so that it passes away in a yawning sort of nonchalance. People are scarcely wide awake, till about dinner-time. But, a few hours after, the important business of the toilette puts them gently into motion; and, at length, the opera calls them completely into existence. But it must be understood, that the drama, or the music, do not form a principal object of theatrical amusement. Every lady's box is the scene of tea, cards, cavaliers, servants, lap-dogs, abbés, scandal, and assignations; attention to the action of the piece, to the scenes, or even to the actors, male, or female, is but a secondary affair. If there be some actor, or actress, whose merit, or good fortune, happens to demand the universal homage of fashion, there are pauses of silence, and the favourite airs can be heard. But without this cause, or the presence of the sovereign, all is noise, hubbub, and confusion, in an Italian audience. The hour of the theatre, however, with all its mobbing and disturbance, is the happiest part of the day, to every Italian, of whatever station; and the least affluent will sacrifice some portion of his daily bread, rather than not enjoy it.'[17]

All the writers of the time saw opera as a kind of celebration, a need similar to that for the air we breathe. If they do not all share the same opinion about the merits of a castrato or a woman singer they are all in unison when they paint this colourful picture of Italian society and make comparisons with their own countries. 'In France we go to the opera in order to follow the work,' wrote Coyer, 'there they go for conversation or to visit each other in the boxes. They only listen and go into ecstasies when the arias are sung.'[18] This pinpoints the great divide between the two nations; French opera attached prime importance to recitative, that unique art of declamation in music which very often made the dramatic quality of the recitative equal to that of the aria, so that the difference between them was not always clear. Goldoni, for instance, while staying in Paris, went to the Opéra in the Palais-Royal to hear a French work. He was amazed to hear all the recitatives accompanied by the orchestra and at the end of the first act asked his neighbour why they had heard no arias. The latter replied, in some astonishment, that there had already been six: Goldoni had not even recognised them!

In Italian opera, by contrast, the recitative was essentially performed *secco*, or dry, that is accompanied by the harpsichord only, and was of little interest. Since there were very few choruses, despite the many crowd scenes mentioned earlier, and very few vocal ensembles, it is obvious that Italian opera depended most of all on the innumerable arias which displayed the rich vocal range of the castrato or the woman singer. The dramatic aspect of the work was in fact not very important. The audience followed with great difficulty, reading by candlelight, the resumé of the complex action taking place before their eyes, whose intricacies they largely failed to grasp. Their interest lay elsewhere: they wanted to be delighted, transfixed, swept away to the limits of consciousness by the smooth and sensual notes sung by a castrato with an ethereal and crystalline voice. They wanted to swoon with pleasure, the fleeting pleasure brought to them, beyond their wildest dreams, by the conventional three-part aria. This was the audience that persuaded composers to write more and more arias suitable for the display of virtuosity. Dr Burney noticed that the Italians never forced themselves to applaud something they did not like, but when a singer moved them 'they seemed to be dying of pleasure too deep for their senses to bear.'[19]

So all the rest of the opera was only small beer, ideal for chat and gastronomic pleasures. That is why we must keep a sense of proportion about that 'lack of attention' often criticised by foreigners, we must see it neither as pretence nor lack of interest in music, but rather as a kind of perfectly sensible self-selection of auditory delights. Charles de Brosses, like many others, failed to understand it: 'The pleasure these people take in spectacle and music seems much more obvious through their presence than through the attention they pay to them. Apart from the front rows, where there is a degree of silence, even in the pit, it is not good form to listen, except at the interesting moments.'[20] There was the same tirade from Espinchal after listening to Paisiello's *Pirro* (Pyrrhus) at the San Carlo: 'They only listen to one scene in the entire opera ... The rest of the time is spent in visits from one box to another, as is usual in Italy. There is a lot of noise in the auditorium, with everyone talking loudly, except during the principal ballet. Then there is total silence and they all listen and watch.'[21] It was agreed more or less unanimously that the presence of the ruling family acted as a kind of anaesthetic on an audience that was constantly in a state of tension. At those times people were more attentive, although they never entirely stopped chattering. Some aristocrats had mirrors placed all round their boxes so that they could glance at the performance throughout their conversations, even if their backs were turned to the stage. Naturally the departure of the king or prince acted like a kind of alarm bell in the apparent lethargy of the spectators. Beckford was present one evening at a dazzling performance by the castrato Marchesi at the San Carlo, in the presence of the royal family, and he later described this curious evening: 'While the court was present, a tolerable silence reigned, but the moment His Majesty left (an event which took place at the beginning of the second act) every tongue was loosened and the rest of the evening was no more than a buzz of conversation and pandemonium.'[22]

At the end of an aria or the lowering of the final curtain the Italians gave full rein to their enthusiasm and appreciation: they stood up, applauded as loudly as they could, threw verses to the castrato in homage, loaded the *prima donna* with flowers or little sonnets praising her, they stormed and shouted until they obtained the encore of one aria or a whole scene. When the audience left the pit looked like a battlefield, littered with papers or a miscellaneous array of objects. It was time to go and take supper, often on the premises, not returning home until a late hour of the night. At the very end of the twentieth century this same tradition, far from disappearing, remains cheerfully in place at the San Carlo. If people no longer eat in the boxes as they did in the past, a private and highly exclusive club still serves dinner during the (interminable) entr'actes, right in the middle of the theatre, a few yards from the royal box.

This feeling of celebration, this baroque taste for the juxtaposition of pleasures, was virtually a way of life in the eighteenth century and was to be found in all social and religious behaviour. When Count Espinchal attended a solemn funeral service in Naples, he found the church magnificently decorated and those attending enraptured by the sounds of the orchestra which was directed by Paisiello. The whole thing was more like a fête than a funeral mass. As for the Abbé Coyer, attending a ceremony for the entry of a young girl into a convent renowned for the severity of its enclosed rule, he could hardly believe his eyes. The church was like a ballroom where mass was being cele- brated at every altar as the 'victim' was sacrificed; 'and as she was clothed in her nun's habits,' he added, 'sonnets and refreshments were distributed to the congregation.'[23]

5
The Road to Fame

They sing like nightingales, they make you lose your balance and take your breath away.

RAGUENET

In the fierce and superhuman struggle lived out by the young castrati during their studies, how many of them reached the top rank? In addition to disasters as exceptional as the plague of 1657, which carried off thousands of Neapolitans, including a hundred *figlioli* in the Conservatorio della Pietà alone, many children, due to illness, exclusions or flight, did not complete their studies.

Others were unable to achieve a musical career because their voices had not survived the effects of castration and had merely become unpleasant or excessively low, sometimes disappearing completely. Charles de Brosses wrote, not without irony, that they were left with nothing in return for the exchange, a 'totally unprofitable deal'. In the best of these cases the boys were destined for the priesthood or for a hypothetical retraining in instrumental music. Sometimes they could only seek out work for which they were ill-prepared and some of them even became vagabonds or drifted into delinquency. The great majority of those who were able to sing were recruited by the innumerable choir schools which officiated every Sunday, and sometimes every day, in the great cathedrals and parish churches. This was a very extensive and fairly variable outlet in the sense that it was just as likely to lead to fame as a soloist in a large choir school as to oblivion and poverty in a third-rate choir.

There remained the top band of students, in reality the narrowest, estimated by contemporary observers as about ten per cent of all the Italian castrati trained on Italian soil. A large proportion of these young men, with soprano or contralto voices, were engaged by the many Italian or foreign theatres. If they did not acquire international fame they often followed a fine career which earned them a certain reputation locally. As for the most outstanding, the future sacred monsters—possibly 1 per cent—the regal entry to the greatest European theatres was immediately open to them.

The choice of a name

By a strange custom, which was lost in the nineteenth century, the castrati, like many women singers and even composers, took an assumed name. The purpose was different from that of twentieth-century actors who change their names for one that is more aesthetically pleasing or more 'commercial'. In most cases the assumed names had emotional origins; sometimes they were merely imposed by the public and adopted by the young singer for the rest of his career. This custom affected nearly all the castrati, with the exception of the first among them, who were born in the early seventeenth century, or of the very last, at the end of the eighteenth or the beginning of the nineteenth, who usually kept their real family names.

Since pseudonyms were fashionable, some castrati elected to adopt one for themselves at the end of their studies or at the start of their professional life; in this way they chose to pay homage to a person or a family who had had a particular influence on their life as a singer. Giovanni Carestini, who had been protected during his studies by the Cusani, a noble Milanese family, took the name 'Cusanino'. Stefano Majorano, as we have seen, received his early musical training from the teacher Caffaro in Bari, and for this reason decided to call himself 'Caffarelli'. The Italian-German Hubert (or Uberti) studied at the Conservatoire of Santa Maria di Loreto in the class of the famous Nicolo Porpora, whom he acknowledged by taking the name 'Porporino'. The same was true of Gioacchino Conti, a pupil of the famous Domenico Gizzi, whom he immortalised by assuming the name of 'Gizziello', and also of Angelo Monanni who called himself 'Manzoletto' after being the pupil of the castrato Manzuoli. Carlo Broschi, who had also followed the teaching of Porpora, was protected during his stay in Naples by the three Farina brothers, enlightened music-lovers well known in Neapolitan high society; through gratitude towards them he took the name of 'Farinelli', although his compatriots, the Italians of the south, continued for a long time to call him *il ragazzo* or *il bambino*, the little boy. We should mention here that the Italian language of the period cheerfully accepted a few variations in the spelling of proper names, in particular where vowels were concerned. It comes as no surprise therefore to find that in old documents names are spelt indiscriminately: 'Farinello' or 'Farinelli', 'Caffariello' or 'Caffarelli', 'Gizziello' or 'Egiziello', 'Pacchiarotti' or 'Paccherotti'. In the same way the architect Vanvitelli, in a letter of 13 July 1756, spoke of 'Farinelli' while on 24 July he wrote 'Farinello'.

The other assumed names were mainly bestowed by the public themselves and then adopted for good. The diminutive form of a name or a first name sometimes endowed

the pseudonym with an emotive character: in this way
Matteo Sassano became 'Matteuccio', Giuseppe Appiani
'Appianino', Francesco Pistocchi 'Pistocchino' and Nicolo
Grimaldi 'Nicolino'. Certain assumed names, probably
given when the singer was very young, retained a pleasing
childhood connotation: Antonio de Nicolellis was 'Cicillo',
Francesco de Castris 'Checco', and Antonio Rivani
'Ciccolino'.

A singer's native town might also provide him with a
new name: Francesco Bernardi, who was born in Siena,
became famous under the pseudonym of 'Senesino',
Domenico Cecchi took the name of his birthplace,
'Cortona', the contralto castrato Melchiorri, born at
L'Aquila in the Abruzzi, became *L'Aquilano* and shared
this assumed name with another—*Cacciacuori*, meaning
'slayer of hearts'. Some women singers and composers were
also given the name of their native town or district as their
assumed name: the Saxon composer Hasse was called *Il
Sassone*, Gluck became *Il Boemo*, the Bohemian, Galuppi
de Burano *Buranello*, Miss Davies *L'Inglesina* and Elisabeth Duparc *La Francesina*. Some assumed names were
likely to be less satisfactory to the person concerned, such
as *La Bastardina* given to Lucrezia Agujari because she
had been born illegitimate.

Several castrati retained all their lives the name of a
character whom they had brought to life admirably on the
stage: the canon of St Peter's in Rome, Tommaso Inglirami,
sang the role of Fedra so well in the opera of that name
in the palazzo of Cardinal Ruffo, that he remained Fedra
for ever. In the same way Francesco Grossi was so dazzling,
in Venice in 1678, in Cavalli's *Scipione Africano* that everyone called him 'Siface', the name of one of the protagonists.

All these assumed names usually followed the castrati's
Christian names and their own surnames in the programmes, on the posters, in the memoirs of the period and

even in handwritten letters. For example, one can read in these 'Carlo Broschi, known as Farinello'. These assumed names, where they exist, will always be used in the chapters that follow.

Débuts in public

It is astonishing to realise the very precocious age at which some castrati first appeared in public: Nicolino was twelve, Ferri and Farinelli fifteen, Caffarelli sixteen, Matteuccio seventeen. It was not unusual for young castrati to make their débuts in the middle of their studies because their personal teacher or chapel master had realised that they possessed higher than average abilities compared to other children. This happened in the case of the twelve-year-old Nicolino, for whom Provenzale had created the role of a young page in his opera *Stellidaura Vendicata* at the Teatro San Bartolomeo in Naples, and in that of Matteuccio who, although still a student with the Poveri di Gesù Cristo, had already given proof of his talent at seventeen, during Holy Week in 1684. His name had spread through Naples and people fought to hear him or employ him; the viceroy wanted him for his palace chapel and the Archbishop demanded him for the Treasury of San Gennaro in the cathedral.

The majority of the young castrati were more or less obliged to participate in church music before approaching the stage. This allowed them to make their débuts 'quietly' and to complete the religious vocal training often acquired in choir school when they were very young. Pasqualini had joined the boys' choir of San Luigi dei Francesi at the age of nine and Marchesi, after his castration, had begun his career in the choir of Milan Cathedral when he was ten. Ferri was already in the service of Cardinal Crescenzi at the age of eleven and was singing in the Orvieto

Cathedral chapel. When he was thirteen Rubinelli belonged to the ducal chapel in Württemberg, Bernacchi, at fifteen, was in the choir at San Petronio in Bologna and Nicolino, at seventeen, was in that of San Gennaro in Naples. Later débuts, however, did not prevent the castrati from spending some time in church choirs. Aprile became known at twenty in the Naples Royal Chapel, Guadagni at twenty-one in the basilica of San Antonio in Padua and Pacchiarotti at twenty-seven in San Marco in Venice, where he became friendly with his teacher Bertoni. These first steps in the church obviously took place throughout the whole of Italy, from north to south, in the places where the singers had studied but also in the areas where they had been born.

The youthfulness of the castrati when making their débuts was due to the length of their studies and the early age at which they began them. Many were trained in classes, in choirs or by individual teachers, and were not bound to work through a precise number of apprentice years—they made their début when the *maestro* judged them to be ready. In Naples, as we have seen, they were obliged to respect a contract of six, eight or ten years and could not enter professional life before the contract came to an end, apart from exceptional evenings authorised by the rector of the conservatoire. After entering at the age of eight or ten, they emerged between sixteen and twenty at the latest. Caffarelli, for example, was one of the youngest to leave, at sixteen, Matteuccio was nineteen and Aprile twenty.

The young men usually made their débuts on the stage after making them in the church, sometimes the same year. According to a well-established tradition the castrato-beginners were used in female roles. This was a kind of transition period before the big heroic roles to which they were destined while at the same time advantage could be taken of their youth, their fresh-sounding voice, their feminine charm and that kind of hybrid sensuality they possessed, which people found particularly attractive. The Italian public had unlimited love for these young men with their beribboned costumes and powdered wigs who gracefully interpreted Alvida or Angelica and gave long, elaborate curtsies at the end of the performance. Some singers, like Andrea Martini, even had to confine themselves all their lives to this type of character, for their lack of vocal power did not allow them to play the great heroes of *opera seria*. In the eighteenth century these female roles often belonged to the repertoire of *opera buffa*, that new comic vein which was to strike a mortal blow to the old *opera seria* and, indirectly, to those who best interpreted the spirit of it—the castrati.

Rome was a vital centre for the castrati beginners. For more than a century women were forbidden there to appear on the stage, and only castrati, falsettos or tenors in disguise could interpret female roles. In this way Siface made his début in the Teatro Tor di Nona, Caffarelli at the Teatro Valle in an opera by Sarro, Rauzzini at the same place in the female role in a short opera by Piccini, *Il finto Astrologo* (The Feigned Astrologer) and Marchesi at the Teatro delle Dame in the female roles of three comic operas. Other castrati experienced identical débuts in cities where female singers were, nevertheless, allowed on the stage, such as Genoa for Bernacchi, Naples for Matteuccio or Venice for Pacchiarotti and Guadagni.

Farinelli's official début took place in Naples, in the palazzo of the Prince de la Torella. This evening was to affect his life permanently, for in addition to revealing him to the public it allowed him to meet the man who was to become his close friend for life, the poet Metastasio. The latter had been asked to compose a poetic work to celebrate the arrival in Naples of the viceroy's nephew; his offering was *Angelica e Medoro*, his first creation, which Farinelli interpreted superbly. This was the unforgettable meeting between a poetic genius of twenty-two and a vocal prodigy of fifteen, both at the start of their dazzling careers. The two men, as we shall see, wrote to each other regularly for much of their lives and called each other 'twin'. Metastasio immortalised this evening in 1720 in two simple lines. *Appresero gemelli a sciorre il volo/ La tua voce in Parnasso, e il mio pensier* ('Your voice over Parnassus, twinned with my thought,/Learnt at the same time to unleash their flight').

Farinelli, like all the others, had first won the hearts of a local public. But the fame of these exceptional voices spread like wildfire throughout the Italy of the time. The castrati, like the divas and the film stars later, were much talked about in the principal states and were soon offered the much sought after roles of a *primo uomo*.

Vocal prowess

Leonardo da Vinci said that music was the least important of the arts since, unlike architecture, painting or sculpture, which are durable, a note of music, however sublime it might be, died as soon as it was born. Of course we still have the scores which fascinated past generations, but what can we say about the voices? Is it not guesswork if we try to 'describe' the vocal qualities of Madame Saint-Huberty or Madame Pasta, even though we know what a woman's soprano or contralto voice sounds like? The problem is insurmountable when we come to those voices quite unknown to the modern ear, those of the great castrati of the seventeenth and eighteenth centuries, the only ones that interest us, since the pallid if moving recording made between 1902 and 1904 by Alessandro Moreschi, a modest religious castrato far removed from the golden age of his

counterparts, gives us only an infinitely small part of the
'whole'.

So we have only the testimonies of the period to help
us pierce the mystery and comprehend the incomprehen-
sible. But what testimonies, what warmth, what feeling
throughout two centuries of memoirs and musical history!
'No hyperbole, no excess of the poetic pen can suffice to
praise such merit,'[1] wrote Bontempi on the subject of Ferri.
Alessandro Scarlatti, when describing the castrato Francischello, could not believe that 'a mortal could sing so
divinely' and wondered if in fact it was 'an angel who had
assumed the shape of Francischello',[2] for his performance
surpassed anything he had been able to imagine in a human
being. Baron Grimm was no less carried away when he
heard Caffarelli at the Louvre on St Louis's day: 'It would
be difficult to give any true idea of the degree of perfection
to which this singer has brought his art. The charm and
love which can convey the idea of an angel's voice and
make up the character of his, combined with surprising
facility and precision, exert over the senses and the heart
an enchantment which those least responsive to music
would find hard to resist. It can also be said that no mass
was heard with as little attention as that one, although
the most profound silence reigned in the chapel.'[3] As for
Beckford, he wrote at the end of the eighteenth century,
'In the midst of all that splendour [the Teatro San Carlo]
Marchesi sang the poorest piece of music imaginable in a
voice that was possibly the clearest and most triumphant
in the world.'[4]

These four accounts, among scores of others, cover the
two golden centuries when the castrati were part of opera.
The descriptions are only a pale reflection of reality, for
emotions stirred by music throughout a lifetime cannot be
expressed in words. Indeed, no description could convey
the atmosphere of that evening in 1776 at Forli, when Pac-

chiarotti played Arbace in *Artaserse*, with a libretto by Metastasio. He interpreted admirably the role of a son who was going to his death, sacrificing himself on behalf of his father. The entire theatre was in tears and the orchestra was so moved that it gradually stopped playing in the middle of an aria by the singer. Pacchiarotti came forward to the front of the stage to ask what was happening. The *maestro* could only manage to say: 'I am weeping, signor.'

One cannot speak of 'the' castrato voice, for each man possessed 'a' voice of his own, more or less wide-ranging, colourful, agile, powerful. Some were *soprani* (Cusanino, Caffarelli, Rauzzini...), others *contralti* (Senesino, Guadagni...); some fascinated the public by their astonishing 'florid' technique, others overwhelmed Europe by the sensitivity and pathetic quality of their voices and their acting. Generalisations, which might tend to fit all the castrati into the same mould, should be avoided.

These voices led to such a craze among the public because they corresponded to a very widespread taste in the seventeenth and eighteenth centuries for the upper registers, the only ones which allowed the singers to excel in the 'florid' style. This is why the castrati always shared stardom with women sopranos, except in the Papal States. Tenor voices came a long way behind while basses hardly counted. In an opera such as Alessandro Scarlatti's *Pompeo*, eight out of eleven roles were sung by high voices—four by castrati and four by women. Three of the latter were in fact masculine roles and could have been sung perfectly well by other castrati, and there remained three natural men's voices.

Why was the baroque era not content with women's voices? Their prohibition in the Papal States did not explain everything, neither did the very pronounced taste of the period for all that was artificial, created by the hand of man—trees, gardens, fireworks or castrated singers. It is

probably because the voices of the castrati differed somewhat from those of women. They possessed some other
quality, perhaps, even some additional quality which justified their presence and their near-supremacy for two centuries. Sexual ambiguity, which will be mentioned again
later, certainly constituted one of their strongest points.
In addition they possessed considerable vocal advantages.
Several hours of work each day for years gave these singers
a capacity for respiration which, in conjunction with the
development of the rib cage, endowed them with a truly
amazing and powerful control over their breathing. Sacchi
was right when he said of Farinelli that he possessed 'what
is most important, an extraordinary power of inhalation
and exhalation.'[5] Further, as we have seen in connection
with the operation and its consequences, the particular
location of the castrato's larynx and the increased proxim-
ity of the vocal cords to the resonators reinforced this
impression of fullness, 'brilliance' and clarity which so fascinated their listeners. Lastly, the castrato's vocal cords, as
a rule shorter than those of a normal man but longer than
those of a woman, and above all more muscular, were
likely to produce an intermediate sound in which the best
characteristics of a child's voice and a woman's voice were
fused together. But it is essential to recall once again that
all the castrati were different and even if the operation
brought about a certain number of physical changes it did
not necessarily bless them with a sublime voice.

The vocal range of the singers evolved greatly during
the seventeenth century, not because those of the latter
part of the century were better than those of the early
years but because the composers, seeing their immense
vocal possibilities, exerted great pressure on them and
demanded more acrobatic achievements in the low or high
register. The early seventeenth-century musical scores did
not take the singers higher than G4 for the sopranos and

C4 or D4 for the contraltos, with the exception of the very high C demanded by Luigi Rossi in his *Castello d'Atlante* in 1642. There was nothing remarkable about such tessituras. During the second half of the century sopranists and contraltists aimed respectively at C4 and E4, which obliged them to blend together the chest and head registers. This was only the start of more and more exploits; they were to continue throughout the eighteenth century with singers whose voices rose cheerfully from low to medium and high, moving evenly and smoothly from note to note. Cusanino went from C3 to C5 (or high C), Pacchiarotti from B below middle C to C5, Marchesi from G2 to C5 and Farinelli from C2 to C5, even to D above C5. Even more exceptional (but not necessarily aesthetic!) was the very high F sung by the castrato Domenico Annibali, which he surely had little opportunity to use. In one totally unique case, that of Luca Fabris, vocal exhibitionism proved to be quite simply lethal. One evening the *maestro* Galuppi asked his disciple for a note so high that it gave the young castrato a heart attack and he died instantaneously! Apart from such useless exploits the range of the principal singers covered more than two octaves, almost three in the case of these last named. Mancini, writing about Farinelli, said, 'His voice was regarded as a marvel for it was so perfect, so powerful, so sonorous and its range so rich in both the high and low registers, that its equal has never been heard in our time.'[6]

A glance at the scores of the period shows that the roles written for the castrati included only rarely the extremely high notes just mentioned. The public enjoyed being amazed by virtuosity but was not interested in the exhibitionism of a counter-tenor. By choice they definitely preferred low notes sung by a high voice, for they were warmer, more sensual, endowed with a far superior emotional quality. In fact, and this was the privileged area of the castrato, the composers favoured the medium register, the most suitable for rendering the *affetti* and for emphasising the warmth and smoothness of these incomparable voices. Most of Farinelli's arias range between A2 and C4, the average range for a contralto castrato who does not want to endanger his voice. But it is true that an exceptional aria such as *Qual guerriero in campo armato*, written by his brother in *Idaspe*, caused him to pass from G2 to C5 through all kinds of leaps, trills and elaborate vocal exercises, down a series of descending *volées*, like a peal of bells. It was the cadenzas in fact, which the singers could handle freely on their own, just as they chose, that revealed best of all the most imaginative of their exploits, all the more so since the singer, in order to satisfy the audience, had to devise a progression throughout the three sections of the aria (A-B-A), add more ornamentation to the second cadenza than to the first and then even more to the third than to the second. In doing this he was not merely satisfied with displaying his virtuosity but gave proof of his good musical taste. The vocal art had to be continually creative and not frozen in notes written down on paper. So a knowledge of how to devise and perform ornamentation proved total mastery of this art.

In this way *virtuosismo*, inseparable from baroque art, gradually developed during the seventeenth century, reaching its climax during the first half of the eighteenth, considered to be the end of the baroque period proper. The castrati, as the finest products of an art devoted to acrobatics and artifice, inevitably followed this evolution.

The studies they had worked through, whatever their seat of learning, had revealed to them all the secret techniques of baroque ornamentation, which has now more or less vanished. These included *virtuosità spiccata*, which consisted of separating the notes in the trills, singing *gruppetti*, rapid *volées* and *passaggi*, in a real firework display.

L'agilità martellata was one of the fundamental aspects of this technique, consisting, according to Mancini, of a descending or ascending leap, followed by several repetitions of the second note, sung in a percussive manner. Lastly came the *messa di voce*, the favourite display of many castrati; it consisted of starting a note *pianissimo*, gradually inflating the sound to a climax, then reducing it and letting it die away. The English diarist John Evelyn, who heard Siface in 1687 in London, had to concede the miraculous nature of this technique: '. . . indeede his holding out & delicatenesse in extending & loosing a note with that incomparable softenesse, & sweetnesse was admirable.'[7]

Farinelli excelled at this, and it was said he could prolong the note for one entire minute without taking a new breath. 'First he took a deep breath,' wrote Sacchi, 'then he controlled the breath so carefully that he could hold the note much longer than one might have expected, singing loudly and then softly in an inimitable way.'[8] His brother Riccardo had in fact written an aria 'made to measure' for him, entitled *Son qual nave che agitata*, which began with a very beautiful *messa di voce* extended by several bars of trills and detached notes. If his contemporaries are to be believed, he could hold a note five times longer than a normal singer.

One of the first pieces of advice that teachers instilled into their students from the sixteenth century until the end of the eighteenth concerned birdsong. They must listen to it attentively in order to reproduce it afterwards. This was both an end and a means, strictness in study and a consecration in front of the public. Birdsong in fact included all the 'ingredients' of *virtuosismo*, in particular rapid trills with detached notes, and ability to reproduce it was the demonstration of a consummate art. As early as the middle of the sixteenth century Zacconi said, 'A number of notes are added and must be sung very quickly, they are notes which give great joy and pleasure, as if one were listening to so many well trained birds which delight our hearts with their song and let us enjoy contentment.'[9] Many arias used the bird theme, allowing the castrato to display his technique, especially in the flowery cadences added to the theme. The aria *Quell'usignolo che innamorato* (This nightingale in love) by Girolamo Giacomelli was a model of the genre. The castrato Balatri tells in his autobiography how he was invited one day to sing before Bishop Schönborn and was allowed to choose the aria he preferred. The castrato stated that his repertoire was unlimited and that he could sing 'until there was no aria left'; he was asked then to sing his favourite melody and he inevitably suggested the one he was asked for everywhere, the 'Nightingale', adding, 'Of all the melodies that I have written, however outstanding, I have only one that sounds like the nightingale; and without boasting I can say that I alone have been able to imitate that song.'[10] Then, to use his own expression, he began to 'nightingalise', exhibiting all he could do. The bishop-prince offered to engage him at any price, but Balatri refused, promising only to return to Würzburg soon.

The most varied ornamentations found their rightful place in the three-part arias which had developed during the second half of the seventeenth century: an A theme was followed by a B theme before the first part A was repeated as a whole. In order to avoid any monotony the first theme, already ornamented during part A, could be used for all possible fantasies when it was repeated. The castrati stopped at nothing as they gave free rein to their imagination, ornamenting the original theme just as they wished. Ferri earned the admiration of his listeners through the clarity of his voice, the rhythm of his trills, the unbelievable length of his *passaggi* which he extended with a long and very fine trill without taking a new breath, then with another *passaggio* even louder than the first. There was no sign of movement in his body and Bontempi said he looked like a 'statue'. Marchesi, taking only one breath, could execute a perfectly clear and loud chromatic trill, over six or seven successive notes. Grosley states that if the audience demanded it, a castrato could repeat the same part of an aria five or six times. 'It is in these repeats that the singer exhausts all the resources of Nature and Art through the variety of nuances he adds to every note, to the modulations and to everything concerned with expression.'[11]

All the singers would insert into their performance the most dazzling arias full of vocal ornamentation, even if these arias, which came from their personal repertoire, had no connection with the work in question. They were called *arie di baule* (portmanteau arias) because the *virtuosi* carried them in their luggage and used them again and again in all circumstances, with the sole aim of appearing brilliant. Marchesi introduced the bravura aria from Sarti's *Achille in Sciro* into everything, for it displayed his voice superbly. Farinelli had included his brother's aria (*Son qual nave*) in the London performance of Hasse's *Artaserse* for, in addition to the very fine *messa di voce* which opened the aria, he performed, without any obvious signs of breathing, fourteen consecutive bars of vocalises, ending with an interminable trill. As these examples show, the agility of the voice only worked when it was accompanied by exceptional breath control, which was preached by Tosi at the start of the eighteenth century: 'All the beauty of the *passaggio* lies in its precision, its detached notes, the gradual dropping away of the sound, its evenness and speed. All agile singing should be supported by a strong chest and with this should be linked the control of the breath and the lightness of the vocal organ so that each note can be heard distinctly, even when sung with maximum speed.'[12]

As the theorist Mancini emphasised, Farinelli excelled in this art of breath control: 'The art of holding or renewing the breath with so much restraint and skill, without anyone ever being aware of it, was born and died with him.'[13]

Mastery of this kind allowed the castrati to perform a balancing act, an exercise for which they had a particular affection—at least those who were capable of it: this was the competition between their voice and a wind instrument. It was not merely a question of being accompanied by an orchestral soloist, following the conventional plan of *opera seria*, the trumpet for a warlike aria, the horn for a hunting aria . . . The singer had to prove that his voice had the same agility, the same power, the same capacity for holding notes as a trumpet, working through improvisations which included all the difficulties of the ornamentation technique. Competitions of this sort took the public's breath away and sent audiences into a state of euphoria which Grosley described as 'a foretaste of the joys of paradise'. Once again this kind of 'bravura duel' suited Farinelli more than anyone else. Burney described a particular evening in 1722 when the 27-year-old castrato began to compete with the trumpet: 'After the two musicians had each amplified one note separately, each demonstrating the power of his lungs and seeking to outdo the other in brilliance and strength, they had to perform together a crescendo and a trill, in thirds, which was held for so long that both seemed exhausted, and in fact the trumpeter, who was out of breath, stopped, thinking that his opponent was as exhausted as he was and that this would be an indecisive battle; then Farinelli, with a smile, showing that he had merely been amusing himself with the other all the time, suddenly, without drawing breath, began again with renewed vigour and not only amplified and trilled the note but performed the most rapid and difficult divisions, interrupted only with applause.'[14]

However, this form of vocal exhibitionism had not ousted the expressive type of song, which had always survived through certain types of aria. During the second half of the eighteenth century this expressive type partially eclipsed the other and replaced it, due to the influence of a new generation of singers and composers. Already a certain number of earlier castrati—Farinelli, Caffarelli, Gizziello—had considerably changed their style during the second part of their career. When Farinelli had reached the peak of his 'acrobatic' period he had received the following advice from the Emperor Charles VI, a discriminating music-lover and an excellent judge in the matter: 'You sing more slowly than the slowest, more rapidly than the most rapid . . . In future it would be fitting for you to walk like a man and not a giant. Adopt a more simple style and gradually you will win hearts.'[15] The singer, who was too modest and too intelligent to be vexed at this, took the advice literally and decided to modify his style a little.

For him, as for his successors in the new generation—Guadagni, Pacchiarotti, Tenducci, Rubinelli, Rauzzini and Crescentini—subtlety, finesse, expressiveness, grace, moderation and the understanding of the role were now to predominate over vocal exploits. In the same way as the 'pathetic' song had always had a place in the earlier period, virtuosity would certainly not be totally banished since it was in an integral part of the music of the period and provided a source of expression and emotion. Even Algarotti, regarded as a reformer in the middle of the eighteenth century, recognised the necessity for it: 'As for the *passaggi (di virtuosità)* reason demands that they should not be used except for words which express passion or movement.'[16] Mozart himself, after the actual baroque period, was to use this virtuosity to confer a highly individual expressive quality on the arias of the Queen of Night.

After 1750, however, despite the durability of the *chant*

orné, the castrati of the time concentrated the extraordinary power of their voices on something new, a simple and 'natural' expression of feelings addressed to the soul more than to the mind. Brydone was one of the first to hear Pacchiarotti in Palermo, in 1770. This young 30-year-old contraltist enchanted him through the novelty of his singing: 'He excels in the pathetic, too much neglected today in many theatres: it seems to me that he adds more colour and expression to his *cantabile* and moves his listeners more deeply, precisely because he himself has a more sensitive soul than all the singers I have heard in Italy. He speaks truly to the heart, while nearly all those who sing today intend merely to divert the imagination.'[17] Farinelli also reached the height of his fame by performing arias in the pathetic style, based on the medium or low registers of his voice to the exclusion of the very high notes. The emotional power contained in slow vocalises, the long drawn-out notes and the type of abandon found in arias such as the andante *Pallido il Sole* or the adagio *Per questo dolce amplesso* made the whole of Europe faint with pleasure before they later made Philip V of Spain take an interest in life again.

Gaetano Guadagni was another contributor to this vocal renewal. In his case virtuosity was far from being a major advantage. The entire character of this *virtuoso* with the superb contralto voice lay in the subtlety, dignity, sobriety and expressiveness of his singing and acting. For him Handel had rewritten an aria from *The Messiah* and composed his *Foundling Hospital Anthem*. But above all Gluck offered him, as though on a plate, the score *par excellence* of the vocal renewal, with the role of Orfeo which consisted entirely of simplicity and restrained emotion. In this way one of the greatest castrati of the eighteenth century initiated a reform which would, however, soon remove his peers from the stage.

The castrati on stage

In 1639 Maugars, Cardinal Richelieu's musician, saw the Italian castrati and wrote from Rome: 'It has to be admitted that in these musical stage works they are incomparable and inimitable, not only through their singing but also in the way they express in words, postures and gestures the characters they naturally represent well. Their style of singing is more lively than ours, they have certain inflexions of the voice that we do not have.'[18] Coming from a Frenchman, the compliment was fitting, even if totally justified since Maugars was speaking of the two great names of the seventeenth century, Loreto Vittori and Marc'Antonio (Pasqualini).

In fact all the castrati were not necessarily both good singers and good actors. Some, like Aprile, had a weaker and more uneven voice, but much good taste and expression in their acting; others compensated for poor acting through a very fine voice. It is true that very few of them had been trained for the stage, for the art of drama was not included in the syllabus, no more in Rome or Bologna than in the Neapolitan conservatoires. Only the singer's innate gift for moving on stage could count, and some of them did not possess that gift. Moreover, the length of the traditional baroque *aria da capo* hardly allowed the singer scope to avoid a rather static style of acting. How could anyone vary his dramatic performance while singing an aria such as *Quell'usignolo che innamorato*, which consisted of only six lines and could last a good quarter of an hour?

Some singers, in fact, through whims or pride, scorned any attempt to improve their performances on stage and merely behaved as they chose. The architect Vanvitelli, for example, said that Mazzanti sang well but acted like a clumsy oaf, so much so that he wanted to go up on stage and punch him. In 1765 the French traveller La Lande wrote, without naming anyone, 'The great actors in Italy, the leading virtuosi [= castrati] do not always take the trouble to act themselves: when they do, it is often in a way that is highly familiar and not very respectful towards the spectators; they greet the people they know, even in the middle of their performance, unafraid of displeasing the audience whose indulgence has permitted this abuse for a long time; it can also be attributed to the scant attention paid to the performance if there is an unbearable noise either in the pit or the boxes.'[19] It is true that the French were usually harder to please than their neighbours about foreign stage settings and acting. They tended to think that if the Italians were well ahead in the vocal domain, they were far from equalling the noble gestures and dramatic understanding they themselves had inherited from the great French lyric tragedy of which they were proud.

But some castrati deserved praise. After making rapid progress during their early years in the theatre and spurred on by contact with the public, they succeeded in giving superb renderings, through facial expression and gestures, of the inner passions and dramas they were living through. These singers, whose social origins were often humble, even acquired through experience much subtlety, taste and distinction which frequently led them to be compared to princes; the heroic grandeur of the characters they portrayed was only equalled by the nobility of their acting.

Nicolino was typical in this way, possessing as he did such a powerful gift for personifying the slightest expression and emphasising the slightest gesture. Burney described him as 'an actor who, through the grace and accuracy of his acting and gestures, does honour to the human figure; through his acting he brings out the character he is incarnating in an opera, and does the same to the words through his voice. Every limb and every finger

contribute to the role he is playing, so much so that a
deaf man could follow the meaning through him. There is
hardly a pose from ancient statues that he does not adopt
himself. He performs the most ordinary gesture in a way
suited to the grandeur of the character and maintains
princely attitudes, even when handing over a letter or
despatching a messenger.'[20]

The roles performed by the castrati certainly demanded
good posture, fine presence and noble bearing. These stars
of baroque opera, these 'half-godlike, half-human beings',
played the heroic roles to which they seemed destined:
Caesar, Scipio, Pompey, Cyrus, Alexander or Achilles
belonged to them twice over since they were the favourite
protagonists of *opera seria* and all the composers re-used
without any scruples the same libretti, containing the same
plots from mythology or ancient history. During the eighteenth century a subject such as *L'Olimpiade* was set to
music by Vivaldi, Pergolesi, Federici, Traetta and Cima-
roso, to mention only the leading composers, and the libretto for *Armida* was taken up in turn by Sacchini, Sarti,
Jommelli, Mysliveçek and Gluck. The principal records
were beaten by the libretti of Zeno or Metastasio, which
experienced unprecedented popularity, especially *Didone
abbandonata*, *Alessandro nelle Indie* and *Semiramide
riconosciuta*. It is understandable that the Abbé Ortes
wrote to Hasse that the *opera seria* was 'warmed-up broth',
even if the public accepted it very happily: an old libretto,
used twenty times over with a new score, was wonderfully
well received, while an opera performed the previous
season had no chance of success the following year.

Metastasio and the other poets had to follow the golden
rule for a good librettist: they had to render, in fine verse,
both a good story and what Eximeno called 'the expression
of the most tender feelings and the most violent passions
of the human heart'. In practice the most difficult thing

was to share out the principal male roles, taken by castrati or even by women, since the vogue for high voices out-stripped all other dramatic considerations: an opera was based only on soprano and contralto voices, accompanied by one or two tenors. The poet and composer had the thankless task of constructing their story with voices that were more or less the same while respecting the absurd demands of the principal singers. The leading castrato (*primo uomo*), the leading female singer (*prima donna*) and the leading tenor must each sing five arias of a different kind: pathetic, *cantabile* (tender feelings), spoken (express-ing agitation or passion), *demi-caractère* (serious but less dignified or less pathetic) and a bravura aria. Between these fifteen arias the composer had to insert four arias for the second castrato, four for the *seconda donna*, and three for the possible remaining characters.

Opera seria was always a work *a pezzi chiusi* ('closed' pieces), that is to say composed of a series of arias and ensembles fairly independent of each other and much more valuable through their own intrinsic beauty than through their musical and dramatic link with the rest of the work. The order of the arias caused an endless problem: the mel-odies sung by the second singers were intended to enhance the value of those sung by the first, a *virtuoso* or a *prima donna* must not leave the stage after certain tragic situations without singing an aria, just as one singer could not be left on stage after an aria sung by another. Neither was there any question of killing the hero. 'It is a rule in Italy,' said the Président de Brosses, 'that there must never be any bloodshed on the stage ... through the murder of one of the principal characters, not even when the plot includes the most appalling deeds in the world ... The people who are killed are totally subordinate.'[21] The contracts signed between entrepreneurs, librettists and performers set out all these demands, then one day an impresario would ask the librettist to entrust a supplementary aria of this or that type to the *primo uomo*, and the next day this same castrato would write insisting that he must always enter on horseback, even into a room within a palace.

Once these details were settled Achilles could finally leave Scyros and Alexander could set out for India. It is fairly difficult for us to form a precise idea about the behaviour of the singers on stage, for the descriptions by their contemporaries vary. Italians and foreigners have left us highly contradictory accounts. The French were surely the hardest to please. Misson expressed his revulsion for these 'cripples' with girls' voices and feeble chins who attempted to perform 'rodomantades', all brag and bluster. The Abbé Labat could barely tolerate these singers 'as fat as capons' who opened a large mouth 'producing a thin voice that was a mere thread and going through endless contortions in order to lend more grace to their roulades.'[22] Espinchal wondered how people could accept the illusion of Caesar's death when the role of Mark Antony was taken by a castrato. The Swedish writer Grosley seemed hardly more convinced. 'Moreover I was unable to share the pleasure derived by the Italians from these effeminate voices. They emerge from bodies which are so little in keeping with them: these bodies are made up of parts which fit so badly together; their movements in the theatre are so heavy and clumsy that I would always have preferred an ordinary voice in an ordinary body to the most marvellous *musico*.'[23] The English diarist Addison agreed with him: 'The subjects are often based on some famous deeds by the ancient Greeks or Romans, who sometimes appear rather ridiculous, for who can easily hear without suffering one of those ancient and proud Romans utter cries through the mouth of a eunuch?'[24]

More unusually, some Italians chose to criticise the castrati's acting, or rather their lack of stage reality. 'What would the Greeks and Romans say,' wrote Tragiense in the middle of the eighteenth century, 'if they saw Agamemnon, Pyrrhus, Hector, Seleucius, Cyrus, Alexander the Great, Attilius Regulus, Papirius Cursor, Caesar, Nero or Hadrian played by a castrato with the face and voice of a woman, with feeble effeminate gestures, languid from habit, who becomes seductive when he is angry, pleasing when he wants to appear frightening and amusing when he tries to express grief ?'[25]

This criticism, very rare on the part of the Italians, was in fact submerged in the ocean of praise which had brought about the triumph of the castrati for more than two centuries. Their strength lay elsewhere, and certainly not in the over-intellectual attitude of many foreigners. It mattered little to the Italians that Scipio was a soprano and Pompey a contralto, that Hydaspes fought for twenty minutes with a make-believe lion while vocalising in all keys, or that Narcissus fell in love not with himself but with the nymph Echo! All these operatic conventions had been accepted for a long time and the Italians thought that it was only those French Cartesians who chose to assess and dissect what was dramatic and what was not. The Italians, and along with them many foreign courts, went to the theatre with only one aim: to enjoy themselves, to enjoy the performance, the matchless voice of the *musico*, his gestures, his escapades and his whims, his confrontation with the *prima donna*, his struggle with the 'cruel monster' or his feigned terror in the 'fearful wood'; they wanted to enjoy everything. For the Italians the crucial word 'enjoyment' swept away all prejudices and discussions concerning castration, the dissolute morality of the singers and the pseudo-absurdity of these heroes of antiquity with their high voices.

In the satisfaction of this unlimited desire for overwhelming emotions and sensual pleasures the *virtuosi* knew no equals; the great castrati possessed simultaneously masculine presence and feminine grace, they were equally at ease in vocal fireworks and the heartrending expression of pathos, their voices were both flexible and agile, tender and powerful. As a result they had no difficulty in captivating their audiences and making them weep. An indescribable sensuality emanated from their acting and their asexual voices, causing men to shiver and women to faint, creating that moment of vertiginous delight that might partially compensate the singers for what they had lost.

It is understandable that once foreigners had heard the voices of the leading castrati in Italy, in the supercharged atmosphere of the theatres, they might change their minds. Grosley himself, who had ridiculed these 'effeminate voices' and bodies 'badly fitted together', had to make this admission later after having heard the aria *Misero Pargoletto* from *Demofonte* by Metastasio and Hasse: 'The French people present at this performance forgot the clumsy appearance of the castrato who was playing Timante, along with the contrast between his voice and his great height, his vast arms and legs, and mingled their tears with those of the Neapolitans.'[26]

Escapades and temperaments

The public today often attack great singers who refuse to go on stage unless they have drunk a certain mineral water or a particular type of tisane. The public forget that frequent performances, accumulated fatigue and the degree of concentration necessary can easily lead to minor tantrums of this sort. With two or three exceptions the great castrati of the seventeenth and eighteenth centuries were no more capricious than the women singers who performed beside them or the divas of today. They too had their moods, their weaknesses and their financial demands. The much talked about, long-standing image of the castrato as arrogant and capricious by nature makes no sense, although it can be explained by the inevitable abuses by some singers and by the often exaggerated criticisms in the satires and lampoons current at the time; if you didn't like the castrati that was enough to transform them very quickly into monsters.

However, it cannot be denied that the success of these singers, which might be very rapid, could easily go to their heads. They had been born into poor or very minor bourgeois families and brought up in strict, austere schools and conservatoires where there was no scope for originality in behaviour or dress; then, in all their youth and strength they burst upon the Italian stage, they were adored by the public, they could wear rich clothes and live in luxury. This was enough to turn the heads of several singers. Matteuccio, for example, had left Naples worshipped by 'his' public, but had not taken advantage of the fact. After travelling and experiencing other triumphs he returned as a hero, acclaimed by the crowd but also intoxicated by such an easy life. The memoir writers and the press did not hesitate to point out the fact. Confuorto wrote in his *Giornale di Napoli*: 'This eunuch, since his return from Germany, has become inordinately proud and takes no heed of any person, even a great one.'[27] One day the Viceroy summoned him to his presence. In order to avoid going Matteucio pretended he was ill and provoked the sovereign's wrath. The Queen, who was more diplomatic than her husband, made the castrato come, requested him to present his excuses and things went no further. Disobedience to the sovereign could have serious consequences.

Anecdotes of this kind are not rare for it is true that certain singers were not overendowed with modesty. A poem of the period satirised a *parvenu* castrato for beating his valet unreasonably because he had not addressed him as *illustrissimo*. This arrogance towards servants was also directed at composers and the public. One day a castrato complained to the composer Galuppi that he had not written a good enough part for him and on purpose he bungled his finest romantic aria before a full house. Galuppi was angry, turned towards the audience and announced that he would sing it himself in order to prove how good it was. The audience, who relished the scene, applauded the *maestro*'s courage even if his voice was not splendid. The castrato, somewhat put out, addressed the audience directly: 'Ladies and gentlemen, I did not want to sing the romance simply because it meant nothing to me to do so, but I can sing it better than he can. Silence, listen!' He sang sublimely and received an ovation from the spectators who were not put off by one display of tantrums.

A similar attitude could easily be found in the most elevated spheres, involving princes or sovereigns, even the Pope himself. In Senegaglia, at the beginning of the nineteenth century, the castrato Velluti provoked a near-diplomatic incident. The theatre was so brightly illuminated by poor oil lighting and tallow candles that the heat and smoke affected everyone's breathing. The Princess of Wales, who was present at the performance, had requested that the opera should start with Act II. Velluti, seeing the danger from this smoke, flatly refused to sing. To crown it all he stated categorically, 'My throat deserves a Queen!' After the performance had been suspended for a long time Velluti, under pressure from the authorities, finally agreed to begin but took good care, as he came on stage, not to make the usual bow to the Princess. In the same way Senesino was dismissed by the court at Dresden for refusing to sing an aria that he did not like.

An equally entertaining incident took place in Rome when Pope Benedict XIII died. At the Teatro Aliberti the

castrato Carestini ('Cusanino') was in the process of singing his great aria *lasciatemi* (leave me), when he was told
of the Pope's death and was asked to stop singing as
a mark of respect. Carestini, far from allowing himself
to be silenced by the news, continued to sing with more
skill and humour, concentrating on the word *lasciatemi*,
so relevant in the circumstances. The audience, who
also did not want any interruption to such a fine evening,
gave him an ovation with much repetition of '*Evviva
Carestini!*'

Behaviour that consisted of mere pretentiousness and
passing whims among the castrati as a whole developed into
a permanent life-style for the two phenomenal characters
Caffarelli and Marchesi. The former had few personal
assets, apart from his voice, one of the finest of the century.
He was somewhat antipathetic, violent, arrogant, incom-
parably vain and more given to tantrums than a spoilt child.
His perpetually disrespectful attitude was largely responsible for bequeathing to posterity the unfortunate public
image of the castrati which has already been mentioned.
Insulting in turn sovereigns, impresarios, singers and audiences, he committed excesses in both the theatre and private
life which no one would have tolerated if he had not been
the great Caffarelli. He was the archetype of those singers
attacked by Benedetto Marcello in his famous satire *Il
Teatro alla moda*. The moment he went on stage he would
pour scorn on the public, go up to a box between two
parts of an aria in order to converse with a lady and behave
as though he were in his own salon; he would take snuff
during the orchestral *ritornello*, refuse to sing with his partners if he did not want to, laugh at them openly while they
were singing their aria or would answer them with an echo
and make the audience roar with laughter.

If Caffarelli was always sure of himself he did not always
live up to his reputation as a singer and could not avoid

some bitter changes in attitude, as happened in Vienna where he caused great displeasure. Metastasio was no doubt less objective since he was the close friend of Farinelli, his rival, but he did not hesitate to criticise his 'out of tune, strident and uncontrolled voice', his bad taste in classical works and he even added: 'In the recitatives he looks like an elderly nun, for everything he sings has a tearful quality of lamentation which leads you from pleasure to boredom.'[28] In fact Caffarelli was so humiliated by his setback in Vienna that he was forced to show more modesty and submissiveness.

Composers and poets had to grovel before him, satisfy his slightest wishes and, by tradition, pay him their humble respects when they were summoned to collaborate with him in a theatrical production. In fact this is what Gluck refused to do, when his *Clemenza di Tito* was first performed in Naples. The composer had already had so many problems with singers that he could not humiliate himself before Caffarelli. The *virtuoso* was offended at this, discussions took place and finally, by some unknown miracle, the singer consented to offer his respects to 'the divine Bohemian'. Perhaps because Gluck had stood up to him the two embarked on a lasting friendship. Burney too found little cause for complaint about Caffarelli and left us a more or less flattering portrait of him. He met him one evening in Naples at the house of Lord Fortrose. The castrato arrived half-way through the evening, in very good humour, and for once readily agreed to sing, accompanying himself on the harpsichord. Burney noticed a few weak notes but admitted to being won over by the grace and expressiveness in the *virtuoso's* performance.

The excesses of Luigi Marchesi repeated in a way the well-known tantrums of certain castrati during the late seventeenth or early eighteenth centuries, but all this belonged to the past and was outmoded by the years 1790–

1800. The other soprano castrati had already adopted a simple style of acting along with modesty and the search for realistic and straightforward emotion, which contrasted strangely with the vanity and prancing gait of Marchesi. The singer was endowed with a face of extreme beauty, two magnificent bright eyes and a perfectly proportioned body; his voice had a wide range, going from flute-like soprano notes to the more 'virile' tenor ones. In fact he was not really antipathetic and even showed himself rather bold in refusing twice over to sing before generals when they ordered him to do so. One of them was none other than Bonaparte and the singer came within an inch of being sent into exile.

As can be imagined, Marchesi had absolutely no interest in the tender and pathetic arias which had created the reputations of Guadagni or Pacchiarotti. He only liked singing bravura arias, *arie di tempesta*, for he liked to dazzle with the most astounding vocal acrobatics. He relished ornamenting a melody in a hundred different ways, just as he fancied, his speciality being *passaggi* with sixteen double crotchets to a bar, adding vibration to the first in each group of four and expressive nuances to the remaining three. Like Caffarelli he was the obvious butt of Marcello's satire, who laughed at those interminable vocalises by the castrati during which the *maestro al cembalo* (at the harpsichord), predecessor of the modern conductor, had ample leisure to take his pinch of snuff.

Marchesi's most absurd (and most notorious) demands concerned his entry on stage. He insisted that the impresarios and composers should allow him to make his first appearance, whatever the opera, at the top of a hill, carrying a sword, a gleaming lance and wearing a helmet crowned with white and red plumes 'at least six feet high', as Stendhal described it. Marchesi insisted too on beginning with the words *Dove son io?* (where am I?) and then after an inevitable trumpet fanfare he would sing loudly *Odi lo squillo della tromba guerriera!* (Hear the sound of the war-like trumpets!); after that he invariably sang his 'portmanteau aria', *Mia speranza pur vorrei*, composed by Sarti and later included in *Achille in Sciro.* Slowly the singer would descend the steps to the stage, his weapons gleaming and the plumes on his helmet nodding, and come down to the footlights to receive the ovations of the jubilant spectators, intoxicated with splendour and beauty. Did this prove the bad and perverted taste of the Italian public? Certainly not. The opera was first and foremost a source of physical pleasures. The audience enjoyed having their breath taken away by thrilling action and an irresistible voice, they asked for nothing more. Surely theories and reasonings counted for nothing in the rapture of a single moment?

Fortune and honours

Nearly all the great castrati, like the great women singers, were extremely well paid and amassed large fortunes. The passion of the European public and the royal or princely courts for their singing even led to a continuous rise in salaries from the end of the seventeenth century. Most of the castrati knew very well how to make money out of their talent and how to raise the bidding.

All the same, not all of them were the millionaires of their day. It should not be forgotten that many of the *virtuosi* lived on their earnings and, since the opera seasons in Italy were very short, they could not exist for the entire year on such limited incomes. They had to travel in order to make up the losses caused by the months of inactivity. Since the situation abroad varied greatly from one court to another and the singers frequently had to pay their own travel and accommodation expenses, they were often left with no more than modest profits when they moved on.

Vanvitelli, for example, in 1754 noted in connection with one of the greatest singers: 'Caffariello [. . .] received less than 4,000 ducats, which hardly pleased him, for the journey costs something, maintenance and clothing cost something; he could not have had much left.'[29]

To end these general remarks, it should be remembered that being a castrato did not necessarily bring in a salary higher than that of other singers. True, the castrati came first, but they had to share stardom and high fees with the great women singers of the time, who were just as popular in the eighteenth century and in many cases were even better paid. The State Archives of Naples have preserved all the receipts and expenses for the carnival seasons since the creation of the San Carlo theatre in 1737. In 1739, for instance, during a season which included traditionally four great operas, the singer Vittoria Tesi headed the salary list with 3,396 ducats; next came Anna Maria Peruzzi with 2,768 ducats, third came the castrato Caffarelli with 2,263 ducats and finally the castrato Mariano Nicolino (not to be confused with Nicolo Grimaldi, known as 'Nicolino') with 1,838 ducats. These fees, which were very high for the period, merely emphasised the startling contrast between the payments made to singers and those made to composers. During that same season Porpora received only 200 ducats for setting to music the opera *Semiramide*, while Riccardo Broschi had only 30 ducats for composing the third act of *Demetrio*.

During the following carnival season it was by contrast Senesino who received most money, namely 3,693 ducats, and then, far behind, came Maria Santacatanea (1,108 ducats) and the tenor Amorevoli (1,053 ducats). To give an idea of the scale of these salaries, the records show that the castrati earned 460 times more than the copyist, who received only 8 ducats for the same season. If we multiply the minimum wage of today by the same amount, we can understand the dizzy heights reached by the fees of the most popular singers.

The Teatro San Carlo undertook to arrange accommodation for the leading performers and supplied them with a few rooms. The archives have preserved documents relating to the renting of two apartments in the Conservatorio della Pietà dei Turchini for the producer and the castrato Mariano Nicolino. The question of lodging arrangements for the singers was a real headache for the impresarios, for the *virtuosi* sometimes arrived with a tribe of cousins and nephews, while the *prima donna* would not travel without her dogs, cats or parrots.

The steep rise in salaries had often surprised contemporary observers. In the seventeenth century people had been so amazed at seeing 120 sequins* being given to a woman singer for one carnival season that the nickname 'Centoventi' (120) was given to her, and stuck. At the beginning of the eighteenth century the least important singer demanded 200 to 300 sequins and in 1740 Caffarelli received fees of 800 sequins plus a benefit performance worth 700 sequins, sums which had never been reached before. At the end of the century, disregarding general price inflation, Pacchiarotti obtained 1,000.

The singers, and above all the castrati, were the main financial worry for an impresario. It was better to economise on all the other expenses rather than fail to acquire one or two of the great names of the day. These latter represented luxury 'merchandise' so valuable that they were not only paid well but watched over carefully to keep them in good shape. In Rome the theatrical entrepreneurs kept them almost under lock and key to preserve them from any chill or accidents. Despite this, the fees paid to the castrati and the musicians plus the expenditure on stage

* The sequin was a gold coin of the period.

effects meant that many of these impresarios went bankrupt.

These same organisers had also to face up to the black-mail practised by certain *virtuosi*. Siface, on his way to the opera in Naples, let it be known that unless he was paid 800 ecus for two operas instead of three, he would go no farther than Rome. He presumably got his way because he fulfilled his contract as arranged. On another occasion Cusanino demanded a fee of 800 doubloons and maintained that he was even being accommodating for he was worth at least 1,100. In the end Caffarelli, who for once only asked for 500, was employed in his place.

Most of the Italian and European courts made all allow-ances for the castrati and ensured they would receive the payments they deserved. Certain princes pursued these young castrati relentlessly and then exchanged them between themselves. The electors of Bavaria were famous for their passion for sopranists. In this way, thanks to their 'scouts', they recruited the castrato Vincenzo del Prato, who sang in Stuttgart, and attached him to themselves for twenty-five years in Munich. It was there that the singer created the role of Idamante in Mozart's *Idomeneo*. Much earlier, at the start of the seventeenth century, the Duke of Mantua expended considerable energy in order to surround himself with young singers. Thanks to his henchmen they came to him from everywhere. The correspondence of this court reveals the many contracts that were arranged. On 9 June 1604 a Venetian noble recommended to him 'Paolo, a Spanish eunuch singer', who lived in his house and offered to come to work for His Highness. Without being asked twice the Duke received him on 20 June. In 1607 he was sent a certain Giovanni Gualberto, 'a young castrato'. Two years later a Florentine tried unsuccessfully to obtain two castrati who belonged to the court of Mantua, while a relative of the Duke, Ercole Gonzaga, permitted his young sopranist Pittorello to sing during a ballet staged at the residence of the Marchese di Caravaggio. It should also be remembered that it was the Duke of Mantua who had caused the French page Pierre-Valentin to be abducted and sent to Venice for castration. Three years after this episode, while the young man was indulging in escapades all over Italy, an actress, Anna Vittoria Ubaldini, thought it worthwhile to tell the Duke of Mantua that she had found a boy with a superb voice, but this could not have been 'Valentino' for he was only eighteen and had not been castrated; to which she hastened to add: 'But that can still be done!'[30]

The court at Turin accorded high status to its *musici armonici*, among whom there was always one castrato who received the best salary and as a result enjoyed the highest social standing. In about 1650 Chiarini received 2,250 livres, while the best instrumentalists only got 1,275. Ten years later Charles Emmanuel II had the contraltist Rascarino brought from Genoa for his sister's wedding and hastened to keep him in his service with an annual salary of 1,800 livres. In 1689 Cortona was invited to Turin for the carnival and the following year it was Siface's turn. A century later Marchesi was named *musico* at this same court, with a very good salary and permission to travel for nine months each year.

Apart from France, which held the record for meanness, a fact that will be mentioned again, all foreign countries showed great generosity towards the castrati: London, Vienna, Lisbon, Moscow and the German courts offered them good money, as they did women singers and instrumentalists. As a general rule the mere fact of being Italian guaranteed musicians abroad fees twice as high as those paid to local performers. It can be imagined how much jealousy this could cause, and more than one castrato fell into an ambush at night and was beaten by rivals who showed little understanding.

Sarah Goudar, who was always critical of the *virtuosi*, declared that England had been 'the first country to pay a eunuch £2,000 sterling per year to sing arias'.[31] She regretted the example given to other countries by England and almost rejoiced in the Lisbon earthquake, without which 'the eunuchs would have seized all the gold from Brazil'. It is true that the English were among the most generous: £1,000 per season for Caffarelli, £1,500 for Farinelli, Senesino and Cuzzoni, representing astronomical sums for the period. At the beginning of the nineteenth century no one could give less than £2,500 to Velluti!

But these sums were only the tip of the iceberg. The English were accustomed to showering their famous guests with gifts and payments in kind. These presents, given by the nobility and the gentry, were then listed in detail in the London gazettes, with the names of the generous donors: a pair of diamond buckles given by . . . , a diamond ring given by . . . , a banknote enclosed inside a luxurious gold box, a gold snuffbox carved with the legend of Orpheus charming the wild beasts, and so on. Caffarelli had the gift of irritating the English through his tantrums and his bad humour, but Farinelli, as in all countries through which he passed, was their beloved son. On the evening of his last performance he received, in addition to gifts, presents of money from all prominent members of the aristocracy: 200 guineas from the Prince of Wales, £100 sterling from the Spanish ambassador, £50 from the ambassador of His Imperial Majesty, from the Duke of Leeds, the Countess of Portmore, Lord Burlington . . . Such largesse meant that Farinelli at least trebled his income and his official earnings of £1,500 were easily turned into £5,000 each season.

This was the envied fate of the most famous performers. Other singers, who were less well known, did not leave with considerable fortunes and there was no danger, as has sometimes been alleged, that they would have palazzos

Eighteenth-century engraving celebrating the great singers of the time, including many of the castrati, in a collection of portrait medallions. *Photo: Bibliothèque Nationale de France - Paris*

Carlo Broschi, known as Farinelli, the most famous of the castrati. Portrait by Bartolomeo Nazari, 1734. *Photo: Royal College of Music, London*

Theatre set by L.O. Burnacini for Antonio Draghi's opera *Il Fuoco eterno* (1674). The scene is the interior of a Roman senate house and shows the use of perspective which was the forte of the Italian stage designers. Contemporary engraving by Matthäus Küsel. *Photo by courtesy of the Board of Trustees of the Victoria & Albert Museum, London*

Antonio Bernacchi, castrato. From an engraving by G. Van der Gucht. *Photo: Hulton Deutsch Collection Limited*

Giovanni Carestini, known as Cusanino. Mezzotint by J. Faber, 1735, from a painting by George Knapton. *Photo: Royal College of Music, London*

George Frideric Handel, who adapted the Italian style of opera for his own compositions and included many castrati roles. Painting by Balthazar Denner, 1728. *Photo by courtesy of the National Portrait Gallery, London*

Above: Engraving by William Hogarth satirising Handel's opera *Flavio* (1723). The singers are the castrato Senesino, the soprano Cuzzoni and the bass Berenstadt. *Photo by courtesy of the Board of Trustees of the Victoria & Albert Museum, London*

Francesco Bernardi, known as Senesino. Mezzotint by Alex. Vanhaecken, after Thomas Hudson. *Photo: Royal College of Music, London*

Venanzio Rauzzini, who retired to Bath at the end of his operatic career spent largely in London and Dublin, one of the few Italian castrati who did not return to their native land. Stipple engraving by Robert Hancock after a painting by J. Hutchisson.
Photo:Bibliothèque Nationale de France - Paris

Queen Christina of Sweden, the most enthusiastic royal patron of the castrati. Detail from a painting by Pierre-Louis Dumesnil the Younger (1698-1781): 'Queen Christina of Sweden and her court'.*Photo: Giraudon/Bridgeman Art Library*

Facing page: Farinelli (centre) with his lifelong friend Metastasio (left), the singer Teresa Castellini and the painter himself. Jacopo Amigoni (1692-1752), Italian: 'Portrait Group:The Singer Farinelli and Friends' c.1750-52. Oil on canvas, 172.8 x 245.1 cm, Felton Bequest, 1949. *Photo: National Gallery of Victoria, Melbourne, Australia*

Luigi Marchesi, known for his unruly temperament on stage. Engraving by L. Schiavonetti after a painting by R. Cosway. *Photo: Bibliothèque Nationale de France - Paris*

Giovanni Battista Velluti, the last of the operatic castrati, as he appeared in the opera *Il Trajano*. From an engraving. *Photo: Bibliothèque Nationale de France - Paris*

G.B. VELLUTI

built on their return to Italy. The castrato Balatri, for example, confirmed that generous gifts were received but regretted that less famous singers were not paid also in hard cash. When he appeared in London he was amazed by the number of watches, rings and swords given to him but found it somewhat unkind that he received no actual money at all. If the singers left London more often than not with empty pockets this was because life in the capital was particularly expensive. The performers spent a lot of money on accommodation, if not on gambling. They often incurred debts and left very quietly.

Everywhere else the sums of money paid were more than worthwhile, sometimes even exceeding the hopes of the singers. Balatri was amazed to receive 4,000 florins for ten months in Vienna and 1,000 florins for singing in the Elector Prince of Bavaria's chapel, although he was far from overworked there. For one season Matteuccio obtained the remarkable sum of 3,000 ecus for appearances in the Emperor's chapel. The great female singers, too, showed themselves to be just as demanding as their friends (or enemies) the castrati. One day La Gabrielli was engaged by the Tsarina of Russia, and demanded 5,000 ducats! The sovereign reeled on her throne at this and exclaimed that none of her field-marshals received such a sum. Without flinching La Gabrielli replied, 'Very well, Your Majesty has only to make her field-marshals sing!' And Catherine II paid the 5,000 ducats.

In addition to fees and gifts many castrati were honoured by the sovereigns themselves and received high distinctions. Nothing was too good for them. In 1645 Ferri had the signal honour of being summoned by Queen Christina of Sweden, while he was in the service of the Polish court. The two countries were at war. Christina demanded a truce and begged the King to lend her for two weeks the sopranist who was the talk of all Europe. She then sent her own royal ship to Poland to fetch him, and hostilities ceased provisionally. Ferri, like Nicolino and Guadagni later, received the envied title of Knight of the Cross of St Mark, and a medal was even struck in his honour. One face showed his head, crowned with laurels, while the other revealed a dying swan on the banks of the Meander river beneath a lyre descending from heaven.

In 1657 Atto Melani, who acted as a secret agent for Cardinal Mazarin, received in Paris the title of Gentleman of the Bedchamber. Matteuccio found himself doubly rewarded by the Emperor of Austria and the King of Spain. The latter conferred on him a high office at the Hôtel de la Monnaie in Naples, for the duration of his life and also for 'another life after his own'. In the absence of any descendants the sopranist named Doctor Domenico Terminiello as his successor. As for the Emperor, he awarded him a title of nobility which allowed Matteuccio to style himself thereafter as 'Marchese Sassano'.

In 1739 Senesino had the honour of singing in the Palazzo Pitti in a duet with the Archduchess Maria-Theresa, the future Empress of Austria. Farinelli, after so many good and loyal services to the court of Spain, was named Commander of the Order of Calatrava, a decoration only awarded previously to the grandees of Spain. In another field it was the castrato Tenducci who in 1784 became director of the Handel festivals in Westminster Abbey.

The most entertaining incident of all took place at the beginning of the nineteenth century, involving one of the last castrati, Girolamo Crescentini. Napoleon, who had been captivated by his voice in Vienna, had him brought to Paris for his court theatre and awarded him the cross of the Crown of Lombardy, an honour given only to the best officers. The latter were much displeased at seeing such a distinction awarded to a singer, that is a common mountebank, and a castrato at that! They were ill-advised enough to complain about it one evening in front of Madame Grassini, the other great performer at the court theatre and a friend of the castrato. Upset at hearing such remarks about Crescentini, she stood up and cried, with her little Italian accent, 'But you forget his *wownd*!'

6
The Castrati and
the Church

On Good Friday morning I went to the Sistine Chapel to hear Allegri's famous *Miserere*, sung by sopranists, unaccompanied. It was truly the music of angels.

Madame VIGÉE-LEBRUN

The Church always maintained a somewhat confused and ambiguous attitude towards a subject as delicate as castration. It firmly condemned this mutilation and those who practised it, but always protected the castrati to the extent of being the last institution to make use of them, even at the start of the twentieth century. The number of its choir schools certainly allowed it to favour the proliferation of sopranists and on several occasions authorised it without question, because singing of any kind celebrated the glory of God.

Robert Sayer (or Sayrus, in Latin), the English Benedictine moralist of the late sixteenth century, who spent his last years in Venice, dying there in 1602, said, 'The voice is a faculty more precious than virility, since it is through his voice and his reasoning that man is distinguished from animals. If therefore it is necessary to suppress virility in order to enhance the voice, it can be done without impiety. Now the voices of sopranists are so necessary for singing the praise of God that they are beyond price.'[1] A little later a Sicilian Jesuit, Tommaso Tamburini (1591–1675), explained that castration was legal, 'on condition that there is no danger of death and that it is not performed without the boy's consent. The reasons given are that eunuchs serve the common good by singing the divine prayers much more sweetly in the churches; and also that the preservation of the voice should certainly be considered by the boys as an advantage not to be neglected, since through this voice they improve their way of life, and throughout their entire existence they obtain financial support and the patronage of the nobility.'[2] Statements of this kind, which certainly reflected the opinion of many churchmen, were nonetheless denied by many casuists who referred back to ancient texts in their condemnation of all castration without valid medical reasons.

The Popes and castration

The relationships between the Papacy and the practice of castration form a long story full of changing attitudes. Apart from the eunuch singers who took part in the Byzantine religious ceremonies, the Western Christian world seems to have been content for its church music to be performed by children and falsettos, reflecting in this way the words of the Bible, *Mulier absit a choro* (woman must be absent from the choir). The Papacy did not face up to the problem of the castrati before the sixteenth century: after that it was perfectly well aware of their presence in Spain, and perhaps even in Italy, but did not actually acknowledge the fact.

At the end of the sixteenth century Gregory XIV (1590–1591) tried to enoble the practice of castration but did not have time to do so. Clement VIII (1592–1605) completed what Gregory had not been able to do. He opened the

Pontifical choir to the Italian sopranists, which was more an official recognition of the castrati than a true innovation since the latter were presumably present in the choir from the middle of the sixteenth century, described as 'falsettos'. Clement VIII and his successors were fascinated by these voices, which were still very much in a minority, and acted quickly to replace all the soprano falsettos by castrati, so much so that in 1625 not a single one remained in the Sistine Chapel. From that time the falsetto voice was described as 'artificial' and the voice resulting from the operation was 'natural'.

From all points of view Innocent XI (1676–1689) was one of the least understanding popes. Since he was sour-tempered and systematically opposed to everything he had been nicknamed 'Minga', a Milanese dialect word meaning 'no'. We owe him one particularly famous tragi-comic incident. Since the Church did not permit the marriage of eunuchs, every request of this kind had to go through the hands of the Pope. The castrato Cortona had fallen madly in love with a woman named Barbaruccia and wanted to marry her. He therefore wrote a petition to the Pope, explaining that since his castration had been badly carried out (which was meaningless) he was perfectly fit for marriage. Innocent XI read the letter but remained uncompromising: he merely wrote in the margin, 'Let him be castrated better!'

Despite the somewhat hypocritical hesitations of Benedict XIV (1740–1758) there was evidence of a change of heart during the eighteenth century. This latter pope in fact decided to distance himself from castration and began to talk of 'an unnatural crime the victims of which are young boys, often through the complicity of their parents.' He recognised that the Church was well aware of the origins of the singers it employed but, like all the other popes, and in view of the universal success of the castrati, he avoided the possibility of laws that might militate against castration.

The 'flexibility' of the popes concerning the theory and practice of castration had also allowed the adaptation of the canons of the Church concerning castrati in the priesthood, since many castrati who had not experienced the hoped-for results from the operation turned towards the religious life. During his trip to Italy La Lande was amazed by this attitude: 'Apparently a form of barbarity is authorised in Rome whereby those unfortunates who can no longer rely on their voices are given permission to become priests: according to canon law anyone whose members are not complete would not be in order, but it is said that a form of words can be introduced, which acts as a kind of palliative, but it does not reduce the indecency of this practice.'[3]

During the eighteenth century the Church, as we have already mentioned, excommunicated anyone who performed castration. Benedict XIV began with the decree that 'the amputation of any part of the human body is never legal, except when the entire body cannot be saved from destruction by any other method.' Clement XIV (1769–1775) in his turn forbade any preparation for singing which aimed at giving an artificial voice to young boys; but he never had the courage to exclude the castrati from his chapel, and the conservatoires continued to train them. In order to suppress the passion for this phenomenon he allowed women to sing in the churches and take soprano parts, while in the same way he permitted them to appear in the theatre in the Papal States. These measures did not produce immediate results but it is certain that in conjunction with the current of ideas discernible at the end of the eighteenth century and the decline in the teaching of song in the conservatoires, they probably played a part in the progressive disappearance of the castrati at the transition between the eighteenth and nineteenth centuries.

After the years 1800–1830 and the departure from the stage of the last two great sopranists, the Church was alone in facing the eternal problem of the eunuch singers. After the whole of Europe had relegated them to oblivion, only a few choir schools and the Sistine Chapel continued to welcome them. Condemnation and polemics were no longer in fashion. The question, on the contrary, was rather that of knowing whether one should 'abandon' these 'unfortunates' who, cut off from the golden age of the castrati, found no other refuge outside the Church. This was discussed in so much detail that the entire century went by without any solution being found. During the years preceding the twentieth century Perosi, *maestro* in the Sistine Chapel, fought to have castrati finally removed from his choir. However, he came up against the violent opposition of the sopranist Mustafà, who was very keen to protect the last prerogatives of his peers. But Perosi won in the end, even if it was only in 1902 that Pope Leo XIII signed the order which banished castrati from the Sistine Chapel for ever. Out of courtesy the survivors were not driven out as though unclean: it was found preferable to let them leave as they wished. Alessandro Moreschi brought up the rear in 1913, after leaving us several recordings of his voice.

Music in church

The Italian choir schools, and especially the Sistine Chapel, were very possessive of their castrati; they took care of them, ensured good incomes for them and as far as possible removed from them the temptation to 'look elsewhere'. In about 1780 the churches in the city of Rome alone employed more than two hundred castrati. However, their entry into the great Italian religious centres had not been as easy as it had been in Rome. In Naples, for example, when the castrato-priest of the Chapel Royal, Ottavio Gaudiosi, was appointed canon of the Cathedral, the event caused an outcry from the metropolitan Chapter who maintained that ever since the founding of the church in Naples there had never been any eunuchs among its members. The protest was in vain and Gaudiosi occupied the post for which he had been nominated. The affair proves that the large-scale appointment of castrati at the beginning of the seventeenth century had been truly an unprecedented phenomenon and for that reason was not without problems.

As a general rule the theatres offered serious competition to the Church, for they were enormously attractive to singers and to the castrati in particular. It should be noted that in the chapel of San Marco in Venice the tenors and basses were the best paid singers until the appearance of the operatic theatres. After that the chapel began to pay its sopranists very well indeed, in order to compete with the fees paid by the theatres. However, payments within the Church still remained far below those made to singers in opera, and many members of the chapel refused to stay for this one reason. This is why, in 1765, the number of singers at San Marco was reduced by one third in order to ensure better payments for each of them. Pacchiariotti, for example, received 300 ducats while the tenor Pasini and the bass De Mezzo had only 150. Venice gave sumptuous rewards to the castrati who passed through its cathedral; Rubinelli, Marchesi and Crescentini could boast of having sung before the Doge and of having received from his hands the *Osella d'oro*, the medal of old gold that was struck every year for the Christmas festivities.

Sometimes certain of the chapel singers were requested by the Venetian theatres to sing female roles, and the non-clerical members were invited by foreign cities and courts. In this way Cavalli took the castrato Calegari to Paris and Bertoni had Pacchiarotti accompany him to London. Naturally the procurators were particularly unwilling to authorise their absence, for the chapel was deprived of its good singers for a long time and could never be sure that they would return.

The singers in the Sistine Chapel were almost all clerks or priests. This had not necessarily been the case earlier, and it is known that Paul IV (1555-1559) had excluded married men from his choir, one of them being the composer who was to provide the basic repertoire of the Sistine Chapel until the twentieth century—Giovanni Palestrina. It looks as though the Papal Chapel also experienced desertions and periods of crisis, since a Vatican document of 1761 deplores the fact, blaming 'the multiplicity of theatres and the various princes who invite the *Musici* (castrati) from Rome and Italy, offering them excessive salaries; as a result these singers no longer set much store by the Papal Chapel.'[4]

Despite certain problems of this sort, coming rather late in the day, the Papal Chapel could pride itself on possessing great singers and composers. In 1622 it welcomed the first great Italian castrato, Loreto Vittori, and then, seven years later, Padre Gregorio Allegri who was apparently a mediocre castrato but a man of infinite kindness and a remarkable composer. His *Miserere* was preserved in the Vatican as a unique treasure, and later Popes forbade its diffusion and reproduction. Mozart heard it at the Vatican and copied it down from memory after leaving the Sistine Chapel, though there was nothing exceptionally difficult about that, given the simplicity of the work and the talent of Mozart. All foreign visitors passing through Rome made it a duty to hear the *Miserere*, if the liturgical calendar allowed it. Montesquieu's description of it is close to that of Madame Vigée-Lebrun: 'I have seen the ceremonies of Holy Week. The thing that pleased me most was a *Miserere* so unusual that the voices of the castrati sound like organ-music.'[5] In the course of a historical description of the Papal Chapel written in 1711, Adami lavishes 'eternal praise' on his companion Allegri and his *Miserere*, 'which ravishes the soul of any listener', and then adds, 'the loss of this great man was felt with infinite regret by our entire college.'[6] After him came other important personages: 1660 saw the entry of the tenor Antonio Cesti, famous composer of the opera *La Dori*, then two years later came the contraltist and composer Matteo Simonelli who was to become the teacher of Arcangelo Corelli.

As a general rule the Papal Chapel possessed a choir of thirty-two singers in groups of eight: all the *sopranos* were castrati, while the *contraltos* were falsettos for a very long time despite occasional attempts to replace them by castrati. Siface was the first to sing there in this capacity, but he had to sing soprano although he was a contralto. Some 70 per cent of the singers were Italian and 30 per cent foreign, including 10 per cent of Spaniards. There followed a few Frenchmen and Swiss . . . The majority of the sopranists came from the Papal States, then came natives of the Kingdom of Naples and of Tuscany, all of which corresponded perfectly to the general geographical distribution of the Italian castrati.

All the singers in the Papal Chapel choir joined it at the age of about twenty or twenty-five, resided in the principal Roman parishes and had to leave the choir after twenty-five years of service. They were dependent on the protection of a cardinal and were directed by a *maestro* elected by themselves. Apart from holidays they were entitled to two free days each week, except during major religious festivals, and they rehearsed or sang in services on the remaining five days. Their participation was limited to the services in the Chapel, especially the Papal mass, as well as to some external ceremonies in the city of Rome. Some of them might even be sent more or less anywhere within the Papal States.

In the San Marco chapel in Venice there were between twenty-eight and thirty-six singers, including thirteen *sopranos* and four *contraltos*. In Naples the royal palace chapel was more modest and contented itself with eighteen singers, including five *sopranos* and five *contraltos*. It was there that the two great castrati Nicolino and Matteuccio made their débuts, then left very soon to go on the stage. In the chapel of the Tresoro di San Gennaro in the cathedral the castrati clearly predominated. The list of all the members from 1663 to 1790 included no fewer than forty-five castrati out of sixty-five. Lastly, in Turin, there were two chapels in the cathedral: the chapel of the Innocenti, with six boys who were not castrated, and that of the Cantori where the singing was shared between *choristi*, priests or future priests, and *musici*, lay or castrated. Famous *virtuosi* were called in from neighbouring states for the major festivals.

The theatres in the Papal States

During the years 1585–1590 Sixtus V had promulgated a first decree aimed at preventing women from acting in the theatre, but the opera did not yet exist. This measure did not last and had no consequences during the next few decades. The birth of the opera, followed by its rapid and growing success during the seventeenth century, began to cause conflicts between the public, the performers and the papacy. It is true that on many occasions 'sound moral behaviour' had not been maintained during the performances since the women singers had devoted themselves more to libertinage and debauchery than to the serious exercise of their profession. Since their reputation was not of the best during the course of the seventeenth century more than one pope began to fear for public morality.

The situation remained the same until the arrival of Pope Clement IX (1667–1669), who was well disposed towards music since he was himself the librettist of an opera, *La Baldassarra o la Comica del Cielo*, written when he was still only Cardinal Rospigliosi, papal nuncio in Spain. Anton Maria Abbatini had composed the music. It was performed seven times during his pontificate, in 1668, and the Pope took all possible steps to make it into a real triumph. He asked Bernini to organise the stage effects and Monsignor Lodovico Lenzi to direct the orchestra. The subject was cleverly chosen since it presented a theatrical performance within an opera, with a superb final apotheosis, well worthy of the baroque era, during which a choir of angels accompanied Baldassara to heaven, while the seven Virtues danced a ballet. The Rome press praised these performances: 'This evening Monsignor Rospigliosi's comedy *La Baldassara comica convertita* [sic] was given again, a splendid opera, composed by the Pope, good music, good performers, with rich costumes and fine, graceful stage effects, the inventions of Bernini causing it to appear curious and extravagant.'[7] However, the Pope made no concession to women in this presentation; all the female roles were sung by castrati, accompanied by a few tenors and basses: La Baldassara, Thalia, Urana and Beatrice were performed respectively by the castrati Giuseppe Fedi, Francesco Maria Fede, Damaso and Domenico del Pane.

Clement X showed himself to be even more liberal since he was quite willing to allow women back on the stage. They were unquestionably successful during the opera seasons of 1669 to 1676, in particular at the Teatro Tor di Nona. Their popularity, but also the frivolity and the scenes of collective dissipation that they brought about merely infuriated Clement X's successor, the famous 'Minga' pope, Innocent XI, already ill-disposed by nature towards the race of women. With his accession to the throne decrees multiplied: he forbade women to appear on the stage, prohibited public performances with an admission charge and even did his utmost to prevent free private performances, threatening the castrati who took part in them with banishment from the churches of the Eternal City. The Romans, who were not easily defeated, quickly got round the papal decree by bringing in castrati from outside the Papal States, who were unaffected by the ban, and by thinking up subterfuges which would make public 'commercial' performances look like free private ones. The misogyny of His Holiness even extended to women's clothes described as 'French style', that is, too *décolleté*: he sent his henchmen into all the laundries of the city to confiscate any women's chemises regarded as indecent. Queen Christina of Sweden, who was an exile in Rome at the time, saw this as yet another means of attacking the Pope, which delighted her. She invented a range of clothes dubbed 'Innocentian', which parodied and ridiculed the bans imposed by Innocent XI. She and her court wore them to the Vatican in order to infuriate him all the more.

His successor, Alexander VIII, nicknamed the 'Pantaloon Pope' (after a character in the Commedia dell'Arte), brought a breath of fresh air into this musical and social climate which had been made so dull by his predecessor. During his too short reign—1689–1691—he authorised a return to normality and freedom in public entertainments. The carnivals of 1690 and 1691 were said to be the wildest and most amusing of the seventeenth century. But everything changed very quickly with the arrival of Innocent XII, the 'Punchinello Pope', who was fiercely opposed to both theatres and actresses. He provoked a period of unprecedented anger in Rome, causing satires and demonstrations of hostility against him. The crisis reached its climax in 1697 when the Pope, as a reprisal, had the fine

Teatro di Nona razed to the ground before the indignant Romans.

Nothing changed at the start of the eighteenth century with Clement XI: he simply banned women from singing, even at home, on the pretext that it was 'detrimental to that modesty which becomes their sex so well' and prevented them from working at their household tasks. He decreed therefore that 'no woman, married, widowed or spinster, should learn to sing or act'. He even appealed to husbands and tutors never to allow any music teacher into a woman's house.

Not until the accession of Clement XIV, in 1769, did the situation ease a little. He obliged the theatre directors to ban the ridiculous custom of giving female roles to young boys, men in disguise or castrati. As mentioned earlier, he also allowed women to sing in churches. Before this new situation, for nearly a century, all manner of strange behaviour had been possible. Castrati had moved cheerfully from singing the liturgy to an opera performance in one half-day and young Roman women had passed themselves off as castrati in order to escape the ban and appear on the stage. After all, was disguise not the essence of baroque festivities? This was how one of Casanova's women friends succeeded in deceiving the priest whose task was to examine each new singer: she assumed the clothes and mannerisms of a castrato and fixed an evocative object at the crucial place.

Another practice that made the Papal States different from the other states was the constant use of castrati in women's roles, whereas they generally played the heroic parts of warriors and kings. It is true that many of them began their career in Rome in female parts but immediately went abroad and changed roles. In Rome therefore a large number of castrati were always needed for the leading feminine roles, far more than for masculine roles: it was known as *far da donna*, doing women. In 1698 the French diarist Raguenet saw the contraltist Ferrini and wrote: 'Dressed as a Persian princess, as he was, with turban and aigrette, he looked like a queen and an empress, and it is possible that none more beautiful has ever been seen on earth than he appeared in that costume.'[8]

It is clear that the papal laws also affected the ballets. All the 'danseuses' were in fact men in disguise and the prevailing prudishness even extended to marionettes, as the Abbé Richard stated in 1769: 'Ballerinas are not allowed on the Roman stage. They are boys dressed as women and the police order them to wear little black drawers. The same decree applies to ballerina-marionettes which, in revealing their wooden thighs, might also excite the senses of the seminarists.'[9] Of course this ill-advised prudery brought about no improvements and the 'immorality' said to exist in women could also emanate from men. This earned the reproaches of Tragiense in the middle of the eighteenth century, even though it was a time of some early liberalisation: 'It is true that in certain theatres handsome young boys disguised as women can be seen dancing in their place; but it is also true that their attitudes and movements appear much more licentious or dissolute than those of the women themselves.'[10] Espinchal, like most of the French, was hardly enthusiastic: 'What pleasure can one find in a ballet when the *première danseuse* is a boy?'[11] Baron Pöllnitz felt equally disillusioned by the singers: 'There is nothing more ridiculous than seeing these half-men pretending to be women: they have neither expression nor grace: however, they receive the same applause here as the best actresses do elsewhere.'[12]

All in all, the Roman customs imposed by the Church formed the butt of endless satires and lampoons in the Eternal City as in the whole of the country. The subject was too tempting and the Italians too fond of derision not to take advantage of the situation, as proved by this anonymous eighteenth-century satirical sonnet, preserved in the Palermo Library and included here in a prose translation: 'Can Rome tolerate that in its [Papal] States a rascally castrato actor can imitate a woman in order to entertain priests? Rather, if the priests want to show kindness, they had better castrate the other cardinals instead; like that the College will have no c ...'[13]

The craze for opera and disguise had in fact won over the whole of ecclesiastical Italy in the eighteenth century. In Venice certain priests could take part in opera performances; Saint-Didier tells us how, one evening when he was present, a spectator called out, 'Look, there's Padre Pierro playing the old woman.' Nearly half a century later Nemeiz found that monks were playing in the orchestra at the theatre. In certain Florentine convents comedies with music and short ballets were performed; in one place the novice friars disguised themselves as ballerinas and in another nuns acted the parts of men. During some carnivals the Teatro della Pergola had even organised special operatic performances for monks in the Florentine convents: the performance began earlier for they were not allowed to stay out after midnight and the ticket price was reduced. These were shows, as they said, for 'masks and monks'. Through more or less the whole of Italy monasteries accepted the music of their time: in one place monks sang opera, in another enclosed nuns formed a string orchestra. One day there was even a pitched battle between the nuns in a convent, who could not agree about whether they should perform opera or not: one of them perished in the fight, killed with knife thrusts before being thrown down a well, and there were also several wounded!

7
The Castrati in Society

Mutilation had turned him into a monster but all the qualities
that embellished him made him an angel.

CASANOVA
(writing of Salimbeni)

The castrati and women

In Florence, during the eighteenth century, people enjoyed
quoting a witty remark by a young woman spectator after
listening to the castrato Cusanino: 'He sings well, one has
to say: he's lively and expressive, but one feels there's something missing . . .'

One fact is certain: this 'something' hardly seems to have
traumatised the women of the seventeenth and eighteenth
centuries who, with the exception of French women, were
wild about the castrati, unbelievably so. Their voices were
enchanting, their nobility and refinement on stage were
seductive and they were also perfect Don Juans in everyday
life, in the salons and even in the intimacy of the bedroom.
Scenes of collective hysteria were witnessed everywhere,
comparable to those caused among young people today
by the appearance of pop stars. And the kind of stage
personalities involved leads to a similar comparison: surely
David Bowie, Michael Jackson, Prince or Madonna possess

the same type of androgynous sensuality and eroticism that could be observed, with some adaptation obviously, among the castrati? If eye-witness accounts are to be believed, the men and women of the baroque era fainted with pleasure at the disturbing beauty not only of their voices but of their entire being. Was this merely the attraction of a circus phenomenon? Was it the search by the ladies for a love-life without danger? Or the exceptional power of a voice that numbed reason and led to 'the delights of paradise'? The idealisation of a 'supernatural' being who belonged to both sexes without knowing the limits of either? We shall never really understand the intimate motivations of each spectator, man or woman, in their relationships with the castrati, but the near-universal success of the singers with women is truly intriguing.

During the seventeenth century Vittori, during public or private appearances, drove the crowd into a frenzy. People fought to get into the churches where he was singing and stormed the palazzos where he was singing to the aristocracy. Ferri aroused enthusiasm more overwhelming than anything seen before. When he arrived in Florence a procession came to meet him more than four kilometres outside the city gates in order to escort him and carry him back in triumph. On another occasion, after a performance, a masked figure (was it a man or a woman?) placed on his finger a priceless emerald ring—the singer never knew the identity of his generous admirer.

For these singers, as for their successors, the noble ladies displayed boundless transports of delight: they threw tributes on to the stage, laurel wreaths, couplets or passionate sonnets, and went nowhere without a portrait of their favourite castrato over their hearts. Marchesi, despite his extravagant impulses and his tomfoolery on stage, was perhaps the singer most adored by the fair sex. His youth, beauty and talent, all the deception that he practised with so much skill, sent the ladies into ecstasies. Stendhal tells us that in Vienna Marchesi had become the court mascot—the women wore medallions with his portrait, one round their necks, one on each arm, and two others sewn onto their shoes. Madame Vigée-Lebrun described similar reactions to Crescentini: 'In the end he succeeded Marchesi, whom all the Roman ladies were wild about, so much so that at the last performance he gave they made no attempt to hide their grief: several even wept bitterly, a sight that many people found as entertaining as the actual performance.'[1]

The hearts that the castrati caused to beat faster could form a 'catalogue' of amorous adventures, like that recounted by Leporello in Mozart's *Don Giovanni*. Here now are some of the most striking of them.

The most exclusive: The castrato Bernacchi had a mistress, the singer Antonia Merighi. His devouring passion for this woman led him to isolate the two of them, thanks to certain acts of blackmail. He agreed to remain in Naples only if La Merighi was engaged along with him and in particular if his principal rival, the sopranist Cusanino, was dismissed. The king, who wanted him at any price, agreed to his demands, but the Neapolitan nobility supported Cusanino, whom they valued highly. The king gave way and Bernacchi had to leave Naples on the arm of his lady-love.

The most prudent: The court of Turin had taken umbrage at the escapades of its favourite *musico armonico*, Chiarini. The singer was conducting a stormy relationship with a well-born lady of the kingdom and had every reason to believe that his beloved's family would cause him serious trouble. Prudently, he withdrew from his engagement and left for Paris, where he took part in the first performance of Cavalli's *Serse* and *Ercole amante* in 1660 and 1662. It was also prudence which caused Rauzzini to leave the court at Munich, in order to escape the anger of the many husbands whom he had turned into cuckolds. Within living memory the Bavarians had never seen a man (a castrato, what was more!) turn the heads of so many aristocratic ladies at the same time.

The most amusing: The great Caffarelli often angered his public through his scornful attitude and bad temper, but the women were at his feet, and were at a loss to know how to attract his favours. Among his many amorous liaisons was one which he maintained for a fairly long time with an aristocratic Roman lady. Sadly for them, her husband finally got wind of the affair and one evening tried to take them by surprise. Caffarelli only had time to hide in the garden well, where he remained all night. He caught cold and had to spend a month in bed. Shortly afterwards the husband set a trap for him, but he made a miraculous escape. After that the castrato never went out in Rome without an escort of four hired men, paid for by the young wife, who was still in love. Caffarelli, finding the situation uncomfortable, finally chose to move to Venice.

The most respectable: The castrato Consolino had given rise to much talk during his liaison with the Marchesa Vittoria Lepri, but she threw herself into the arms of a 'monsignore' and thereby dismissed him. A daring lampoon by Pasquino about this affair had then gone round Rome: 'If your natural inclination is only for the pleasures of a man with no nuts, why for heaven's sake did you then choose for your new love someone with nothing in his nut?'[2] Consolino found comfort again in the arms of a noble lady who was much in love with him but very rigid about moral principles: to preserve appearances she demanded that whenever he visited her he should wear the woman's costume he had worn in the theatre.

The most sporting: A Neapolitan marchesa, while listening to Pacchiarotti in Schuster's *Didon abandonnée*, fainted away, and then vowed to the castrato passionate and eternal love. The lady's lover, far less impressed than she was, challenged the singer to a duel, but the latter emerged from it alive, to the great delight of his admirers.

The most tragic: Siface, late in life, had fallen in love with a widow in Bologna, the sister of the Marchese Marsili. The affair gently displeased the lady's family, who hastily made her enter the convent of San Lorenzo in Bologna. The castrato, who was quite undeterred, succeeded in gaining entry to the place and continued his amorous adventure at the point where he had left off. However, he was foolish enough to boast indiscreetly about his exploits to anyone willing to listen. The family reacted quickly and Siface, who was only 44, was assassinated on 29 May 1697 by the Marchese Marsili's men on the road from Bologna to Ferrara. Although this liaison was common knowledge, Confuorto, in his Neapolitan journal, described the event with astonishing reticence, explaining the crime 'by the fact (it is said) that the castrato often went to entertain with his singing a sister of the said Marchese despite the formal prohibition of the latter, and there may have been some suspicion of dishonesty.' Such an account meant that the reputation of the great singer would surely not be tarnished.

We remember only the odd or comical aspects of these stories, but they all reveal some important information about the private lives of the castrati. These are obviously only a few anecdotes among many, and concern only the great singers: it can be assumed that the sexual adventures of the other sopranists, those who were obscure or unknown, were just as numerous, and that they could not all be attributed to fame. As we have seen earlier, castration could reduce sexual desire and render each man's performance unpredictable, but it certainly did not destroy sexuality, as the many amorous adventures we know about serve to prove. How far did sexuality go in each case? Certainly, and fortunately, that will remain a secret for ever, but medically speaking it can be assumed that in the best cases it was more or less normal.

There is one interesting detail found in nearly all their liaisons: the fact that the beloved was a member of the minor nobility or the great aristocracy of the court. Several interpretations are possible. The simplest and most obvious is that through their fame, their behaviour and their fortunes, the great castrati frequented precisely that stratum of society, were received at courts and palaces and enjoyed a flattering reputation. There was nothing exceptional about their meetings with noble ladies. It is known also that through the system of alliances and arranged marriages many young aristocratic women were forced to marry men they did not love, even sullen elderly barons. In that century of frivolity and badinage a liaison with a castrato could offer women enjoyment without disastrous consequences. Finally, for the more cultivated ladies, was there not a kind of intellectualised love in a relationship with a castrato, a kind of love which was idealised and therefore possibly much more beautiful? In the same circumstances a little peasant girl from Apulia or a Neapolitan water-seller would probably have found it pointless. At the same time it must not be assumed that the castrati, as singers and as men, formed the choice morsel, the *petite folie* of an elegant and cultivated society, the only one able to appreciate their talents. Through the public theatres, and not only those attached to the courts, working people had access to the opera, contributed greatly to the triumph of the castrati and often showed themselves to be the most eager and the most demanding during the performances.

The sincere love felt by certain castrati for a woman sometimes led them into marriage and if this occasionally ended in failure it was never the fault of the couple them-

selves but of the society in which they lived. We have
already mentioned the story of Cortona who begged the
Pope to authorise his marriage and was merely told to
have himself castrated better. This was an extreme case,
occurring during one of the worst periods of obscurantism
when the Pope preferred to take refuge behind strict legis-
lation rather than create a precedent. Other cases occurred
during the eighteenth century when the pressure from the
Church relaxed a little and the marriage often took place
outside Italy with Protestant women. The castrato Filippo
Finazzi married Gertrude Steinmetz, a Protestant woman
from Hamburg with whom he lived a life without incident.
Much more dramatic was the secret marriage of Bartolomeo de Sorlisi to a young German woman. Eventually the
truth came out and the couple found themselves the butt
of so much sarcasm and unkindness that the poor castrato
did not have the strength to fight back and died of despair.

Society's hostility and failure to understand also affected
the life of Tenducci, the great sopranist who had taught
singing to the young Mozart for a year, in London. The
details of his story remain obscure but they can be summed
up as follows: in 1766 the singer wanted to marry an Irish
Protestant from Limerick. The marriage took place but
caused an enormous scandal since, according to the spiteful
remark by Ange Goudar, 'the two necessary witnesses
were missing'. The young woman's parents, who were
fiercely hostile, did everything they could to obtain an
annulment of this union. It is less clear if the marriage fell
apart or if it lasted despite the obstacles. In the meantime an
additional problem arose for the couple: the young woman
became pregnant and gave birth to a boy, to the great
surprise of everyone, especially her husband. She probably
wanted him to accept paternity for the child, since Tenducci addressed to her one single discerning remark: 'Faith-
less woman, you can see that this child is not mine, since

I cannot give to anyone what I do not possess myself.' Casanova's version, which is quite different, seems hardly plausible; according to him Tenducci, who had been born *triorchis* (with three testicles), must have been inadequately castrated and therefore capable of begetting children. Obviously, if this were the case, the singer would not have possessed all the characteristics of a true castrato, but that was not observed by any of his contemporaries. Despite the lasting uncertainty about this story one thing at least is clear: thanks to the pressure exerted by the young woman's family the marriage was finally annulled nine years later, in 1775.

For the castrati, women were not only a source of limited romances or eternal love, they were also partners with whom cooperation, thanks to professional rivalry, was often less easy. The history of relationships between *primo uomo* and *prima donna* dates essentially from the eighteenth century. Before that women singers, who were not very numerous, often not very talented and regarded as immoral or dissolute, had not yet acquired the social status and popularity that were to make them into queens of song after 1700. The castrati were constantly forced to share the favour of the public with them and confront them in fearsome vocal contests, if the opportunity presented itself. Sometimes they would even oust them from their top billing by singing the role of *primo uomo*. This is what happened, for example, on the evening when the San Carlo was inaugurated and Vittoria Tesi played the title role in *Demetrio*. In fact nobody was very enthusiastic about the distribution of roles. La Tesi complained that 'playing a man' was harmful to her health and Anna Peruzzi protested at being only *seconda donna*. She was persuaded to accept it by the explanation that her rival was singing a man's part and therefore there was no true competition. A singer

like Maria Maddalena Musi in fact hardly ever sang anything except masculine roles *en travesti* for the whole of
her career.

In other operas the women singers interpreted the great
heroines who backed up the leading roles of kings and
captains taken by the castrati. The eighteenth century produced a very fine succession of exceptional female singers
who followed a prestigious European career: La Merighi,
La Cuzzoni, Faustina Bordoni, wife of the Saxon composer
Hasse, La Tesi, La Gabrielli, nicknamed 'Coghetta' because
she was the daughter of the cook (*cuoco*) of Prince Gabrielli, La De Amicis, Maria Maddalena Musi, nicknamed
'La Mignatta' (the leech) and Vittoria Tarquini, known as
'La Bombace', the favourite of Ferdinand de' Medici.

As a general rule the castrati did not fear competition
from the *prima donnas*, for these men were more numerous, possessed voices rendered unassailable by the very
intense vocal training they had received, and enjoyed a
special place in the hearts of the public. Moreover, the
women singers often made themselves unpopular by their
endless tantrums, their intrigues, their unreasonable
demands and their haughty manner towards men. La Gabrielli, for example, could show generosity and unselfish-
ness, qualities she possessed in addition to her astonishing
beauty and what appeared to be eternal youth, since at the
age of thirty she looked eighteen. This is what made Brydone say that this 'most dangerous siren of modern times'
had made 'more conquests than any other living woman.'[3]
Unfortunately her impossible character very often turned
this 'sacred monster' into a monster that was not sacred at
all. According to Brydone again, this supplied a complete
antidote to the charm of her voice and physique. Her
intrigues at the Austrian court had brought about her
expulsion from Vienna and her attitude when on stage had
made all European theatres lose patience with her. When

she chose, La Gabrielli was capable of giving her entire self, singing with all her heart, displaying a vocal mastery and a gift for tragic acting beyond compare. But such moments were rare, and her capricious and temperamental behaviour spoilt everything. A minor quarrel with her director, a timid whistle of disapproval from a spectator were enough to stop her in her tracks like a tiresome adolescent girl. She would then deliberately sing badly and in an undertone, reinforced with scornful glances at the audience.

Her quarrelsome nature outweighed all her other faults. One day when the Viceroy of Palermo had invited her to a luncheon, to be attended by all the Italo-Spanish nobility, she did not condescend to go. The guests were made to wait, she was sent for and found to be reading in bed, pretending she had forgotten. She sang the opera unwillingly and with only a quarter of her vocal power. The Viceroy scolded her, but the more he threatened the less she sang, arguing that he could make her cry but certainly could not make her sing if she did not want to. The affair ended in prison, where she spent twelve days. Out of bravado she began to give daily concerts in the prison, sang divinely, paid all the prisoners' debts and distributed her money to those most in need. The Viceroy was greatly put out but finally liberated her; she left the gaol to the acclamations of the prisoners and the poor.

She displayed the same impudence in her dealings with the castrati, and the latter felt very uncomfortable with her. Mazzanti suffered from this in 1766, in Naples, when he had to stand up to the domineering diva. She began in the first place by refusing to sing a duet with him, probably regarding him as unworthy of such an encounter. Being forced to sing, she began, in the middle of the duet, to improvise acrobatic flights nicely calculated to destroy her partner. The latter begged her, as soon as he could, to respect the score, to which she replied boldly, in front of the audience: 'Follow me, anyone who can!' She repeated this ham performance every evening, but it did her no good. At one of the last performances she tried to take so many risks in order to humiliate the sopranist that she went completely wrong in her vocalises and left the stage in tears, without completing the duet.

Faced with La Gabrielli and a few other women of the same kind, some castrati admitted to moments of sheer panic. In 1724 Balatri, not, it must be said, one of the greatest castrati, was terrified on finding himself beside Faustina (Bordoni) on a theatre stage. With his usual humour he asked himself, 'When a crane is next to a canary, what can she do?' Fortunately for him, his voice and gestures pleased the audience and he admitted that he had managed to get through the performances as best he could, without receiving the slightest show of scorn from Faustina.

Things were not so simple when Pacchiarotti, who was still rather inexperienced, had to face up to De Amicis in Palermo. When the castrato was in Naples on his way to Sicily he received a formal protest from the singer, stating her refusal to compromise herself with a second-rate beginner. The Neapolitan authorities therefore asked him to give proof of his talent, since only Venice and the north so far knew his worth. At the San Carlo he performed two arias from his repertoire as an examination in *passaggio* work, in the presence of Caffarelli and the composer Piccini. The result of the test surpassed all hopes and people begged him to choose between Palermo and the San Carlo. It would have been a greater honour for him to choose Naples, as this would have added more brilliance to his début in the south, but, out of pride, following the insult from De Amicis, he decided to go to Palermo and accepted the offer from San Carlo for the following two years.

The first encounter between the castrato and the diva could not have been more icy: the 'charming' singer asked him to learn his role, if he was capable of it, for she had no time to waste. Never once did she agree to sing a duet with him during the various rehearsals, saying that the dress rehearsal would be enough. On the evening of the so-called 'première' the royal theatre was full, everyone wanting to see 'their' singer perform the inevitable role of Dido. The first aria sung by De Amicis provoked wild enthusiasm, while that of Pacchiarotti was received with general indifference. De Amicis expected that the duet would destroy him completely and almost succeeded on her first entry, which was applauded by the audience. Pacchiarotti followed her and began to attract the attention of the astonished spectators. Since the public were on the diva's side she performed all the vocal pirouettes she could; the castrato outdid her, using a new style of ornamentation of every type, trills, appoggiaturas, bursts of pathos ... The crowd, overflowing with excitement, yelled for an encore. The two singers took the whole thing a stage further with new effects in pathos, new skill in ornamentation and the evening was transformed into an occasion of unique enjoyment for the Palermo audience.

When she left Sicily the singer to whom Pacchiarotti bade farewell was a changed woman: Madame De Amicis, overwhelmed by his talent and touched by his courage, confessed her embarrassment and showed him all possible signs of her affection and admiration.

Masculine rivalries and friendships

The behaviour of the castrati between themselves was more or less identical with that of the great modern divas and all artistes in general: some knew each other well, appreciated and respected each other, while others were jealous and hated each other. The same was true of the famous women singers of the eighteenth century, with La Cuzzoni and Faustina Bordoni making a typical pair of 'warring sisters'.

There was certainly nothing surprising about the rivalry and jealousy among the sopranists. If they were evenly matched they would be on the lookout for the same contracts in the greatest theatres, they coveted the same honours, the same public acclaim; the youngest and most handsome among them were likewise aware of being observed and envied by those who were less so. Defence of their prerogatives, fear of a reversal in their fortunes and the latent envy that some of them nursed deep in their hearts hardly urged them to welcome their rivals. When they dispersed across Europe this resentment tended to fade, but it revived whenever an 'intruder' was announced in the same city and the same theatre, depending on the contracts signed by the impresarios.

The intransigent attitude of Bernacchi, when he demanded the dismissal of Cusanino as his price for appearing in Naples, has already been mentioned. Pistocchi was hardly more enthusiastic when he saw the famous Matteuccio arrive in Florence, engaged to sing with him a motet by Alessandro Scarlatti at the church of Santissima Annunziata. It is very probable that his illustrious rival far outstripped him during the concert and the rewards they received remain significant. The composer was given a gold snuff-box, Matteuccio many gifts and Pistocchi nothing at all. Rather than display his rancour and attack his rival openly he preferred to conceal the truth and pass himself off to all those who had not been able to attend as the one who had scored the greatest triumph. 'You can imagine,' he wrote to his friend Giacomo Perti in Bologna, 'that curiosity about hearing Matteuccio and myself had attracted to this church all the singers, musicians and persons of talent! The motet as a whole was not well received, neither was Matteuccio, and the teachers were even less enthusiastic. And truly, if I had had to give my opinion that day it would not have been very favourable. Scarlatti assures me that many people told him that Matteuccio had sung too much and was not heard with favour, while I sang too little and was heard with infinite pleasure; and many people also told me the same thing.'[4] A good way to bolster one's morale!

Caffarelli, the most temperamental and difficult of all the castrati, adopted a whole range of possible attitudes towards his colleagues. Searing humour suited him very well; he used it one day to put down a young Florentine singer who was murdering the arias in his repertoire. The impatient Caffarelli asked him who were his patrons: 'Jesus and Music!' replied the unfortunate young man with pride. 'Then commend yourself to the former,' replied Caffarelli, 'for you've little to hope for from the latter!' His fits of anger were not necessarily limited to words but could easily be transformed into direct action. One can imagine the astonishment of the congregation present at a religious service in the church of Donna Regina in Naples when they saw two castrati, Caffarelli and Reginella, fighting like a pair of tramps in the middle of the ceremony. Nobody really knew the reason: was it the haughty arrogance on the part of Caffarelli towards a singer less known than he was, although he was the same age, disagreement between the two men about the interpretation of the melody, or jealousy about the unequal lengths of their parts in the score? One thing is certain: Caffarelli knocked Reginella down and he had to be taken out. Such a deed was punishable by prison, but the name of the guilty party was too famous: as soon as the king heard it he exonerated him.

Fortunately Caffarelli could appear in a better light and recognise the merit of certain colleagues. As we know he had given outstanding support to Pacchiarotti after his 'examination' at the San Carlo. He showed equal under-standing towards Gizziello at the latter's début in Rome. Caffarelli knew his teacher Gizzi, in Naples, and had heard endless praise of the young sopranist. He decided therefore to see for himself and go to Rome to hear him. He jumped into the first mail-coach available, travelled all night and went to the theatre wrapped up in a cloak. Gizziello's talent and beautiful voice exceeded all expectations. Caffarelli was won over and could only join in the cheers from the audi-ence. We can imagine the happy surprise of the young débutant. 'Bravo, bravissimo, Gizziello!' he heard, 'This is Caffarelli saying so!' After that, without any unnecessary delay, the famous castrato returned to Naples as hastily as he had come to Rome.

The meeting between Bernacchi and the young Farinelli took place on the stage in Bologna. The former was forty-two, the latter twenty years younger. It is not known how Bernacchi envisaged this confrontation with a young cas-trato who was already the talk of Italy, but we can imagine that he arrived with the firm intention of not letting himself be impressed by this young débutant who could have been his student. The evening offered the public an exceptional vocal duel. Farinelli sang first and deployed all the vocal agility he could muster, trying visibly to 'attack' the older man. The latter riposted by taking up again, one by one, each of the ornamentations performed by the young singer and adding others even more astonishing. Far from ranging one against the other this memorable contest in Bologna created a firm friendship between them which lasted all their lives. Farinelli, who was too intelligent to despise advice from the best singers, continued to frequent Bernacchi's house and learn from him all he did not know.

The most astonishing incident which took place on stage between two castrati occurred in London in 1734 and became a standard anecdote, reported many times by the writers of the eighteenth and nineteenth centuries. Senesino and Farinelli both found themselves in the English capital; they knew each other by reputation but had never had the opportunity to sing together. This opportunity occurred when Senesino, after leaving Handel, founded the Opera of the Nobility, a rival troupe which included among others Farinelli and La Cuzzoni. It was decided to bring these two sacred monsters together in one opera and make this evening the crowning achievement of the London musical season. The contraltist Senesino played the role of a dreaded tyrant who kept an unfortunate prince, played by the sopranist Farinelli, chained up like a slave. In his first aria the latter had to express his despair and beg his implacable gaoler for mercy. Farinelli sang in such an overwhelming manner, finding such penetrating accents of despair, that Senesino, ignoring the contempt of the public and all dramatic credibility, was moved to tears, threw himself into his partner's arms and embraced him at length. Even if there was something histrionic about such an attitude, it was the first time a castrato was seen to give public proof of his admiration for one of his rivals.

Friendly or affectionate relationships between the castrati and other men are naturally less well known, for they belong to the private life of each singer. The biographies of the most famous castrati reveal no precise case of homosexuality, whereas romantic adventures with women predominate widely. We can of course only discuss the greatest of them and as a result hundreds of life-stories are unknown to us. It is very likely, too, that relationships of this type remained more deeply concealed at such a period. There is only one story, an official one, according to which Cortona, after the Pope had refused to sanction his marriage, actually changed his predilection and became the favourite of Jean-Gaston de' Medici, son of Cosimo III.

However, the possible homosexuality of the castrati formed one of the main topics of debate at the time among Italians and others. Curiously enough, they were often accused of corrupting morals, although those who were mostly in the public eye had no cause to reproach themselves in this respect. It was castration that was on trial and even more so the abuses of cross-dressing, rather than the castrati themselves.

It goes without saying that if the majority of the public admired the *virtuosi*, the lampoons directed against them emanated from a minority of intellectuals fiercely hostile to every deviation in the realm of social morality. For example, some people reproached the castrati for daring to take sexual pleasure of any kind, even with women, since they could not father children, which in any case implied 'impurity'. Ancillon, in his *Traité des eunuques*, accepted that they were great lovers but added somewhat harshly: 'It is certain, however, that a eunuch can only satisfy the desires of the flesh, sensuality, passion, debauchery, impurity, voluptuousness and lechery. Since they are not capable of engendering children they are more sought after by debauched women, because they provide them with the pleasures of marriage unaccompanied by any of its risks.'[5] There then followed a long legal discussion as to whether a man who could not beget children had the right to marry or not. Ancillon was a typical representative of the austere and moralising fringe of his time. In fact the castrati were no more inclined to sexual crime than other men, no more than the women who had emotional relationships with them were necessarily debauchees.

Violent lampoons attacked the 'dangers' of transvestism and were for that reason out of place at a period when carnivals, opera and the other arts elevated sexual ambiguity into a kind of game inseparable from daily life. However, it is true that the papal laws forbidding women from appearing on the stage in order to safeguard public moral-ity, favoured the feminisation of many men, castrati or not, in operas as well as in plays or ballets. This led to endless liaisons between actors and spectators, between protectors and protégés.

Many young castrati in Rome were kept by ecclesiastical personalities such as abbés, priests, or monsignori, and such relationships, in the context of the period, were often far from chaste. The protectors paid court assiduously to their young protégés, visited them in the morning, took them out in the afternoon, were present in their dressing-rooms while they were being made up and dressed, and showered them with gifts and billets-doux. Casanova tells how he saw at the Teatro Aliberti a young castrato who was the favourite of Cardinal Borghese and took supper with him every evening, tête-à-tête. The most minor singer had not only his protector but his frenzied admirers who showered him with impassioned sonnets. Cimarosa gave us an example in verses addressed by a bedazzled poet to the castrato he adored: 'When you sing, your smooth voice/ Swiftly moves from ear to heart/Awaking pleasure, awaking love/And the saddest thoughts flee wandering away.'[6]

The total illusion created by cross-dressing is borne out by many descriptions. 'These unfortunate men,' says Arch-enholz, 'have carried imitation so far that anyone who is not knowledgeable on the subject, seeing them from a distance, could not guess their sex. Since the greatest diffi-culty has been removed by the nature of their voices, they attempt by their carriage, gestures, movements and facial expression to imitate women, in such a way that from this point of view the illusion is complete.'[7] Madame du Boccage told how in Rome, in 1758, people admired 'the attractive Battistini who, disguised as a soubrette, displayed such graceful airs and attitudes that the cardinal Vicaire responsible for inspecting the actors forbade him to act without gloves or to shorten his skirts.'[8]

Montesquieu made the same observation and saw it as bound to encourage loose morals: 'In Rome, women do not appear on the stage; [their parts] are played by castrati dressed as women. This has a very bad effect on morals, for nothing, as far as I know, is more likely to inspire philosophical love in the Romans.'[9] Had Montesquieu actually seen so many examples? Was he not using this as a pretext for condemning castration, an attitude very common among the French at that time? Was he attacking in a more general way Italian behaviour, especially Roman behaviour, as it had been described to him? It was said in France that from the end of the sixteenth century sodomitic love was practised 'in Spain by knights, in France by nobles and pedants, in Germany by very few people and in Italy by everyone.' Henry Estienne also made this commentary: 'Today sodomy is becoming more and more common, because people frequent the countries that see it as a profession and a form of merchandise. Moreover, if anyone examines which Frenchmen are prone to such vices, they will find that nearly all of them have been in Italy or Turkey or, without leaving France, have mixed with people from those countries or at least conversed with those who have learnt from them.'[10] Even the Président de Brosses, on seeing in Rome men dressed as women and in Naples women dressed as men, was afraid that such confusion might often lead to fornication.

The number of young castrati in Rome singing women's roles, the intense pursuit of femininity by several of them and the general passion for cross-dressing among both men and women brought about burning passions. Casanova, for instance, owed one of his best romantic escapades to a woman whom he first knew dressed as a castrato. The young lady, Teresa Lanti, probably received her musical education from the castrato Salimbeni, who lived in her father's house. The great singer had protected her, as well as a young boy named Bellini, whose father had caused him to be castrated. When Salimbeni went to Rome, leaving his young protégée, she decided to pass herself off as Bellini, who had just died, fairly young. Casanova saw her dressed as a castrato and was fascinated by her beauty. 'But I, far from closing my eyes, observed those of Bellini which were black and full of fire, seeming to throw out sparks, I could feel them burning me.' Although Casanova was in love at first with this false castrato he soon suspected the deceit. 'So, despite outside appearances, I got it into my head that the so-called Bellini was no more than a beautiful girl in disguise and as my imagination was in full flight I fell deeply in love with her.'[11] The love story then took its course without trouble, after Teresa had resumed her feminine appearance. Through a taste for disguise typical of the eighteenth century, Casanova toyed with the ambiguity of his feelings right until the very start of their first night of love: just before clasping her in his arms he asked Teresa to put on the castrato's clothes again and look like a man, the way she had done on the first day he saw her.

This escapade inspired Balzac to write a famous short story which is perfectly plausible in the Rome of the baroque period. While Casanova fell in love with a castrato who revealed himself to be a woman, the French sculptor Sarrasine fell madly in love with a sopranist whom he mistook for a young girl. His ardour for his heart's desire was short-lived: he had not counted on the jealousy of Cardinal Cicognara, the protector of the young singer, who simply had him assassinated.

Even Montesquieu, who never ceased criticising Roman morals, had to admit one day how disturbing the charm of certain singers could be: 'In my time, at the Teatro

Capranica in Rome, there were two little castrati, Mariotti and Chiostra, dressed as women, who were the most beautiful creatures I have ever seen in my life, they would have inspired a taste for Gomorrah in people whose taste is the least depraved from this point of view. A young Englishman, thinking that one of these two singers was a woman, fell desperately in love with him and sustained this passion for more than a month.'[12]

Of all the male friendships known to us the finest, the closest and at the same time the most chaste was that between Metastasio and Farinelli, which lasted for their entire lives. As already mentioned, the poet and the castrato made their débuts together in Naples. The friendship born between them that day slowly grew into a deep affection that was strengthened by the singer's absence during the twenty years of his stay in Madrid. Nothing is more moving than their voluminous correspondence, of which unfortunately only Metastasio's letters to his friend have survived. Each line expresses a truly exceptional depth of feeling, a purely intellectual attachment and a wonderment at the very smallest things in life. With constant regularity, sometimes temporarily interrupted by the ups and downs of their lives, this correspondence linked them together and kept them informed about the principal affairs of state, the major achievements in opera and also about the slight cold that one or the other might have caught. Metastasio tried to begin or end each letter with a different phrase. We read for example, 'Very dear and incomparable friend', 'Dear Twin', 'Adorable Twin', 'My amiable little Carlo', 'Incomparable Twin', 'Most amiable Twin'. When Farinelli was too long in replying the poet changed to 'Inhuman Twin', and with that innate sense of drama that ran through his operas he went on: 'Are the words you write so valuable, then, that one cannot aspire to receive them without first sighing after them during several olympiads? Bar-

barian, ungrateful man, Hyrcanian tiger, deaf asp, cheetah, Apulian tarantula! For so many months it has not occurred to you to let me know if you are alive!'[13]

Despite the distance that separated Madrid from Vienna the two friends exchanged gifts. Farinelli sent cases of vanilla, snuff and Peruvian bark. The poet thanked him profusely and then changed his mind: 'But alas! This expression of thanks, brief though it is, already seems too prolix for your virginal modesty: you blush, you lose patience, now you're angry. It amuses me . . .'[14]

Was it friendship, tenderness, affection or love? It is not clear how we should describe their feelings, which is what makes these letters so charming. If some words and phrases seem to the modern reader more indicative of a homosexual relationship, we know that this was not so, and that if there was love it was entirely idealised and intellectual, sublimated by the art which united them. Metastasio in fact spoke quite plainly in one of these letters. 'I cannot express myself better than by telling you I love you as much as Farinelli deserves that love. But let us cease these tender words, lest some malignant person accuse us of some deception, like those that help to console an intolerant desire for honesty, for friendship that is affectionate, true and disinterested.'[15]

From month to month, from year to year, the two men lived 'side by side' through their correspondence. When Farinelli asked Metastasio for his portrait the latter had to be coaxed into it, excusing himself by saying that he hated posing for a painter, but gave in to his friend's wishes, asking, 'who can resist the entreaties of the beloved twin?' On another occasion the poet recommended to the Madrid court a woman singer endowed with a beautiful voice and lovely eyes. The two men later exchanged a long correspondence because Farinelli wanted to bring some thoroughbred horses from Austria to Spain and asked Metastasio to be kind enough to arrange it. After endless bargaining and complications the poet finally despatched sixteen Liechtenstein horses from Vienna to Genoa, from where they left by sea for Spain.

Each letter represents a page from their daily life, each one ending with a repeated proof of their indestructible friendship: 'Farewell, dear twin. Love me as I love you and this way you will satisfy my infinite desire for your love and you will do justice to the tender friendship I have and will always have for you!'[16]

Twins for life, Farinelli and Metastasio remained so almost in death, since they both died in the same year, 1782, within a few months of each other.

The castrati and their relatives

We possess little information about the relationships between the singers and their families, or about their filial feelings. The great castrati not only failed to write their autobiographies, they were somewhat evasive about their origins, which they preferred either to conceal or erase from their memory for ever. The case of Farinelli seems relatively exceptional while at the same time it is perfectly revealing of his character. All his life he showed kindness and generosity and constantly looked after the health and comfort of his mother who remained in Italy during his long years of absence. Through his brother and sister he made certain that she went short of nothing and supplied all her financial needs.

In all other cases the sopranists showed indifference, distrust, even hatred towards their parents. It is true that many had lost touch with them since their operation and their first studies. Family relationships at this period were different from ours today. A father or mother in charge of a large family, living in conditions which were often

wretched and in isolated villages, did not necessarily consider the loss or departure of a child as a tragedy; it was more
of a fatality, a 'blow' from destiny to which they were
resigned, and sometimes it meant one mouth less to feed.
Geographical remoteness, the lack of money and sometimes
a certain indifference meant that they did not try to find this
child again after he had become famous, unless they wanted
to ask him for help. As for the adult castrati, cut off from
their family roots by long studies, then delivered up to a
totally different world which required endless travelling,
they often had neither time nor inclination to return to
their homes. The fame and fortune they had acquired 'dis-
connected' them in a way from their family origins. A
line had been drawn. Some pamphlets even ridiculed those
castrati who, born into the humblest families now excised
from their memory for ever, boasted of noble lineage and
alleged that they counted doctors or lawyers among their
brothers. The situation was even worse for any man who
had not had the compensation of success and had become
bitter towards his father, feeling neither affection nor gratitude towards him. We have quoted in this connection the
violent reaction of Mustafà, a famous singer in the Papal
Chapel, who threatened to kill his father if he were to
learn he had been castrated for no valid medical reason but
simply to make him into a singer.

Any parents who tried to see their son again, ten or
twenty years later, could hardly expect to be thanked and
welcomed with open arms—their son's reaction might not
be the one they expected. One day a man presented himself
to Loreto Vittori and asserted that he was his father,
although the castrato did not recognise him. It is not
known whether it was really he or a profiteer. The man
insisted, and asked the singer to consider the poverty into
which he had fallen, begging him for financial help. Without turning a hair Vittori declared that he would return to

him what was owing, and coldly offered him an empty purse (*bourse* = scrotum). Many singers were to have recourse to Vittori's symbolic gesture. It is known that much later a castrato used a similar argument directed not at his parents but at King Louis XV of France. When threatened with dismissal from Versailles because the court finances could no longer maintain him, he contented himself with an ironic remark: 'It matters little to me if the King dismisses me provided that he reimburses me.'

The State archives in Naples contain statements relating to court cases between singers and their parents, as well as petitions to the King begging him to banish families who were too invasive or too 'greedy'. The castrato Giuseppe Sedoti, a pupil of Porpora, wrote to the King of Naples explaining how he was short of money, and had supported for years, in Naples or Palermo, his brothers, his sisters, his aunt and his parents, whose debts he also paid. Since he could no longer cope with such a responsibility he begged His Majesty to send his parents back to their birthplace in Arpino in exchange for a pension of 5 ducats a month. The King at once took the singer's part and let it be known that his parents had one week in which to leave Naples, under threat of imprisonment, in exchange for which the castrato paid for their journey and the upkeep of their house.

The reunion between Matteuccio and his mother was much more eventful, occurring just when the twenty-one-year-old singer, who was worshipped for his good looks as well as for his silver-toned voice, was starting to find fame and see the ducats piling up. When his mother flung herself into his arms after so many years the young man recognised her impoverished state and did not reject her in churlish fashion. He placed his house at her disposal but, having no wish to share it with her, he promptly requested hospitality from the fathers of Saint Francis of

Paola, near the Royal Palace, who gave him a small apartment in their monastery.

Unfortunately for him his mother gradually revealed herself to be something of a nuisance; people began to gossip in the city when they saw her living a fast life and changing her lovers from week to week. It was not exactly the behaviour expected from the mother of a castrato invited to sing for the Duchess of Medinaceli, wife of the Spanish ambassador and future vice-reine of Naples. In between travels, Matteuccio searched for a solution and found one. As previously mentioned he had been taken up, following his operation in a village in Apulia, by a Neapolitan barber who had brought him to the city, got him into the Conservatorio dei Poveri di Gesù Cristo and then given him moral and material support for ten years. This barber had remained unmarried. Matteuccio made him see the advantage of marriage with a woman who could supply a good dowry and explained to his mother the urgency for an honourable end to the saga. This was how, in 1694, the marriage of Alessandro di Liguoro and Livia Tommasino came to be celebrated. Matteuccio's mother found she had 'married well', for her famous son had given her a dowry of 282 ducats, with which the fortunate barber was able to buy himself a new shop, opposite the Nuncio's residence. Everyone was satisfied, especially Matteuccio who was now able to pursue his career in peace.

The patrons

> *A lato ai regi*
> *Ei siederà cantando*
> *Festoso d'aver fregi.*

> At the side of kings
> He will sit and sing,

Happy to be honoured.
PARINI, *La Musica*

Through their talent and because their voices were sought
out like the most valuable commodities, the castrati came
to mix with monarchs and princes and often felt more at
ease with them than with their families. Their musical and
literary education (sometimes including science as well)
allowed them to converse easily with the great families of
Europe and in this way to rise above their mere status of
singer. Each Italian court possessed at least one castrato
who was permanently attached to it in the capacity of
virtuoso da camera, for its religious services or theatrical
performances. The courts also invited from time to time,
for a carnival season, a very big name from the operatic
stage, paying him generously for just a few performances.
Turin, Milan, Parma, Modena, Florence or Mantua knew
nearly all the great castrati of the seventeenth and eighteenth centuries in the same way as the more prestigious
centres like Rome, Naples or Venice. The same situation
prevailed in the other European countries which appointed
the best singers for public performances, as in London or
Vienna, or for private performances at court as in Madrid,
Moscow or the German states.

Royal munificence provided one of the principal guaran-
tees of success and survival for the castrati during two
centuries. The passion among princes for these singers was
unlimited and contributed largely to spreading the vogue
for castration, so much so that early in the nineteenth century some of them had to take measures to stop this trend.
What finer example, for the father of a young boy, than
the sight of certain singers rising to dizzy social heights?
How could he fail to dream about it on his son's behalf?
Some royal houses even showed remarkable generosity
and fidelity towards a castrato: Farinelli remained at the

Spanish court for more than twenty years, while Ferri spent thirty years in the service of three successive kings of Poland and then of two German emperors.

Of all the patrons, the most generous, the most lavish, the most infatuated with the castrati was Queen Christina of Sweden, during the twenty-six years or so that she spent in Rome after her abdication. Rarely had opera, singers and musicians known a more omnipresent and faithful protector. It is true that her temperament, hard to please and terribly exclusive, made her different from others. Christina was capable of giving everything, but woe to him who betrayed her, or merely disappointed her! Her attitude towards the castrato Antonio Rivani, known as 'Ciccolino', is revealing of her personality. Although Rivani was in the service of the Queen he had gone in 1667 to the court of Charles Emmanuel II of Savoy. Unfortunately he delayed his return. Christina's reply to the Comte d'Alibert was as swift as it was severe: 'I shall never agree to his leaving my service for any other. I wish it to be known that he exists for no one except me, and that if he does not sing for me he will not sing long for anyone at all. Try to express my feelings in a way that will deter other people from making advances to him, for I wish to keep him at any price. And even if anyone tried to convince me that he has lost his voice, that would be of no avail, for whatever his condition he must live and die in my service, or he will come to a bad end.'[17] There followed a somewhat acid correspondence, not always worthy of royal persons, between herself and the Duchess of Savoy.

This passion for the castrati came as no surprise in a person as typically androgynous as Christina of Sweden, whose sexuality had been in doubt ever since she was born. All her life the Queen had allowed seduction and charm to alternate with strength and violence. All her life she had been falling madly in love with men and with women, and all her life she had been by turns Protestant and Catholic, tyrannical and submissive, entertaining and cruel, distinguished and vulgar. No person so hybrid could have failed to be attracted to beings as ambiguous as the castrati. She did all she could to have them in her service or merely to shelter them for a while. While she was in Sweden she had already brought Ferri from Poland in her royal ship. In Rome she negotiated with the Empress of Austria to obtain Cortona, as she did with the Duke of Mantua for Finalino and the women singers Salicoli and Riccioni. At Il Riario, her palazzo on the Janiculo, a true fortress for the Roman artistic world, she surrounded herself with the castrati Vittori and Fede, the *soprani* Ceccarelli and Rafaelli from the pontifical choir, and made the two great names of her time, Siface and Cortona, into her own personal castrati. She also protected Alessandro Scarlatti and befriended Arcangelo Corelli. Lastly it was she who, with the agreement of Clement IX in 1669, created the opera troupe at the Teatro Tor di Nona: there she admitted beautiful young women singers to take feminine roles rather than castrati alone.

Christina stopped at nothing in order to protect artistes, actors and women singers from the devastating authoritarianism of Pope 'Minga'. Apart from the 'Innocentians', the parody-clothes she had created to ridicule the pontiff's decrees, she provided shelter for the women singers banned form the Roman stage and allowed them to sing at Il Riario before an Academy composed of the greatest artistes and learned figures of the period. On the other hand the Queen collaborated with the more understanding popes; she explained to Alexander VII the merits of the theatres and asked him, successfully, to allow theatrical performances all through the year, not just during the carnival season. She also encouraged the building of new theatres since there were so few in 1652.

Compared to Christina of Sweden or Louis XIV, the other patrons seem lacking in panache, but they were no less essential if the singers were to flourish. Francesco II of Este also employed Siface at his court in Modena, while Ferdinand de' Medici received the greatest artistes of his time in Florence between 1683 and 1713 and developed a friendship with Alessandro Scarlatti. The Viceroys and Kings of Naples were also great patrons and favoured the castrati whom they employed continuously in their chapel in addition to the performances at their two theatres, the San Bartolomeo and the San Carlo. Huge sums were employed in the recruitment of the castrati Cortona, Siface and Nicolino, as well as Matteuccio, nicknamed 'the Nightingale of Naples'.

Some of the castrati combined their careers with diplomatic functions. Cortona played a political role in the service of the Medici. Pasqualini, who sang in the chapel, was sent to Paris by the Pope in order to influence Mazarin during the quarrel with Spain. On the other hand Mazarin made Atto Melani, who had come with him from Italy, one of his principal diplomatic agents. He named him 'gentleman of the Bedchamber' in 1657 and sent him on a mission to the Electress of Bavaria. All this did not prevent the castrato from singing in Cavalli's *Serse* before the court. He fell into disgrace through compromising himself with Fouquet but with the Pope's support he was recalled by Louis XIV who held him in high esteem and affection. In the same way his brother Bartolomeo, also a castrato, acted as diplomatic agent for Mazarin but had the misfortune to be indicted in Munich for his intrigues on behalf of the Cardinal.

Satires and pamphlets

From the early seventeenth century until the disappearance of the castrati, many satires circulated about the practice of castration and the singers themselves. The 'anomaly' of their situation, but also the jealousy they provoked in many people made them a prime target, both in Italy and abroad. It would be impossible to quote all the satires and pamphlets published during this period. Some were merely entertaining and in good taste, others attacked the castrati's infirmity in a coarse and cruel way which could only cause hurt and sadness, especially among those whose voices had let them down.

For example, a manuscript in verse from the seventeenth century, preserved in the National Library of Florence, lampooned the previously mentioned castrato Atto Melani. In it the singer is lambasted for his diplomatic and political role, but taken as a whole his vocal qualities receive more attention and the anonymous author concludes with grating humour: 'He who hears you will surely say with astonishment: how can a capon crow like a cock?'

An interesting comedy with dialogue appeared in 1630, entitled *Contrasto Musico*, an 'entertaining work' by Grazioso Uberti of Cesena. It is an educational and amusing piece in which two characters discuss a music school of low standing. Severo is a pedant, a misanthropist and a misogynist who doesn't like music. Giocondo is a bookish man who tries to understand and discuss; he does not follow music in a practical way but is trying to open his ears and his soul. Curiously enough opera is not mentioned, being too recent perhaps, unlike chamber music, musical education or religious music. The conversation focuses inevitably on the subject of castration. The two men are in fierce opposition. Severo condemns those 'inhuman persons, unworthy to be called father or teacher', who arrange operations on boys and render them 'useless for the work of nature'. Giocondo becomes angry with those who practise emasculation, those 'enemies of nature' to whom he can find nothing to say beyond, 'Cut your own off yourself!' The dialogue becomes less relaxed when they consider what judicial measures should be taken. Severo states that the damage is irreparable and that nothing can console the young castrati. Giocondo, however, is less categoric and becomes entangled in Jesuitical reasoning on which certain casuists should rely, alleging that the castrati can be consoled by the words of Isaiah: '. . . neither let the eunuch say, "Behold, I am a dry tree"; for thus saith Jehovah: "Unto the eunuchs that keep my sabbaths, and choose the things that please me, and hold fast to my covenant, even unto them will I give in my house and within my walls a place and a name better than of sons and daughters; I will give them an everlasting name, that shall not be cut off."'[18]

Salvatore Rosa became famous through a series of satires in verse about painting, poetry or war. The one entitled *La Musica* dates from 1640. The author writes ironically about people who make a living from music, the professionals, the *maestri*, the patrons, and displays considerable virulence about castration. In a famous tercet he refers to the town of Norcia which was reputed to be a centre for castration: 'Fine Cornelia law,* where hast thou gone/ Now that the whole of Norcia seems not enough/For the castration of boys?'[19]

He then mocks the success of the castrati:

Da le risa tal hor mi muoio
In veder divenir questi arroganti

* A Roman law from the Republican period prohibiting and punishing castration along with other damage to physical integrity.

Calamità del legno e del rasoio.
E non di meno son portati avanti
E favoriti dalla sorte instabile
Per la dolce malia de'suoni e'canti.

I die of laughter when I see
Their arrogance, those leftovers
From wood and razor.
And yet they are admired
And favoured through changing destiny
Thanks to the charm of their voice and their song.

Later, Rosa criticised those singers who moved calmly
from church to opera:

Chi vide mai più la modestia offesa
Far da Filli un castron la sera in palco
E la mattina il sacerdote in chiesa.[20]

How could modesty not take offence
When eunuchs play Phyllis at night on the stage
And act the priest in church by day.

No less interesting and striking is the poetry of Lodovici
Adimari, a seventeenth-century scholar who divided his
time between the courts of Mantua and Florence. His principal satires were written between 1690 and 1700; the
author, who was a total misogynist, wrote a text entitled
Against the vices of ladies and in particular those of the
women singers. Singers, musicians and castrati are not
spared since, according to him, the world of the theatre is
the world of perversion: 'Africa is better than Europe,' he
wrote, 'for at least there are neither theatres nor concerts
there.'

Being a contemporary of Siface he treated him as *superbo*
more musicorum, castratorum baronfututorum ('as proud
as all those ridiculous castrati sods') and wrote no fewer
than two hundred tercets making fun of the singer's roman-

tic involvement, the cause of his assassination. Since he did not like either Siface, Rivani or Christina or Sweden he added:

S'odon si spesso omai trilli e canzoni,
Che ogni città d'Italia ha più castrati,
Che non ha Puglia e Barberia castroni
Or di musici esperti e sopraffini
Fata sol genitrice, ha per suoi vanti
I Rivani, i Sifaci, i Cavagnini
Avvilita così con suoni e canti,
Gode de'nuovi figli, a contrappone
A molti e prischi eroi pochi birbanti.

We hear so often trills and songs,
Castrati in Italian towns
Outnumber the sheep in Apulia and Barbary.
Italy, mother today
Of skilful and famous castrati
The country is proud of men like Rivani, Siface,
    Cavagnini
And thus debased by these voices and songs
She takes a pride in her offspring
Replacing noble heroes by a handful of rogues.

In a completely different vein some eighteenth-century operas or plays formed an important body of entertaining satires in very good taste. Girolamo Gigli's *La Dirindina*, set to music by Domenico Scarlatti, is a rich satire on opera singers, their behaviour and their abuses, full of humorous allusions to castrati, patrons and artistes without talent. Don Carissimo, an elderly singing teacher, loves his young pupil Dirindina but is jealous of the castrato Liscione whom he considers to be his rival. During a rehearsal between Liscione and Dirindina, Don Carissimo makes a mistake and on listening to the young woman singing the words of Dido he sincerely believes she is expecting Liscione's child and is planning to commit suicide—the two young people are in paroxysms of laughter. In the end Don Carissimo attempts to unite them in a legitimate marriage.

To crown everything, in a city so prone to ambiguity and relaxed morals as Rome, Scarlatti's amiable and entertaining comedy was actually banned because of its immorality! However, it was revived the same year in a theatre in Lucca.

Many other comedies celebrated the world of the theatre and all the temperamental behaviour of the actors and singers. This was true of *Le Convenienze e inconvenienze teatrali* by the Venetian Simone Sografi, or the very fine play by Goldoni, *L'Impresario di Smirne* in which the author describes with his usual humour the endless worries caused by the envy, jealousy and pretentiousness of the castrati and the women singers.

One of the most racy satires about this theatrical world, and also one of the most famous, was that by the composer Benedetto Marcello, entitled *Il teatro alla moda* (The Fashionable Theatre), which appeared in 1720. With great verve the author gave composers, poets, singers and all those who made a living out of opera a quantity of 'useful advice' which allowed him to attack, through exaggeration, the most common vices in the theatre of his time.

To the castrati he gave the following 'advice': 'He will always complain about his role, alleging that "it was not right for him, that the arias are not in keeping with his superior talent", etc; then he will refer to an aria by another composer and will state that at such and such a court, at such and such a great lord's residence, "this aria (modesty apart) received approval from everyone and he was asked to sing it again *as many as seventeen times during the evening*." On stage he will sing with his mouth half-closed and his teeth clenched, he will do all he can to ensure that nobody understands a single word; during the recitatives he will observe neither full stops nor commas. When on stage with another performer who, following the demands of the libretto, will address him by singing an aria, he will take no notice; he will greet the masked spectators in the boxes, smile at the instrumentalists and the extras so that the audience will clearly understand that he is a Signor Alipi Forconi, *musico*, and not Prince *Zoroaster* whom he is playing. While the *ritornello* of his aria is being played he will walk about, take a pinch of snuff, tell his friends he is not in good voice, that he has a cold, etc. When he sings he will not forget that he can linger over the cadenza as long as he wishes and add ornaments and *gargouillades* just as he pleases; during this time the musical director will abandon his harpsichord, take snuff and wait until the singer condescends to finish . . . If the singer is playing the part of a slave, or a prisoner in chains, he will appear well powdered, wearing a coat covered with precious stones, a very tall helmet, carrying a sword, wearing very long and very shiny chains that he will rattle constantly in order to excite pity from the audience . . . If the modern singer has to act out a duel in which he is wounded in the arm he will still go on making lavish gestures with his wounded arm; if he has to drink poison he will sing while holding the cup in his hand, he will turn it round and round as though it were already empty . . . He will pay court to all the actresses as well as their protectors and will live in the hope that thanks to his talent and his exemplary and well known modesty he will finally obtain one day the title of *marchese, conte* or at least that of *cavaliere* . . .'[21]

Less amusing but equally corrosive is the ode that Parini entitled *L'Evirazione* (*Emasculation*) and renamed *La Musica* because the publisher had been ashamed of printing the original title. The author attacks the social customs existing between 1756 and 1783 and reserves a few caustic stanzas for the castrati. Fifteen or so of them attack with dramatic bitterness those parents who handed over their sons to torture:

> *Ahi! Pera lo spietato*
> *Genitor, che primiero*
> *Tentò di ferro armato*
> *L'esecrabile e fiero*
> *Misfatto onde si duole*
> *La mutilata prole!*

> Ah, may he perish,
> That father who, first,
> Armed with his knife,
> Attempted the loathsome
> Cruel deed that crippled
> His suffering son.

One stanza, which has become an anthology piece, was taken up by all those who rebelled against castration, especially during the nineteenth century:

> *Aborro in su la scena*
> *Un canoro elefante*
> *Che si trascina a pena*
> *Su le adipose piante*
> *E manda per gran foce*
> *Di bocca un fil di voce.*[22]

> I hate to see on stage
> An elephantine singer
> Who barely drags himself about
> On fleshy swollen legs
> Emitting from his big wide mouth
> A thin and tiny voice.

Here as elsewhere the lack of grace and lightness on the part of the singers 'fattened up' by castration was certainly a permanent subject of mockery. Among other examples, an Englishman jeered very amusingly at the appearance of Farinelli, observed near St James's Park in London. This final quotation is more valuable for its provocative anecdotal quality than for its credibility, since all portraits and descriptions of the singer show us a different man, more slender and trim: 'If thou art in the environs of St James', thou must have observed in the Park with what Ease and Agility a cow, heavy with calf, has rose up at the command of the milkwoman's foot: thus from the mossy bank sprang the divine Farinelli.'[23]

8
European Journeys

Were you there when the castrato Caffarelli sent us into raptures?
DIDEROT

The castrati constituted an essentially Italian phenomenon in the sense that they were recruited and trained only in that country. Examples of German, English or French castrati remain the exceptions for they do not correspond to any tradition firmly rooted in their countries nor to an educational structure truly adapted to their 'case'.

In contrast, the principal European music-lovers, who often formed a select, aristocratic and cultivated public, were very receptive to castrati as they were to everything that came from Italy concerning the opera: vocal style, dramatic libretti, productions, baroque settings with décors based on perspective, and so on. During the seventeenth and eighteenth centuries, what would musical life at the courts of Sweden, Russia, Germany or Spain have been like without Italy? True, each country 'digested' or absorbed in its own way what it received from her: Lully created French opera by starting from Italian opera, Handel adapted the *opera seria* in the Anglo-Saxon world and the German composers employed the principles of *opera buffa* in their *Singspiel*. Italy, however, merely exported her musical output as it was, like highly-priced merchandise, and the castrati, like Stradivarius violins, were part of the package.

Perpetual travellers

Some castrati left Italy when they were very young as a result of campaigns by the recruiting officers who worked for foreign courts. In this way Balatri left very early for Russia and Rubinelli sang when he was thirteen in the ducal chapel of Württemberg before making a triumphal début in Stuttgart. As a general rule all the others went abroad only after taking their first steps in Italy, either in church or on the stage. For many of them a tour through the different Italian capitals actually represented a vital stage in their progress: it was there that their first contracts and their first triumphs awaited them; there that foreign impresarios heard them and made them offers of appearances in public theatres or residence at royal courts.

The endless European journeys made by some castrati are astonishing, for conditions of comfort and safety can only be imagined. The opera seasons, which were relatively short in some towns, allowed them to move about frequently and take advantage of the free months to go abroad. Since these contracts were often renewed, the singers never stayed very long in one place, one or two years at the most. Long stays like those made by Ferri in Poland or Vienna, Senesino in London or Farinelli in Madrid were much rarer. As a result the chance timing of their engagements made them return frequently to Italy, especially for periods as vital as carnival time, between Christmas and Shrove Tuesday. In this way the singers travelled considerable distances throughout Europe.

Siface, at the start of his career, visited all the Italian cities before going to London. He came back to Modena for the marriage of the Duke's sister to James II, left again for Paris and London before ending his travels in Modena and Naples. Tosi passed through virtually all the courts of Europe, while not neglecting the principal Italian cities. Senesino, after the inevitable Italian tour, went from Naples to Dresden, from Dresden to London, from London to Venice and then to London again, before ending up in Venice and Naples. Bernacchi went constantly from the different Italian capitals to Mannheim, Vienna and London. Cusanino added to these same destinations Bavaria, Berlin and St Petersburg. Caffarelli broke the records, going to or from Rome, Venice, Milan, Turin, Rome, Milan, Bologna, Venice, Naples, London, Naples, Madrid, Naples, Vienna, Venice, Lucca, Naples, Turin, Paris, Naples, Lisbon and finally Naples. Marchesi travelled at astonishing speed, going all over Italy before leaving for Russia by way of Vienna and Warsaw. In St Petersburg he took part in the inaugural performance at the Hermitage Theatre (in Sarti's *Armida e Rinaldo* in 1786), returning to Milan via Berlin. He then stayed three years in London, divided his time between Venice and Milan, made short stays in Vienna and ended his career in Milan.

Balatri remained a somewhat exceptional case. When he was in Moscow he was invited to accompany the Tsar's ambassador who was leaving for Tartary to meet the Khan. The memoirs of this little known singer, the only ones we know of written by a castrato, form a wonderful text of several thousand rhyming lines. In it Balatri reveals very beguiling humour and imagination and in the process does not neglect to hand himself a few bouquets. But behind these jokes lie a deep sadness and a sense of futility and loneliness that touch the reader. Each of his amusing tirades is preceded or followed by a flood of invective against the 'World', that is to say Destiny, or Fate. His talent consists in constantly hiding his unhappiness and emerging from embarrassing situations by means of a pirouette.

The Khan asked him to sing and probably appeared taken aback by such a voice. Balatri re-creates the scene for us in a fine tirade which deserves to be quoted in full:

Incomincia dal farmi domandare
Se maschio son o femmina e da dove,
Se nasce tale gente (ovvera piove)
Con voce e abilitade per cantare.
Resto imbrogliato allor per dar risposta:
Se maschio, dico quasi una bugia,
femmina, men che men diro ch'io sia
E dir che son neutral, rossore costa.
Pure, fatto coraggio, al fin rispondo
Che son maschio, Toscano, e che si trova
Galli nelli mie parti che fanno nova,
Dalle quali i soprani son al mondo;
Che li galli si nomano Norcini
Ch'a noi le fan covar per molti giorni
E che, fatto il cappon, son gli uovi adorni
Da lusinghe, carezze e da quattrini.[1]

He asked me first if I am
Man or woman, where I came from,
If people like me are born
with this voice and skill, or rain down
from the sky. In confusion I reply:
If I say 'man', I lie,
'Woman' I certainly shall not say
and 'neuter' would make me blush.
But finding courage I reply
That I'm a man, from Tuscany, and
In my country there are cocks
Who lay eggs and hatch out sopranists;
These cocks are called Norcini,*

* Inhabitants of Norcia, a town where castration was practised.

The brooding goes on for years,
And once the cock has become a capon
The eggs win flattery, love and wealth.

Vienna and London

It may seem surprising today that all the countries which
did not practise castration, at least officially, adopted the
castrati singers so spontaneously and loved them with the
same passion as the Italians themselves. The vogue for
opera seria abroad was certainly the main reason. There
was also the example provided by some sovereigns, often
women, who were infatuated by the castrati; they included
Christina of Sweden, the Electress of Saxony, the Empress
Catherine of Russia, Leopold I and Maria-Theresa of
Austria.

Vienna proved to be one of the cities most receptive to
the castrati and even showed unreserved enthusiasm for
them. We have already described those besotted ladies of
the court who decked themselves out from head to foot
with miniature portraits of the castrato Marchesi. Even
without such paroxysms, the capital of the Empire and the
Germanic world in general had always opened their doors
wide to the castrati; Ferri spent no fewer than twenty years
in the service of Ferdinand III and then Leopold I during
a period that was particularly glorious for Viennese musical
life. 'Nothing in the whole of music,' wrote the poet Wil-
helm Heinse, 'is as fine as the fresh young voice of a *castrato*, no woman's voice has the same firmness, the same
strength and the same smoothness.'[2]

Metastasio was surely no stranger to this Austrian infatuation for he had spent fifty years in Vienna. It was there
that he had written most of the hundred and sixty or so
opera libretti which the eighteenth century was to make
its own. In them he followed the reforms of Zeno and

concentrated the 'psychological action' in his works on a series of arias specially composed for the castrati of the time. That said, and despite his affection for his 'dear twin', Farinelli, he had not concealed the anxiety and disapproval he felt at the behaviour of certain castrati who spoilt operatic works by their abuse of ornamentation. All the same, it must be said that Metastasio, as well as the composer Hasse and the castrati Caffarelli and Farinelli, had taken *bel canto* to the highest point of 'virtuosismo' and technical perfection before they all died within a few years of each other.

At the end of the eighteenth century Gluck added further reforms to Metastasio's drama, reinforcing the clarity of feeling and analysis of the human heart sought by the great poet, while he also continued the simplification and expressiveness of a musical language which would enhance the text. It was in Vienna that he created his masterpiece *Orfeo e Euridice*, in 1762, with the castrato Guadagni in the role of Orfeo. Mozart himself made use of castrati. Apart from his friendship with Tenducci he chose the castrato Vincenzo del Prato to create the role of Idamante in his Munich production of *Idomeneo*. In the same way he reacted with delight when he heard Rauzzini singing in Vienna and offered him the role of *primo uomo* in his *Lucio Silla*, in Milan, before composing the motet *Exultate Jubilate* especially for him.

The English capital was the other centre of activity for all the great castrati in their European journeys. In the eighteenth century, especially thanks to Handel, it became a magnet of great importance. Many castrati stayed there for periods lasting from a few months to several years.

The love story between the English and the castrati began late but it was what one might call love at first sight. The situation was unusual: unlike most other people the English public had never been able to hear voices of this sort during the seventeenth century. Some castrati had come to London but had confined themselves to private gatherings. In 1667 Samuel Pepys, the London civil servant who was only saved from anonymity by his *Diary*, heard without much enthusiasm two Italian castrati during a soirée at Lord Bruncker's. The *virtuosi* must have constituted a phenomenon that was too shockingly new and these singers may not have been very talented, since Pepys wrote this not very flattering commentary on them: 'Here came Mr Hooke, Sir George Ent, Dr Wren, and many others; and by and by the music, that is to say, Seignor Vincentio, who is the maister Composer, and six more, where of two Eunuches (so tall that Sir T. Harvy said well that he believes they did grow large by being gelt, as our Oxen do) ... and I confess, very good music they made; that is, the composition exceeding good, but yet not at all more pleasing to me then what I have heard in English by Mrs. Knipp, Captain Cooke and others. Nor do I dote of the Eunuchs; they sing endeed pretty high and have a mellow kind of sound, but yet I have been as well satisfied with several women's voices, and men also [...] their motions, and risings and fallings, though it may be pleasing to an Italian or one that understands the tongue, yet to me it did not ...'[3]

Twenty years later, in 1687, it was Siface's turn to visit London. The great castrato appeared only in the Royal Chapel and in private salons, so the wider public could not hear him. Another Londoner, John Evelyn, was at first delighted by his voice when he heard him in January in the Chapel: 'I heard the famous Cifaccio [sic] (Eunuch) sing in the new Popish Chapell this afternoon, which was indeed very rare, & with great skill. He came over from Rome, esteemed one of the best voices in Italy, much crowding, little devotion.'[4] In April his impression of the singer changed somewhat when he was able to see him at close quarters, in Samuel Pepys' drawing-room. He thought the voice admirable but found the man 'a mere wanton, effeminate child; very Coy, & proudly conceited [...] who much disdained to shew his talent to any but Princes.'⁵

The wider public had to wait for the very beginning of the eighteenth century before they could get to know the castrati. It was a real shock to them when they heard, a few months apart, the first two castrati engaged on British soil. The attraction of novelty and the pronounced taste for the exotic among the English, as it was said at the time, cannot explain everything. These voices surpassed all that they were used to hearing, mainly the singing of counter tenors: in future no expense would be spared to bring the most famous castrati over from Italy. The first of them to come was not, however, one of the most famous, although that in no way detracted from his qualities. Valentino Urbani was to be known to posterity especially for the medley of works by Bonocini and Alessandro Scarlatti, put together by Pepusch and performed at Drury Lane Theatre in 1707. Following a custom usual in London and the German towns the opera was sung half in Italian and half in English. The same policy was adopted the following year at the Queen's Theatre, with Scarlatti's *Pirro e Demetrio*, arranged for the occasion by Nicolas Haym. This time the castrato role was sung by Nicolino, one of the greatest names in Italy. Urbani had disturbed and moved the public. Nicolino's performance struck them like a bomb, and from then on the English public swore only by castrati. In 1710 Mancini's *Idaspe fedele* was given with the same singer, all in Italian this time. Finally, in 1711, an important date in London musical life, Nicolino created the first role written by Handel for his adopted country, Rinaldo, performed along with Urbani and Francesca Vanini Boschi who had already sung his *Agrippina* in Venice.

Once Nicolino had left to go into retirement in Italy, Handel was given full authority to recruit singers on the continent. He went to Dresden, where Senesino was singing, and hastily engaged him along with other performers. The cost was certainly high, a little too high for the English impresarios, but Handel needed a great name if his future compositions were to succeed. It worked out well for him since Senesino remained in London for eleven years, in two periods of eight and three years, performing in nearly twenty-five of Handel's operas and oratorios, including *Giulio Cesare, Tamerlano, Scipione, Alessandro, Admeto* and *Siroe.*

After Senesino the festival of song offered to the public continued with the arrival of Carestini, Bernacchi, Gizziello, Annibali, Caffarelli and Guadagni, who all participated in the first performances of works by Handel. It was Caffarelli who had the honour of creating *Xerxes* (Serse), and singing for the first time the famous largo *Ombra mai fu.* Of all the singers with whom Handel had dealings— usually fairly stormy—it was Guadagni who pleased him most. Handel appreciated his intelligent approach to a role, the simplicity of his art and his deference towards the creator of the work, an attitude very rare at the time. A sincere understanding was established between the sixty-four-year-old master and the young castrato of twenty-four. For him Handel wrote the superb aria in the *Foundling Hospital Anthem* and consented to transpose one of the arias from *The Messiah.* Guadagni was the castrato who collaborated with Handel for the shortest period of time but also the one who, musically and emotionally, had most influence on the composer, ten years before his death.

Farinelli, who spent several months in London, has not yet been mentioned because he was the only singer to go there directly on behalf of a troupe who were Handel's rivals. Senesino was not sympathetic towards Handel, a feeling which had grown stronger over the years. He therefore decided to create a new troupe, the Opera of the Nobility, based at the King's Theatre in Lincoln's Inn Fields. This rival troupe was supported by the Prince of Wales and relied principally on compositions by Porpora. That is why they welcomed Farinelli, the most famous disciple of the Italian master, as well as Bertolli, Montagnana and, later, La Cuzzoni. Apart from works by Porpora the troupe divided their time between singing creations by Bononcini, Alessandro Scarlatti and Hasse. Farinelli, who had always needed much coaxing to come to London, agreed to do so when the theatre offered him an escape clause. It was there, in Hasse's *Artaserse*, that Senesino fell into his arms in the middle of a performance. The London public gave Farinelli a triumphal welcome, comparable to those he had received more or less everywhere in Europe. His presence on the stage drove the audience into a state of near-frenzy. The spontaneous cry from an English woman spectator during a performance: 'One God, one Farinelli!' spread through the whole of England and was reproduced in a famous engraving by Hogarth.

In fact the Opera of the Nobility enterprise really needed Farinelli, Senesino or La Cuzzoni, for purely Italian operas, as opposed to those arranged by Handel, were far from enjoying universal support. The great master remained extremely popular with the public and part of the aristocracy. In November 1736 a pro-Handel English lady wrote to her sister: 'With such a group of singers, and by giving gloomy Italian operas which nearly send you to sleep, they think they can do better than Handel who has La Strada, singing better than ever, Gizziello, who has made great progress since last year, and Annibali who unites the best qualities of Senesino and Carestini, and acts with supreme taste!'[6]

When he saw fierce rivalries starting to break out between the theatres, Farinelli pretended he was ill and took French leave. Burney in fact thought he could detect in his voice the first evidence of a decline, although the singer was only thirty-two. In any case it was better for him to leave covered in glory, laden with gifts and money, rather than see fate turn against him in quarrels which made everyone uncomfortable. London was the typical case of a city where people enjoyed battles between two opposing factions: politics, religion, theatres and singers supplied ideal basic material for this bipartism which was rooted in the English mind. The rivalry between the two outstanding women singers of the century, the mezzo-soprano Faustina and the soprano Cuzzoni, had led them, one evening in 1727, to have a fight on the stage. London audiences were delighted. A pamphlet by John Arbuthnot attempted a humorous analysis of the real problems: 'Today you are no longer asked the same questions as in the past, namely: are you for the High or Low Church, are you Whig or Tory? Are you for the court or the landed gentry, for King George or the Pretender? You are asked now, are you for Faustina or Cuzzoni, Handel or Bononcini? That is what draws good London society into heated quarrels; and if the sweet notes of the opera had not done much to modify and diminish the native ferocity of the British, bloody crimes would have been committed.'[7] In fact, not only the two queens of song but the entire aristocracy were at each other's throats through intermediaries. The Countess of Pembroke led the Cuzzonisti clan while her rival, the Countess of Burlington, protected the Faustinisti supporters. Like all the women singers of the time, these two had been severely criticised by the moralists who saw in them only perversion and indecency. Ambrose Philips had described La Cuzzoni very harshly as 'a little stage siren', 'worthy seducer of an idle age', 'corrupter of all manly art', and had concluded, 'Let us live as we want to live, leave us, the British, rough and free!'

Such attacks and divided opinions did not spare the castrati either. Not everyone in England found pleasure in the same things, and some people did not warm to these new singers who had come to 'corrupt' traditional singing and sound morals. When Nicolino left the country an anonymous spectator lashed out against him: 'Away with this object of pleasure and shame for our nation! May Great Britain no longer be corrupted by frivolous trilling. Let such a race of singers return to that country where lust and dissolute behaviour prevail. May your eunuch's voice ring out there . . . Away with your accursed singing! Great Britain wishes to assert her liberty!'[8]

The English enthusiasm for the castrati was not affected by such remarks, it even spilled over into the period long after the Handelian era. Tenducci and Rauzzini had very successful careers in England and Pacchiarotti, at the end of the century, re-created the greatest moments of Senesino or Farinelli and made the whole of London weep during the few seasons when he accompanied his Venetian teacher Bertoni. Philippe Egalité, who was living in the capital, never missed a single performance by the castrato and was overcome on each occasion. His attitude even led to one of those mass movements of which only the English are capable. Everyone knows that during the London première of *The Messiah*, fifty or so years earlier, King George II stood up, moved by admiration, apparently, on hearing the Alleluia chorus. The entire audience followed his example and custom decrees that in England today this still happens when the famous chorus is sung. In the same way Philippe Egalité began one evening to hold a white handkerchief in his hand, ready to wipe away the tears that Pacchiarotti caused him to shed. From the next day, and for several months, the audience were careful to equip themselves with immaculate handkerchiefs and wipe the tears away in a unanimous gesture, whenever Louis XVI's cousin raised the royal handkerchief to his eyes. Tradition, tradition!

The French and the castrati

Of all the nations involved with the art of the castrati, France was the only one to differ sharply from the others and adopt a cautious, even downright hostile attitude. True, the Italian castrati were always present at the Louvre, then at Versailles, the least known among them in the chapel choirs and the most famous as personal guests of the sovereigns. True, Louis XIV, Louis XV and Marie-Antoinette expressed genuine admiration for them. True, some musicologists, *philosophes* and travellers were capable of appreciating and praising one or other of these singers, but as a general rule the attitude of the French remained the same: castrati were not acceptable, castration was utterly shocking and the vocal results, with a few exceptions, left the listeners unmoved or made them laugh. Balatri was amazed when he saw the audience at a private concert in Lyon begin to laugh out loud after listening to him for thirty seconds! He had never been received like this throughout his travels and was so mortified that he only remained in the hall because he was persuaded to do so.

This hostility extended to the whole of Italian music. We have only to remember the animosity towards Mazarin and the Italian operas which he attempted to impose on Paris, or Lully's deliberate wish to create an opera in the 'French style', quite distinct from its Italian counterpart. We should remember the *Querelle des bouffons** which,

---

* The 'War of the Comedians' - a public quarrel arising in 1752 from an opera by Pergolese, *La Serva Padrona*, which caused a political split between those who favoured French opera and those who preferred Italian.

for reasons often other than musical, divided Paris from 1752 onwards, or again the hostility between the supporters of Gluck and Piccini, which was ended in 1779 by the competition between the two composers to write an opera based on *Iphigénie en Tauride*. It is true that France was in serious competition with Italy, in the sense that it was virtually the only nation to create its own theatrical music, rather than merely importing it from across the Alps.

In this bitter feud between the two nations the castrati were in the front line. They were so closely identified with the type of Italian music that had formed them, propelled them towards fame and exported them that they suffered both from its domination and its possible setbacks. Most French people condemned nearly everything to do with them. Jean-Jacques Rousseau blamed those barbaric parents who 'allowed their children to undergo this operation for the enjoyment of pleasure-loving and cruel people who dare to seek out the singing of these unfortunate men.'[9] Sarah Goudar, who had become French following her marriage, attacked 'the nation of eunuchs' and what it produced. 'It is humiliating for the most enlightened century there ever was to see the deplorable state to which operas have been reduced, especially the Italian ones, in which the least drawback is possibly that of seeing Alexanders, Caesars or Pompeys order the destiny of the universe with the voices of girls.'[10] La Lande went back to the sanctity of nature: 'It is better for human nature,' he wrote, 'to be accustomed like us to find pleasure in voices that are natural, male, radiant, in possession of their full power, it is custom alone that decides our pleasures; our custom is better and our pleasures more natural.'[11]

There were so many criticisms that it would be impossible to quote them all, but this is why a letter from Charles de Saint-Evremond, dating probably from 1685, has often provoked astonishment among researchers and musicologists. It is in fact a very rare example (especially coming from a Frenchman!) of open encouragement for castration. During his exile in England the famous writer met Madame Mazarin, the niece of an Italian cardinal, who came from Rome and was therefore accustomed to the art of the castrati singers. She had a young French page named Dery, whose voice earned the admiration of London high society. His mistress, who was just as captivated as her guests, had only one idea in her head, which was to arrange an operation for him so that he could keep this voice. It may be assumed that she begged Saint-Evremond to find the right words to convince the page, who had been nicknamed 'the French boy'. This letter deserves to be known not so much for its proselytism as for the shock arguments that it employs. 'My dear child,' wrote Saint-Evremond, 'I am not surprised that so far you have felt an insurmountable aversion to the one thing in the world that matters most to you. Clumsy and coarse people have been talking to you bluntly about having yourself castrated: an expression so ugly and so detestable that it would have revolted anyone less sensitive than you. As for me [...] I shall try to obtain what is best for you in a less unpleasant way, and shall indicate as gently as possible that you must have yourself "rounded off" by means of a minor operation which will ensure the delicacy of your complexion for a long time and the beauty of your voice for ever [...] Today you can speak to the King in a familiar way, you are embraced by duchesses, praised by all high-born people. When your voice loses its charm you will be merely the comrade of Pompey and perhaps you will suffer the scorn of Mr Stourton [respectively Madame Mazarin's negro servant and page]. But you are fearful, you say, of being less liked by the ladies. Forget your fear, we no longer live among half-wits. The advantages that follow the operation are widely recognised today and if Monsieur Dery in his natural state could have one mistress, Monsieur Dery when rounded off could have a hundred. So that means you are certain of having mistresses, which is a very good thing. You will have no wife, so you will be exempt from something very bad. You will be happy at having no wife, happier still at having no children! Monsieur Dery's daughter would get herself pregnant, his son would get himself hanged and, what is most certain, his wife would make him a cuckold. Protect yourself from all these calamities by one swift operation; you will remain devoted entirely to yourself, proud of such a small advantage that will make your fortune and cause everyone to be your friend. If I live long enough to see you when your voice has broken and your beard has grown, you will have to endure severe reproaches. Prevent them, and believe that I am your most sincere friend.'[12]

Such a display of style and inventiveness in the service of castration is exceptional. Even the Italian intellectuals, although captivated by castrati, would take good care not to leave such explicit documents behind them. Other French people usually adopted a very different attitude. Castration was certainly held in contempt and the castrati themselves remained misunderstood. The reasoning, Cartesian French mind had difficulty in adjusting to the fantasy, extremism and irrational aspect of these singers and their music. For the French they were merely 'eunuchs', 'capons'—in a word, abnormal people; the myth of the castrato, the 'angel musician', already so well known across Europe, escaped them completely. What is more, they were unable to dissociate the Italian *virtuosi* from the music they interpreted. While they often agreed in recognising the beauty of certain voices, they could not tolerate their torrents of roulades, trills and endless vocalises.

In fact the French made little effort to understand what

the castrati brought to the art of singing, what dimension they conferred on their characters when on stage, and what considerable progress they brought to vocal technique. As from the eighteenth century France was considerably behind its neighbours as far as the quality of its singers was concerned. Although the void due to the absence of castrati is not the only explanation for this backwardness, it is one of the most revealing phenomena connected with it. The staggering technique of the castrati in fact obliged all the other Italian singers to progress in tandem and constantly to reassess themselves. This competitive edge was lacking from the French stage and many foreigners had difficulty in adjusting to French singing. Casanova thought that the great French singer Nicole Le Maure was mad when he heard her 'shouts' on the stage and Baron Grimm could not believe his ears: 'Singing,' he cried, 'a term shamefully profaned in France, applied to a method of forcing sounds out of the throat and shattering them against the teeth by a convulsive movement of the chin; we call that shouting.'[13] As for Mozart, he said more or less the same thing when recalling the singers of the Académie Royale, who, in his view, uttered howls 'through their noses and throats, with all the power of their lungs.' At the start of the nineteenth century France was a good half-century behind Italy, and the art of song did not make real progress until the arrival of Rossini and the great vogue of the Théâtre-Italien in Paris.

In fact the castrati, without drawing much attention to themselves, had been continually present at the French court since the reign of Louis XIII. One of the first to perform in the royal chapel, under Richelieu, had earned for all his kind a euphemistic description worthy of the *précieuses*. While this castrato, Bertoldo, was singing a psalm, Madame de Longueville turned to her neighbour and cried, 'My goodness, Mademoiselle, how well this *cripple* is singing!' The term spread rapidly round the court and in this way allowed all the castrati to be renamed without risking any offence to over-chaste ears.

Most Italian castrati came to France under the influence of Mazarin, who imported the new transalpine opera and its singers. This was how Paris saw the arrival of great names of song such as the castrati Pasqualini, Atto and Bartolomeo Melani. Louis XIV was impressed by this troupe and even more so by the splendour of the opera they presented. Unfortunately Mazarin had gone almost too far: more than 300,000 écus were spirited away by the production of Luigi Rossi's *Orfeo*, providing very useful ammunition for his enemies. The 'mazarinades' which attacked his policies did not fail to lampoon these vast and costly operas which had come from abroad, as well as their ridiculous castrati who were foreign to French taste. The Fronde not only drove out Mazarin and the court—it conducted open warfare against the Italian performers. Luigi Rossi was forced into hiding, Torelli, the famous producer and creator of theatrical machinery, was imprisoned and some castrati only just escaped lynching.

The rebellion ended, Mazarin returned and with him the troupe of Italian musicians. The court heard six works altogether: Rossi's *Orfeo*, Caproli's *Nozze di Teti e Peleo* and a pastorale and three operas by Cavalli: *Egisto*, *Serse* and *Ercole amante* (Hercules in Love), the latter presented for the marriage of Louis XIV. The audiences admired the glamour of the spectacle, the visual enchantment provided by the stage effects, the grace of the ballets imposed on Cavalli to satisfy French taste, but the music did not please and in private people continued to sneer at the 'cripples': to see that a princess's waiting-woman was in reality a prince disguised as a woman, whose page was a woman dressed as a man, was deeply upsetting to French audiences.

However, there were signs of some development in taste and people gradually became accustomed to these strange singers. By 1639 Maugars had realised that the contact with the Italians was looking positive and that travelling or mixing with foreigners could be a way to musical success. Much later, at the end of Louis XIV's reign, violent disputes broke out between the Abbé Raguenet, a ferocious defender of Italian voices, and Jean Lecerf de La Viéville, sworn enemy of the castrati who were 'old and faded early in life', and that ultramontane music which he described as 'an elderly sophisticated coquette, covered with rouge, white paint and patches'. His rival, on the contrary, envied the Italians: 'What advantages do they not possess over us in opera, through their castrati, countless in number, while we do not have a single one in France', adding shortly afterwards, '[their voices] are clear, they are touching, they move us to our very souls.'[14]

When Raguenet wrote that France did not possess 'a single one' he meant of course that the country had no French castrato nor even an Italian one of international repute. That did not prevent the royal chapel from employing a few castrati and from 'lending' them sometimes to the opera for secondary, usually female roles. Louis XIV had never wanted to get rid of the castrati; on the contrary he had allowed them to blend into the band of singers and musicians who took part every day in religious ceremonies. The chapel included male sopranos who were known as 'trebles whose voices had broken', castrati called 'Italian sopranos', counter-tenors who replaced contraltos, tenors and basses. It was only at the end of his reign that female sopranos appeared.

These Italian castrati enjoyed total security and some material comfort. Several asked to become naturalised French subjects. Louis XIV even showed great esteem for some of them. Bannieri (or Baniera) was one of his favourites, for he had been protected when young by Anne of Austria and brought up along with him. It was this singer who, as already noted, had had himself castrated by his own choice by a relative who was a surgeon, to the great despair of Louis XIV. He had a house built at Montreuil, where all musicians had their 'country estates'; this place became the meeting point and ideal country home for the Italian castrati. In 1704, with the collaboration of the royal musicians, a statue of Louis XIV was unveiled at the end of the garden, proving the high esteem in which the monarch was held. The castrato Favalli, who arrived in 1674, was also much favoured by the King 'because of his beautiful voice and the pleasure his singing gave him',[15] wrote Benjamin La Borde. Louis XIV showed his appreciation by granting him the right to hunt over all the land owned by the captains of the royal hunt, and even in the park at Versailles.

As a general rule all these singers ended their lives in the Paris area without having accumulated great riches— they bequeathed the little money remaining to them to their household or to young castrati who were arriving. Recruiting officers from the court went abroad regularly in search of them. The King and possibly part of the court liked them, they lived straightforward honest singers' lives at Versailles without being totally separate from the other musicians, but they were cut off from the wide public and from the vast European movement which was carrying so many castrati towards brilliant careers.

Even women did not console them for their isolation. On seeing these men, even the famous ones who appeared in Paris, women either mocked them or remained cold. The first castrati to arrive in France, convinced they could impress the ladies and add to their catalogue of conquests, had no success. Unlike many other women, Frenchwomen could not understand how anyone could prefer 'the half rather than the whole', and hastily sent these secondhand hidalgos packing. This attitude was satirised by an anonymous poet:

> I know several braggarts
> With cockscombs and proud expressions
> Who well deserve the name
> of Caponhouse.
> A cockscomb today is not enough
> And the most simple girls
> Care little for it
> If other bits are missing.[16]

The unfortunate Balatri recounted with another kind of humour his wretched soirée in Lyon with a lady of high society who organised a concert in her salons. He was honoured as if he were 'Charlemagne's cousin', but he was not allowed to embrace any of the radiant young girls round about him. No doubt none of them wanted a castrato as companion for an evening. 'None of those young girls,' wrote Balatri, 'is over twenty, and I have to have a nymph with only seven teeth in her mouth! Whatever anyone says, these are true misfortunes!'[17] Balatri saw reason and consented to spend the evening with his antique Venus, 'as old as sixty Easters and Holy Years.'

Women were not the only disappointment for the *virtuosi* on French soil. Money was another. No castrato could think of any country meaner than France. When crossing the Alps, or the English Channel on their way back, all the castrati could forget the largesse they received elsewhere. It is true that the monarchs enjoyed receiving and honouring the 'gods' of the Italian opera. The Dauphine, Louis XIV's daughter-in-law, listened to Siface; Louis XV, who had no passion for music and even less for what came from Italy, heard Caffarelli and Farinelli with immense pleasure. In 1786 Marie-Antoinette, as an Austrian accustomed to castrati, summoned Pacchiarotti, took him to her private apartments and marvelled at his singing. She asked him to return to Paris in three years' time, after his stay in London, without suspecting that 1789 would bring her many other preoccupations!

Siface never had any luck with the French and must often have cursed their reluctance to open their purses. When he sang at Versailles for the first time he was not paid at once. He made it clear that he would not leave the château until he had received what was due to him. The Dauphine was so angered by his attitude that she asked him to leave for London and call for his fee on the way back from England. He had a similar problem in Rome when he sang to the French Ambassador to the Holy See. As he left Siface realised that instead of jingling doubloons he was being offered only a few sorbets for his pains. No doubt he was expected to feel pleased that he had sung before a French ambassador.

Farinelli, as usual, was more fortunate in money matters and long before he left for Madrid had already earned the title of 'Singer to Royalty'. Louis XV received him in the Queen's apartment and listened to him with such obvious pleasure that he astonished his courtiers, who were accustomed to more reticence in public and less enthusiasm for an operatic aria.

Unfortunately the King's generosity was not enough to satisfy Caffarelli, far from modest as we know and accustomed to the most sumptuous gifts. Louis XV had summoned him to entertain the Dauphine during her pregnancy. The singer was given a rented house at Versailles, a carriage and pair belonging to the King and a table with seven or eight place settings and servants in royal livery. Despite all the other gifts he received Caffarelli never had enough and demanded reimbursement for the smallest fraudulent expenses. Shortly before his departure the sovereign sent him a gold snuff-box which he rejected with scorn, alleging that he had received thirty more beautiful and that this one did not even carry the monarch's portrait. It was explained to him politely that the King only gave his portrait to ambassadors. 'Only to ambassadors!' replied Caffarelli. 'Well, let him make them sing!' His remarks were repeated to Louis XV who found them rather amusing and took no offence, understanding no doubt what kind of person had made them. The Dauphine, on the other hand, was not at all amused by the singer's brand of humour. Shortly afterwards she offered him a diamond, accompanied by an official-looking passport, and asked him to leave France within three days, adding mendaciously, 'It is signed by the King; this is a great honour for you.'

The Goudar couple remain a perfect example of the French attitude towards the castrati. Ange Goudar had been born in Montpellier in 1708 and enjoyed a certain reputation as a man of letters and an economist. He married an Irish Catholic named Sarah, who had been a chambermaid and then a serving girl in a London tavern. Casanova had known her while she was following this second career. Sarah had only two good qualities—her beauty and her strong character. Her husband, a typical example of the parvenu trying to climb up the social ladder as fast as possible and worm his way into its leading echelons, realised how he could profit from a wife who was sufficiently seductive and ambitious to further his plans. He trained her in accordance with his own ideas, giving her a kind of superficial intellectuality and began to travel with her wherever his ambition took him. As from 1770 all the romantically-minded aristocrats of Europe knew the 'beautiful Madame Goudar'.

Their two stays in Naples were some of the best periods in the lives of these two adventurers. In order to earn a little publicity Ange pretended that Sarah was an Anglican, although she was a Catholic. He arranged a full and osten-tatious ceremony in which his wife was converted to Catholicism, which caused a great stir in Naples and opened many doors for the couple. Ange, who stopped at nothing, had no scruples about throwing his wife into the arms of Ferdinand IV of Bourbon, who found her a mis-tress much to his taste. Protectors of this sort allowed them to open a gaming-room (which was forbidden) in their superb villa at Pausilippo: many great Neapolitan families emptied their pockets there and filled those of the Goudars. Such a situation could not last for ever. One day the Queen found a note from Sarah to the King in which, Casanova tells us, she had included these few words: 'I'll wait for you at the same place and at the same time with the impatience of the cow waiting for the bull.' The august sovereign did not need to read the note twice before exiling Ange and Sarah from the kingdom.

The story of the Goudars would be no more than a tale of two adventurers if it did not include a bitter feud against the castrati, through various writings which were signed by Sarah but probably thought out and drawn up by Ange. In publishing them under his wife's name the husband guaranteed his *bella Inglesa* a kind of notoriety which could only rebound a hundredfold on the couple. On the other hand it was under his name that a very interesting and judicious essay on economics appeared: *Naples, what must be done to make this kingdom flourish.*

In a series of letters addressed to the Earl of Pembroke and entitled *Remarques sur la musique et la danse* followed by a *Supplément aux Remarques*, Sarah (we will leave her the authorship since no more is known about it) tried to settle her differences with Italy, the 'nation of eunuchs'. With surprising anger and verve she attacked one by one the different castrati of the time and repeated many of the arguments against them current in France at the time.

Her caustic attitude was not lacking in humour when she recounted anecdotes: 'A French lady,' she wrote, 'asked a young Italian woman one day about one of her admirers who was like my cat (castrated). What did she do with such an animal? She was told in reply, '*Lo tengo per non guastarmi la vita*—I keep him so as not to waste my life.' You can see from that, my Lord, that women are so ingenious today that they turn something that's no good for anything into something useful.'[18] Some of these witticisms, which are meant to be amusing, verge on banality: 'They say that the eunuch Phocius possessed universal genius; perhaps he was not really a eunuch, or if he was it can be presumed that during his time the sciences were castrated.'[19]

She is easier to follow when she analyses the evolution of the phenomenon of 'eunuchism': 'Women had to be given monster-like creatures to protect them; and to prevent these monsters from also becoming new instruments of crime the faculty for committing any was removed from them: an unfortunate result of vice which forced chastity to destroy part of the human race in order to preserve the virtue of the rest.'[20] Sarah, in fact, was one of the few people who asked the fundamental question in clear terms: 'Must we mutilate men in order to give them a perfection they did not possess at birth?',[21] a question through which this enemy of the castrati seemed to admit that they could achieve a certain degree of perfection.

Her prolific writings lead to various conclusions. First of all, in her detailed analysis of each castrato Sarah (or Ange?) includes many mistakes: they were pointed out one by one by Paolo Manzin and other musicians in a *Réponse à l'auteur des Observations en langue française sur la musique et la danse*, published in 1773. Sarah states that Gizziello surpassed all the singers of his time, although he was a contemporary of Farinelli and Caffarelli whom he certainly did not surpass. She praises Gizziello's acting, but this was not his major talent, he was compared in fact to a 'singing statue'. In the same way she described as second-rate a castrato as talented as Salimbeni, who obtained one of the best salaries ever paid at the court of Berlin. Lastly, she threw out criticisms which were painfully flat: 'Manzoli sang a great deal but he only sang notes.' Her detractor had no difficulty in answering her: 'What do you want him to sing—sequins?'[22]

It is less easy to forgive her for the scorn she directs against the castrati in general. True, when considering them individually she recognises the fairness and humility of Farinelli, the honesty of Gizziello, the gentleness and moderation of Aprile, the innocence and modesty of Luchini, 'the noble and fine soul' of Guadagni. But as soon as she moves away from particular cases she cannot free herself from that disdain shared by many French people of her time; she dwells heavily on the 'girl's voice' of that *primo uomo* who is only 'half a man', and when after her detailed study of castrati she goes on to examine tenors, she is only too happy to add: 'That's enough about eunuchs, let us now speak about men.' In his *Réponse* Paolo Manzin, who defended the castrati without being one himself, is astonished by so much spite: 'Everyone knows what castrati are, and there was no need to express your scorn for people you have so often courted, and they are not guilty of the defect for which you reproach them, it belongs to the past.'[23]

Equally interesting is the socio-economic approach taken by the couple in which one can clearly see the hand of Ange Goudar. With a prophetic attitude that foreshadows the mentality of the nineteenth century the Goudars argue not only as many French people did but also as economists. They are hardly typical of the eighteenth century for whom the concept of 'utility' and 'profitability' in art had no real meaning. What did the audiences of the seventeenth and eighteenth centuries care about the cost of an auditorium, the money spent on a production, the magnificent gifts bestowed on a castrato! All that counted were the glamour of the festival, the emotional power of a single moment, the magical pleasures of a unique evening. The age of patrons had nothing to do with the complicated accounts of the future business bourgeoisie; the arts, and in particular music, the most fleeting of them all, lived only by the largesse of the 'prince', and nothing was too splendid to serve them. Ange and Sarah did not understand that. They saw castration as producing only 'bodies that are dead for the economic State', and chastised the Italians who were the only people to practise music at the expense of posterity; they did not allow that a singer could be paid a thousand times more than someone of use to science and the economy; they deplored the fact that the cost of music was too high for the States to bear, while this money could solve many problems. According to them the 700,000 livres spent each year on the opera in Paris would save the lives of 2,000 people dying of hunger. This analysis, especially if one looks at it with 'modern' eyes, is certainly not lacking in foundation, it is even visionary from certain points of view, but it foreshadows simultaneously the end of a world and the end of a state of mind according to which generosity and a passion for art were more important and attractive than productivity and the calculation of profit.

In the last analysis, what shocks us most about Ange and Sarah Goudar is not their acrimony towards the castrati, even less their fight against castration which is only the echo of a legitimate and more or less generalised opposition at the end of the eighteenth century. It is above all the constant discrepancy between what they said and what they did. They perpetually preached sound morality, they condemned, took offence, put forward truths and counter-truths, while their own lives were a mere tissue of compromise, intrigue and scandal. Ange acted the part of the upright economist who flew to the help of nations, but he dabbled in shady business and relished the ambience of luxurious gambling dens. Sarah refused to reveal to us the morals of theatrical people (and of castrati in particular!) for she did not want to 'record for posterity the filth of the century',[24] but she collected lovers in order to replenish her own household coffers.

Farinelli in Spain

On reading through the musical literature of the seventeenth and eighteenth centuries it is amazing to discover that one castrato, and one only, was able to escape all the criticism and malice directed at his fellows. Some castrati, as we have seen, proved to have a legendary vocal talent unfortunately counterbalanced by personal qualities that were all too human. Others were the most decent of men while their voices, at various moments in their career, earned them sharp reproaches or contradictory opinions.

Carlo Broschi, known as Farinelli, is a unique case in the history of the Italian castrati since he was the only one to evoke a unanimous response rallying unconditional approbation from the great and the humble, from men and women, from Italians and foreigners, including the French and . . . Sarah Goudar! The 'divine Farinelli', as Charles de Brosses could not refrain from calling 'the greatest castrato in the world', had the gift of gathering round him the entire music-loving West of the eighteenth century; through his countless admirable qualities as well as through the dazzling beauty of his voice and technique, he was able to attract everyone who came near him and became for his century what La Malibran and La Callas were to the nineteenth and twentieth.

In earlier chapters we have referred to Farinelli's origins among the minor nobility of Apulia, to his studies with Porpora, his successes in London and his correspondence with Metastasio. At fifteen he was heard for the first time in Naples, at twenty-five all the courts and opera houses wanted him, and at thirty-two, after London and Paris, he was the undisputed idol of music-loving Europe. At this stage in his life Farinelli had everything on his side. He was tall and handsome, with a face of rare refinement combining strength and grace, kindness and nobility. In addition he possessed personal qualities which were admired by everyone. Unpretentious and modest, courteous, respectful of others, he displayed generosity, altruism and a sense of honour which were out of place in the theatrical world of his time. He was loyal to his impresarios, elegantly gracious towards his partners on the stage; he did not squander the considerable sums he earned, but lived quietly in order to preserve his voice and avoided romantic adventures.

All this was nothing beside his vocal prowess, the real reason for his overall triumph. Farinelli was classified as a 'sopranist', but his voice ranged over nearly three octaves and was totally at ease in the contralto register. Like many castrati he preferred the medium range, for it allowed him to emphasise the mellow quality and warmth of his voice, to express more fully the deepest emotions, tenderness and controlled passion. At the start of his career he had been principally a bravura singer, a specialist in the technique of ornamentation that was taught in Naples. Later his faculty for expressing to perfection passion and languor, vivacity and frivolity, had earned him praise from the most obstinate detractors of the castrati.

Farinelli had reached this point at the age of thirty-two, when his life changed in the most unexpected fashion. Although all the theatres wanted him, he chose to accept an invitation from the Queen of Spain, Elisabeth Farnese, who was very anxious to obtain his cooperation since she was convinced that his singing would relieve the king's neurasthenia. She was of Italian origin and had probably heard Farinelli sing during an earlier stay in Italy when she had gone to visit her father. Was she merely adopting the idea of Queen Marie-Anne of Neubourg, who had summoned Matteuccio to attend Charles II, for the same reasons, from 1698 to 1700? Was she deeply convinced of the improvement that might result from what was literally 'music therapy'? The fact remains that the greatest of the castrati acceded to her request and left London for Madrid, via Paris, without suspecting then that he would devote twenty-two years of his life to the Spanish court and would never, so to speak, see the spectators of other countries again.

Philip V, a grandson of Louis XIV and the first Bourbon ruler of Spain, had reached an acute level of exhaustion and depression. Nothing now could arouse him from his attacks of melancholy when he would stay in bed for several days without seeing anyone or washing himself. For more than twenty years he had been prey to fits of madness during which he would scratch and bite himself, strike the Queen and believe himself to be bewitched, dead, or changed into a frog. The first meeting between the 'angel' and the 'demon' took place one evening in August 1737. The Queen had asked Farinelli to sing from a room adjoining the King's bedroom. The effect was startling. Philip, who previously could find no diversion in anything, now appeared radiant. His face regained its composure, his smile returned, he asked for Farinelli and offered him anything he might want in gratitude for the intense delight he had just experienced. As his sole reward the singer asked that the King should get up, shave and take his place again as head of state. Gradually Farinelli became the sovereign's indispensable 'drug'. Every morning the king told him he would expect him that evening in his apartments, except for the evenings when he was preparing himself for Holy Communion the next day. Farinelli would present himself after dinner and spend a long evening with Philip V, chatting, singing, playing the harpsichord and even praying. Posterity has seized on the story that every evening for nine years the castrato sang the same four or five arias. This seems to have been a legend that merely reinforced the 'supernatural' and miraculous aspect of Farinelli's singing. He possessed a huge repertoire and what was more he had a genius of improvisation during the ornamentation that he added. His art could not be reduced to a few arias, however bewitching they were. Moreover, during these daily meetings the King was seeking not merely a singer but also a friend, a confidant, someone who could listen to him and understand him.

The King's metamorphosis impressed his entourage. He recovered a taste for life, rediscovered a kind of gaiety, signed any document without reading it but at least showed that he existed. He had blind confidence in Farinelli: he relied entirely on his judgement, his greatness of soul and his keen sense of diplomacy. For nine years Farinelli supported Philip at arm's length and did all he could to fight off the royal melancholy, without of course being able to prevent recurrences, which became more and more frequent, of the attacks of madness. Philip would stay in bed all day, get up at two o'clock in the morning to eat or go fishing and insisted on trying to mount the horses he could see on his tapestry. Yet the King's death saddened the singer. Fortunately for him Farinelli had enjoyed excellent relations for several years with Philip V's successors, Ferdinand VI and Barbara of Braganza, the most timid, the most ugly but also the most courteous and most loving couple in the kingdom.

It was only then that the castrato, occupying the same rank as a minister or a Grandee of Spain, was able to win a little independence. It must be said that in Madrid he encountered fertile ground. From the beginning of the century and especially after Philip V had visited Naples, Italian art had reigned supreme at the court. Painters, sculptors, poets and musicians at this court emulated that of Naples to a fantastic extent. During the reign of Philip and Elisabeth Farnese music had become a real passion. One of Farinelli's main tasks was to reorganise the Buen Retiro operatic theatre in Madrid. He brought in the famous designer of stage effects, Giacomo Bonavera from Bologna, created stage effects himself, supervised the moral and physical well-being of the singers and staff, introduced the libretti of his friend Metastasio and the music of Courcelle, an Italian of Franco-Belgian origin. He reserved his own voice for the royal couple (perhaps also because it was no longer secure from public criticism); he himself never sang in this high place of Madrid opera, but summoned and welcomed with the greatest benevolence all the great names of Europe: the castrati Gizziello and Caffarelli, the women singers Teresa Castellini, Vittoria Tesi, Colomba Mattei and Regina Mingotti, the tenor Raaff and the bass Montagnana. The production of Hasse's *Artaserse*, with Gizziello and Castellini, was one of the most glorious moments of Farinelli's career; at the end of the performance the King solemnly presented him with the Cross of the Order of Calatrava, which was reserved for the highest dignitaries in the kingdom.

In addition to the opera and his vocal performances in the royal apartments, Farinelli also exercised considerable political and administrative functions. In the absence of the King and Queen he welcomed important guests, acted as a privy councillor, received eminent personalities and directed major works such as the interior decoration of the palaces of the Buen Retiro and Aranjuez, or the draining of the river Tagus, which at that time was marshy and stinking; he had the ground improved and the river bed cleansed before arranging the building of luxurious small boats for the royal family which allowed them to sail over the fresh water near Aranjuez.

The castrato's disinterested kindness surprised all the observers of the time. One anecdote alone sums up the simplicity and modesty of the man. One day a little tailor brought him the coat he had just made for him. The tailor was so overwhelmed at having worked for the greatest singer of his time that he refused payment and wanted only one thing: to hear the divine voice which the singer reserved for the royal family. Seeing that the young man was determined, Farinelli gave way and for him alone displayed all the marvels of his art. After which he asked the man to give way in his turn also: he persuaded him to accept a purse which contained more than double the sum due.

As time passed Farinelli's incorruptibility became proverbial. How often had people tried to 'buy' him, this man who shared the intimacy of the royal family every day? Louis XV, through the intermediary of his ambassadors, had in vain offered him tempting sums in an effort to obtain information. Several great dignitaries had tried to make Farinelli accept the post of Viceroy of Peru, as well as a considerable financial reward. It was a waste of time, for the singer scorned honours so deeply, especially when they were accompanied with money. If a Spanish noble sent him a casket full of gold in exchange for a service he hastily returned it to him first before considering what he could do to help him. Many people benefited from his personal fortune, starting with the Italian artists and singers living in Madrid or who had escaped the Lisbon earthquake. To everyone he was the 'Father of the Italians'. The painter Amigoni and especially Domenico Scarlatti and his family were rescued from trouble through the singer's influential role and generosity.

Farinelli's stay in Spain, which began in 1737, much more from a sense of duty towards Philip V than for personal pleasure, had become, twenty years later, a source of happiness thanks to his friendship with Ferdinand and Barbara and the responsibilities, worthy of a Prime Minister, that had been conferred on him. The service he had rendered to the health of the two kings—Ferdinand, from the age of thirty-five, revealed the same symptoms as his father— seemed to have brought him more satisfaction than a brilliant career in the theatre. The death of Queen Barbara in 1758 struck the first blow to his years of happiness: Farinelli was deeply saddened, but the King did not recover from it and sank into despair. When he died, a year after his wife, the singer lost everything that attached him to his land of exile.

The arrival of Charles III, who had been reigning in Naples before succeeding his half-brother, was a decisive moment for the castrato. The Queen Mother Elisabeth, banished from the court during Ferdinand's reign, was frankly hostile to him. He was given to understand that in future he would receive his salary but would enjoy none of his past prerogatives. The most painful thing for him was the announcement of the total change that Charles intended to enforce in Spain: he was a perfect example of the 'enlightened despot', full of new ideas; he intended to break with the ancestral traditions of the Spanish court and sweep away the Italian influences that reigned in Madrid. Did people not use the term 'Farinellism' to describe the artistic and musical vogue which had influenced two decades of Spanish history? After Charles III had declared further that 'capons are only fit for eating', Farinelli realised what he must do. He collected together all his souvenirs, jewellery, musical instruments and scores and made his way north. At Saragossa he awaited the arrival of the new king, paid his respects, took leave of him and then set off on the road to Barcelona before sailing away.

9

In the Evening of Life

This soul shines through all Pacchiarotti's features and . . . now that he is seventy, makes him still sublime when he decides he will take the trouble to sing a recitative.

STENDHAL

At this stage in the life of the castrati it is difficult not to think of the least significant among them, the 'obscure', the mediocre, all those whose operation had been a futile exercise that had relegated them to the shadows, and whose solitude and melancholy were accentuated by their retirement. Many castrati resented this 'vacuum' of the last years; even Farinelli, although he had been so deeply admired during his life and was the best supported during his old age, suffered permanently from this sadness. One can imagine therefore the feelings of the men who after all these years possessed neither fortune nor honours nor even the satisfaction of having taken the vocal art of their time to the farthest known heights. The stage to be passed now was only a little less difficult for the greatest singers, those who could mitigate their solitude by training young castrati or receiving eminent personalities from the aristocratic or intellectual world of their time.

Farewell to the public and the return to roots

Surprisingly, we find that the great majority of castrati were quite ready to give up singing before singing abandoned them. As a rule they made their farewells to the public at the height of their fame, usually between the ages of fifty and fifty-five, although their voices could still perform marvels at a much later stage in life. None of them have recorded for us the reasons for their decision: was it due to physical and not vocal exhaustion, after so many journeys across Europe? Or was it the fear of disappointing the public or the difficulty of fending off competition from much younger men, whose physical appearance often played an important role in such a contest? Or personal and exceptional circumstances such as Caffarelli's decision, more or less, to leave the stage (and not the Church) because he had narrowly escaped the Lisbon earthquake by going that day, as though by some miracle, to visit Santarém?

These farewells were made in two stages. First came a series of performances which ended the man's career as an opera singer, then, during retirement, a few isolated and late appearances in private gatherings or churches. For their final departure from the stage they usually chose some large theatre dear to their hearts—Senesino in Naples, where he had shone during his youth, Rauzzini and Rubinelli in London where they ended their careers covered in glory, Marchesi at La Scala in Milan where he had assumed his first 'masculine' roles . . . In 1792 Pacchiarotti returned to the city which had witnessed his début, Venice, and was fortunate enough to participate, during his last appearance, in the inauguration of La Fenice, the third large Italian theatre to be built in the eighteenth century after the San Carlo in Naples and La Scala. It was at this period that Madame Vigée-Lebrun heard him: 'I was present also at the last concert given by Pacchiarotti, that famous singer who was a model of the grand and beautiful Italian method. He still possessed all his talent, but since the day I have mentioned he has never sung in public.'[1]

With the exception of Rauzzini, who had passed a great deal of time between London and Dublin and retired to Bath, or Balatri, who was to die in Munich, all the castrati wanted to return to their home country. Salimbeni alone did not have time to do so; he fell ill in Dresden, tried to return to Italy and died on the way at the age of thirty-nine. Many chose to retire to the town or village where they had been born. In fact it was a return to roots in a community which in the past had imposed on them a destiny as glorious on the professional level as it was painful on the human one. All resentment, it seems, had vanished and they returned to their native region as internationally known artistes, enjoying great fame among their fellow town- or country-dwellers, but never immune from the solitude and progressive oblivion imposed by time.

Through personal conviction a few singers preferred to enter the religious life: Vittori, who had always divided his time between the operatic stage and the Sistine Chapel, became a priest at forty-three. Tosi became one at the end of his life, as did Pistocchi, who retired to a monastery run by the Oratorians where he devoted himself to composition.

All the others pursued a secular life, enjoying secure material comfort thanks to the large sums of money they had accumulated during their careers. However, while these men without posterity could have turned in upon themselves and lived selfishly while contemplating their fortune and their memories, they often showed remarkable generosity towards their remaining relatives or the community around them. Ferri gave 600,000 écus to one of them; Marchesi, who had perhaps amassed the greatest fortune, constantly helped musicians in need and in 1783 founded the *Pio Istituto Filarmonico*, responsible for organising concerts to help the widows and orphans of musicians. Farinelli gave all that remained to him to his nephews and the servants who had looked after him until the end—he who in Spain had done so much for Italian exiles, now assisted poor families of Spanish origin in Bologna and in particular provided clothing for the children. Matteuccio gave a chapel to the priest who helped him during his last years and endowed the funds necessary for its maintenance. Lastly, Guadagni never stopped distributing the vast sums he had earned and, apart from his house in Padua, possessed hardly anything at the time of his death; for him 'lending' meant 'giving', and many people took advantage of this. One day a ruined aristocrat borrowed from him the sum of 100 sequins, swearing by all the gods that he would return it. 'That is not what I had in mind,' replied Guadagni, 'and if I wanted to have it repaid I should not lend it to you.'

It is true nonetheless that these singers did not live an impoverished existence. They had secured for themselves at least a comfortable house where they could reside in peace and receive their visitors. Rauzzini lived in Italian style in his very beautiful cottage, Perrymead, not far from Bath, while Guarducci lived in English style at his house in Montefiascone, near Viterbo, where Dr Burney visited him, finding a totally British décor in very good taste. Matteuccio retired to a large apartment in Naples, Guadagni built himself a house in Padua and Farinelli a small country-style palazzo outside the walls of Bologna. Before leaving for Spain he had bought a piece of land beyond the Porta delle Lame and then, working from Madrid, had commissioned and supervised the building of the residence in which he hoped to end his days. It was there that he spent more than fifteen years surrounded by his souvenirs.

Regrettably the city of Bologna has razed this fine house to the ground, and today a sugar factory stands in its place, in the middle of an industrial estate. Pacchiarotti retired to the palazzo in Padua which had once belonged to Cardinal Bembo. He too chose to live amid an English décor: the English-style garden and the very fine furniture he had brought back from London were there to remind him of his successes on the other side of the English Channel.

Caffarelli, who had not lost his pride and greed, certainly wanted to possess more than everyone else, in particular one thing which was the least easy to obtain, an aristocratic title. Thanks to his vast fortune he was able to buy the domain of San Donato and the entire duchy that went with it, near Otranto in the south of Apulia. In this way he had the satisfaction, in all modesty, of mentioning in his will that he was bequeathing a duchy to his nephew. Since that was not enough he ordered the building in Naples of a palazzo several storeys high. It is still possible to admire this palazzo today, now divided into twenty or so apartments; it is at number 13 in the via Carlo de Cesare, very close to the via Toledo, about two hundred yards from the San Carlo theatre. The Latin inscription that the castrato had engraved on it remains perfectly legible: *Amphion Thebas ego domum* (Amphion built Thebes and I built this house), to which a wag is thought to have added, at the time: *Ille cum Tu sine* (He had got them, you haven't). This was probably not an actual inscription, but a witty remark cheerfully bandied about by the eighteenth-century Neapolitans, but it was too good not to have survived over the centuries. As for the words chosen by Caffarelli, they were no doubt inspired by the inscription of 1698 on the palazzo of Nicolas Altamuro, at Noci, situated in the province of Bari where the singer had been born. There could be read the following words: *Hoc Nicolaus opus non arte Amphion ut alter struxit at Alta lyra saxa stetere Muro*

(This monument was erected not by the art of masons but by Nicolas, like a second Amphion, who built it thanks to his sublime lyre).

The comparison between Amphion and Caffarelli caused much ink to flow. Some saw in it the conceited nature of the sopranist who dared to compare himself to the legendary musician of antiquity, he whose song alone had achieved the building of Thebes. Others imagined that it revealed Caffarelli's nobility of soul, since he acknowledged humbly that while the divine Amphion had been able to build a city, he, through his poor singing, had only been able to build a modest palazzo. Pride or modesty? No matter, Caffarelli had achieved his object, which was to be talked about long after his death.

Old age and the voice

Despite his fame, fortune and properties, Caffarelli had aged badly, physically and vocally. The Neapolitans had been able to hear him, on different occasions, during his long 'official' retirement which lasted nearly thirty years. The man who was regarded in Naples as the 'patriarch of song' had not been able to resist reappearing, despite his vow after the Lisbon earthquake, at concerts, in churches, in the Chapel Royal and even in the theatre. This had only served to disappoint 'his' public, who were used to more perfection. The architect Luigi Vanvitelli heard him during the years 1762–1764 and was most put out, even furious, that the singer dared to appear before the public and sing 'like a bleating goat' (*capronescamente*) while displaying a body that was far too obese and inadequately clothed. 'He sang,' added Vanvitelli, 'like an old castrato who understands music, but he looked like a big goat with a hard and ugly voice, and that is how people admired the relic of the man who in the past was the best castrato after

Farinelli.'[2] A year later Vanvitelli offended again and rather spitefully compared the former stage hero to the ruins of the Colosseum 'and nothing more': Caffarelli was only fifty-three! The singer persisted nonetheless but obviously had to accept the situation when he heard disenchanted or spiteful remarks from the good people of Naples. At sixty he decided that in future he would sing only in churches, during special ceremonies.

The case of Caffarelli might appear quite normal but in fact it was an exception and deserves to be considered separately. As a general rule the extraordinary vocal longevity of the *virtuosi* was astonishing. Some doctors believed that the faculty for singing correctly at an advanced age could be explained by the fact that in the castrati the small vocal cords were amplified by adult muscular development and a large rib-cage. As a result the singer needed to make less effort and tired his voice less, despite possessing power and flexibility often superior to other voices. Many seventeenth- and eighteenth-century observers have confirmed that the voices of the sopranists—the best ones, obviously!—seemed to 'last' better than others; they retained a clarity, resonance and childlike lightness which often led to them being described as 'angelic', even when the singer was approaching the last years of his life. When faced with a medical phenomenon as complex as this we must, as always, remain cautious and not see every castrato as an octogenarian with a voice remaining systematically pure and bewitching. Moreover, the evidence from the past did not mention 'miracles' either; the classic expression 'one cannot be and have been' applied to the castrati also, since at seventy they no longer sang as they had done at thirty. But the disturbing thing still is the near-hypnotic emotional power apparently felt by those lucky enough to hear those voices late in the day, for they expressed a kind of fascination due to a supernatural timbre which seemed to have defied the laws of sex and age. When Dr Burney listened to Guarducci singing an aria by Sacchini he even found that his voice had improved and that, despite his age, his power, taste and expression were far superior to what they had been previously in England.

Matteuccio was a perfect example of this astonishing longevity. When he was over seventy he was still singing in a Naples church. His voice had retained its charm, flexibility and power, and Mancini assures us that members of the congregation who could not see him were convinced they were hearing the voice of a much younger man.

Guadagni and Pacchiarotti, the two most noteworthy voices at the end of the eighteenth century, had retired one after the other in Padua. Guadagni had participated until the end in the ceremonies at the cathedral of San Antonio; he died in 1792, the same year that Pacchiarotti decided to take his retirement in that city, at the age of fifty-two. Four years later he was summoned to participate in a formal soirée in honour of Bonaparte. He attended under duress and sang with restraint. Far from taking umbrage the French general, who had already realised that surrounding himself with great artistes was one way of increasing his own fame, called the singer over and made him sit beside him for the whole of the evening. During the years that followed Pacchiarotti worked constantly and perfected his voice, singing in particular the psalms by Marcello who, he said, had taught him 'the little that he knew'.

Stendhal, when passing through Padua, was amazed by the voice of the septuagenarian Pacchiarotti. His conversations with this ageing man impressed him deeply. 'I have learnt more about music in six conversations with this great artiste,' he admitted, 'than through any book: it is soul speaking to soul.'[3]

Pacchiarotti's last public appearance was also the most

moving of all. It took place in 1814 at St Mark's in Venice: the singer, who was then seventy-four, only agreed to make it because it was the funeral of Bertoni, his teacher from the very beginning. The sorrow felt that day by the castrato is understandable, for he was losing the man who had taught him everything, taken him to London and become his lifelong friend. But we can also imagine his emotion, and that of the people present, when he sang for the last time in the cathedral which had seen the start of his career at the age of twenty-five. Pacchiarotti survived Bertoni by seven more years and died of dropsy, begging God to 'welcome him into His most humble choirs'.

Farinelli never stopped singing. Three weeks before his death, at seventy-seven, he was still practising several hours a day, accompanying himself on the harpsichord. Although he maintained he had lost much power since his youth, he still astonished those who came to see him. Out of modesty he did not want to sing before visitors and only agreed to do so in order not to appear uncivil. The Abbé Coyer was fortunate enough to hear him singing in Bologna: 'I heard him: my ears are still full of the sound. You know about the role he played in Spain, where he made great men and ministers jealous. If he no longer lives in the midst of honours he has gained in tranquillity and he is a great pleasure to know.'[4] Fernan Nuñez also paid him a visit and was very moved on hearing him: '[He] sang a little, as he could at his age, and truly he let us see what he had been.'[5] Of all the enthusiastic writings which tell of the last meetings with Farinelli, the most touching remains that of Casanova, who describes the visit to Bologna by the Electress of Saxony in 1775, when the singer was seventy. When she entered his salon she begged him to sing but at first received a polite refusal. She insisted, and for her alone he sang an aria from his glorious repertoire of the past. As soon as the last note had died away the Electress threw herself into his arms and embraced him, crying: 'Now I can die happy!'

Last occupations

Many castrati used their retirement positively in order to listen to young singers, advising and training them, whatever their voices were like. It was the price of their fame, but also reflected the need to create a musical link with the rising generation, particularly when it led to a kind of affectionate relationship with young castrati. How much we should have valued a few snippets of these conversations between *virtuosi* of different generations! It is certainly not hard to imagine the wise counsel on the strictly vocal level that the older singers could give to the younger ones. But on the human level, what account of their life did they give to those making their début? Was it frankly positive or strongly tinged with bitterness? Did the young singers visit their seniors seeking only encouragement for their future careers or wanting words of consolation? In particular, what could be said to those who were emerging as the nineteenth century approached, along with the first measures forbidding the use of castrati and the general collapse of the world that had favoured the triumph of their predecessors?

We should very much like to know, for example, what Pacchiarotti said to the young singers who came to see him in Padua at that crucial period which was in the process of settling the fate of the castrati for ever. We have no more information about the many discussions that Farinelli had held thirty or forty years earlier with young castrati who asked if they could visit him in his Bologna retreat. We know that he received them with his usual courtesy and modesty: he never asked them to sing in front of him, which might have made them ill at ease, but he listened willingly to those who wanted to perform a few arias in order to receive his advice.

Some castrati even used their retirement to teach in a highly official way. Bernacchi founded a school at his house in the via Riva Reno in Bologna. In this way he was following the example of Tosi and his teacher Pistocchi, continuing to make the capital of Emilia the principal Italian centre after Naples for the teaching of song. This school produced famous names such as Vittoria Tesi and Mancini, the future singing teacher to the Imperial Austrian court; from here too came the great Italian tenor Annibale Pio Fabri, who was attached to the Chapel Royal in Lisbon, and the no less famous German tenor Anton Raaff, who was to create the role of Idomeneo in Mozart's opera forty or so years later in Munich.

The castrato Giuseppe Aprile had taken his retirement in 1785, two years after replacing Caffarelli as *primo musico* in the Chapel Royal in Lisbon. He too then dedicated himself to the teaching of song and could pride himself on having had Domenico Cimarosa as a student. He published several collections of *solfeggio* exercises for the voice before retiring to his native town of Martina Franca near Tarento.

The retirement years also provided a privileged moment for meetings with personalities from the literary and artistic world of the period. After so many journeys around Europe and time spent waiting on princes, the castrati now saw great names from this same world hasten to their houses and ask for an interview. To quote only Pacchiarotti, he received in his salon the entire intellectual elite of the late eighteenth century and the start of the nineteenth— the writers Goldoni, Gozzi and Foscolo, the sculptor Canova and the young Rossini . . .

Farinelli was certainly the most sought after; anyone would have done the impossible to spend an hour with him, surrounded by all the objects he had brought back from Spain. He possessed a Stradivarius and an Amati, a viola as well as ten or so harpsichords which he had named after painters. His favourite, called 'Raffaello', had been given to him by Queen Barbara; another was called 'Correggio,' a third 'Leonardo', and so on.

He divided his time between music and the spiritual meditation which he valued above everything else. He prayed every morning while looking through his window at the sanctuary of the Madonna di San Luca, which stood on a hill near Bologna. He had also obtained permission to have an altar in his house so that his personal chaplain could say mass there. Lastly, he liked to go on pilgrimages to different sanctuaries in the district, including Loreto, his favourite.

Each year he carried out a certain number of ritual visits to the Duke of Parma, the Archbishop and various local personalities. Apart from the young musicians who asked if they could talk to him he received at his house the few close friends who remained to him. Padre Martini certainly occupied the first place in his heart: he was not only the great teacher and historian of music in Bologna, but also his confessor and his dearest friend. Apart from the English musicologist and diarist Dr Burney, many times quoted in this book, the principal personalities who asked to be received included Gluck, Mozart and the dowager Electress of Saxony. Joseph II also came to Bologna incognito on his way to Rome. He hastened to invite Farinelli to the inn where he was staying, but the latter had to decline. The Emperor then left for Rome and repeated his request on his way back, when he had the great delight of talking with him alone for an hour or two.

Did Joseph II, like so many others, beg him earnestly to write his memoirs? The interest such a unique document could hold for posterity, coming from the greatest castrato in history, can easily be imagined. Unfortunately Farinelli responded to the entreaties of his circle with a few words only, reported by Giovanni Sacchi: 'For what purpose? It is enough for me to know that I have caused no harm to anyone. It could be said also that I regret I have not been able to do all the good I should have liked to.'[6]

Adored during his lifetime and remaining famous after his death, Farinelli had the unusual honour, along with Maria Malibran, of becoming a character in literature and opera. The English composer John Barnett made him the protagonist of his opera *Farinelli* (1839), while Eugène Scribe wrote a novella entitled *Carlo Broschi* and included the singer among the characters in his libretto (set to music by Auber), *La Part du Diable* (1843).

The age at which the castrati died provoked discussion among many doctors and historians during the nineteenth century. In their view the emasculation undergone by the singers during childhood could have prolonged their life beyond the normal span; such a theory was obviously without foundation, and it was fortunate that the operation had no adverse effect on the health and entire life of the castrati. In fact suppositions of this sort attempted to justify scientifically a reality that was purely accidental. A glance at the age of the principal castrati at death (with the exception of Siface, who was assassinated at forty-four), shows that of the thirty-five greatest names of the seventeenth and eighteenth centuries, nine became octogenarians and twelve septuagenarians—that is to say, nearly two-thirds lived into their seventies and beyond. Seven castrati died in their sixties while the rest lived to ages ranging from fifty-nine to barely forty. The oldest survivor was Atto Melani who died at eighty-eight, while Salimbeni died the youngest at thirty-nine.

Since all age-groups are represented by these figures it is clear that no theory can be advanced. But it is disturbing all the same that even if these statistics are very limited, twenty-eight castrati out of thirty-five were to live beyond sixty, even far beyond, at a period when the expectation of life was only twenty-five to thirty years. This was likely to astonish contemporaries and intrigue future generations: hence the temptation to attribute such records to emasculation itself. In the long run, was there not confusion or assimilation between the longevity of the individual, on which the medical act had no effect, and the longevity of the voice which, as we have seen, could be somewhat exceptional?

We know less about the deaths and funerals of the castrati. None of them formed the object of lavish ceremonies at a national or local level, as occurred during the nineteenth century for many great composers or performers. Usually the great *virtuosi* gave up their souls to God in extreme privacy, supported by a few faithful friends, and sometimes in total oblivion. They were all buried without the slightest pomp in the town where they had spent their last years. Farinelli, one suspects, demanded the most quiet funeral possible. He asked to be laid to rest on one of the hills of Bologna, in the Capuchin church which the Napoleonic troops destroyed, along with his tomb, a few years later.

There is only one more humorous note in this context: the death certificate drawn up by the parish of San Giovanni Maggiore in Naples when the castrato Matteuccio was buried included one surprising detail: 'On 15th October 1737. Matteo Sassano, aged eighty, resident of the Rosariello de Palazzo, *virgin*, buried at the Carminiello di Palazzo.'

10
The Twilight of the Angels

When we [castrati] are no longer there, *bel canto* also can intone its *Miserere*.

ALLEGRI

From the end of the eighteenth century the fate of the castrati was sealed. Even if the most famous of them quietly ended their careers after 1800, the heroic times when their predecessors had incarnated an aesthetic and musical ideal were over. As the new century dawned the castrati found themselves under attack from all sides for reasons both musical and ideological. In spite of this many boys still underwent the operation in the vain hope of acquiring some claim to fame; the collapse of such hopes was to be all the more severe for those young men whose family or close associates had not seen in advance, or not wished to see, the twilight of a dying musical tradition.

First signs of decline

Opposition to the castrati from the *philosophes* and the encyclopaedists had been particularly virulent. The French, as we have seen, disliked their voices, their effeminate mannerisms and everything that they saw as an offence against 'nature'. Voltaire, through his character Procurante (in *Candide*), could not have rendered more clearly the opinion of his intellectual contemporaries: 'Go if you wish to see bad tragedies set to music in which the scenes are only devised to bring together, most inappropriately, two or three ridiculous songs which show off an actress's throat; swoon with pleasure if you wish or if you can at the sight of a eunuch warbling the roles of Caesar and Cato and walking about the stage in clumsy fashion. As for me, I long ago gave up these miserable performances which today constitute the glory of Italy and are paid for so dearly by sovereigns.'[1]

In most contemporary writing the opposition to the castrati was dictated by the eternal feud with the whole of Italian music. The writers of the 'Enlightenment' entered the argument deliberately and aimed straight, concentrating their accusations against the practice of emasculation, unworthy of a modern, enlightened society. Voltaire, in *Candide* again, exaggerated the number of children handed over for castration in order to bring out the sordid aspect of such a practice: 'I was born in Naples [. . .]; there they castrate two or three thousand boys every year; some die as a result, others acquire a voice finer than that of women, and others still go off and govern countries [an obvious allusion to Farinelli].'[2]

Jean-Jacques Rousseau, who had attacked those 'barbarous fathers' who 'handed over their children [. . .] for the pleasure of self-indulgent cruel people', pursued his diatribe with vehemence: 'If it is possible, let us allow the voice of shame and humanity to be heard, the voice that cries out against this infamous custom; and may the princes who encourage it through their requirements blush at the thought of endangering the survival of the human race.'[3] But Rousseau failed to avoid the pitfall of caricature when he attacked the castrati from the musical and humanitarian point of view, making them into real monsters: he sees in them 'the most gloomy actors in the world' who sing 'without warmth and passion', speak 'worse than other men' and cannot even pronounce an 'R'!

It was this lack of objectivity that caused Stendhal to intervene half a century later, with ironic criticism of the economico-demographic reasonings of the French: 'As for the beautiful voices of Italy, the stupid attitude of our little *philosophes* will probably diminish our pleasures for a long time to come. These gentlemen have been preaching the message that a little operation performed on a few choir-boys was going to turn Italy into a desert: the population would die out, the grass was already growing in the via Toledo; and what of the sacred rights of humanity!'[4]

The attack led by the French was coupled with a growing awareness of the moral problems posed by castration. The Church itself began to react: Benedict XIV declared in his important work *De Synodo dioecesana* that the amputation of any part of the human body was not legal except in the case of essential medical necessity. The growth of this argument reflected the progressive disappearance of the Neapolitan conservatoires, the bastions for two centuries of training for the castrati and the most accomplished art of singing. The Conservatorio dei Poveri di Gesù Cristo had closed in 1744, the victim of bad administration and internal troubles. During the following two decades the three other establishments were plagued by the same rebellions by the *figlioli*, the same incapacity of the directors but also by the growing incompetence of the singing teachers. By about 1790 the glorious period of the Neapolitan school of song was already past. Many failed teachers of the harpsichord or the violin liked to think they could teach singing without knowing anything about the vanished art of Porpora or Gizzi. These were the people who were attacked by the theorist Mancini: 'They make their students sing as loudly as possible and ruin some very fine voices through their ignorance about the principles of producing and controlling the voice.'⁵ When Mattei was appointed to the Pietà dei Turchini in 1790, he found the conversatoire in a state of indescribable disorder. The high-grade teaching of twenty or thirty years earlier was reduced to a few rondos and little lightweight songs taken from third-rate scores, earning the contempt of the great Italian teachers.

The city of Naples, more preoccupied with the ups and downs of political life—the Napoleonic epic, the attempt to set up a Parthenopean Republic, the re-establishment of the monarchy—did not react to the death-throes of the three remaining conservatoires. In 1797 Sant'Onofrio, which had only thirty students at the time, was amalgamated with Santa Maria di Loreto; this unstable group of forty students was incorporated in 1806 with the Pietà dei Turchini which for some years had consisted of only ten castrati. It was then that Monsignor Capeciletro decided to dissolve what remained of the old conservatoires, planning to construct over their ruins an institution better adapted to the new era: the conservatoire of San Sebastiano.

The decline in the art of song and its teaching was not the only reason for the disappearance of the castrati. The ideas promulgated by the French Revolution and the armies of Bonaparte were also spreading at the same time, and they were to deliver a final blow to a vocal tradition linked to the Ancien Régime. New society, especially in France, but also in Italy, now thought in terms of 'levy', 'conscription' and 'military bravura', Rouget de Lisle, who had heard a castrato in 1792, had been unable to resist a humorous remark on the subject: 'Our army,' he declared, 'can see little advantage in cannons without balls!' The *Declaration of the Rights of Man* also dealt a blow to those who supported castration, sometimes unconsciously, by proclaiming the physical and spiritual liberty of every man: 'Do not do to another what you would not wish to be done to yourself' (1793, article 6).

In 1798 the Pope revoked the long-standing ban in his States against women on the stage. The castrati did not disappear as a result but they had to face ever-growing competition from women singers, as in all the Italian states. Napoleon made full use of his power to condemn the practice of emasculation in Europe. At his request his brother Joseph, then King of Naples, forbade castrated boys to enter the schools and conservatoires, in order to dissuade Italian society from such a practice. The *Monitore Napoletano* of 5 December 1806 testifies to this: 'His Majesty has been unable to consider without indignation the barbarous practice of creating eunuchs in order to produce women's voices in men. As a result he has ordered, by the decree of 27 November, that in future such people shall not be admitted into the schools at all.' Napoleon flattered himself that he had contributed to the abolition of this custom which he described as 'shameful and horrible'. He even thought he had put an end to it, in which he was wrong: 'I abolished this custom,' he confided to his doctor on St Helena, 'in all the countries under my rule, I even forbade it in Rome, under pain of death. It had entirely ceased, and I think that although the Pope and his cardinals are now in charge, it will not appear again.'[6] Clearly he could not conceive that the entire nineteenth century would still have eunuch-singers.

Some time after the measures taken by Napoleon and his brother Joseph, in 1814 precisely, it was the turn of Francis I of Lombardy-Venetia to exclude castrati from the stage, a measure which put the singer Velluti temporarily in danger although this was soon circumvented. On all sides the ground was becoming shaky beneath the feet of the last castrati. In a quarter of a century a change as rapid as it was inescapable had driven them from their heroic bastion to join the ranks of ordinary singers, suffering from the vogue for tenors and women singers, as well as from the decline of *opera seria* which had been the reason for their existence for nearly two centuries.

However, many music-lovers remained faithful to them and did not hesitate to demand the continuation of a medical practice that was almost universally condemned; how many Italian theatres, it is said, did not resound at the end of the eighteenth century with cries of *Evviva il coltello! il benedetto coltello!* (Long live the knife! the blessed knife!)

The last two great castrati

The careers of Girolamo Crescentini and Giovanni Battista Velluti led the era of opera castrati into its swan-song. These two careers were as brilliant and international as they were isolated in time, since the former singer retired in 1812 and the latter in 1830, when romantic opera was born and had no more dealings with the voices of castrati.

The emasculation they had undergone as children had taken place at a period when many famous castrati were ending their careers in glory. Aprile, Pacchiarotti, Rubinello and Marchesi made their farewells to the stage respectively in 1785, 1792, 1800 and 1805; it was not surprising that some boys were still being castrated at the end of the eighteenth century, despite the success of the other 'natural' voices on which opera now relied. Velluti's operation even seems to have been a doctor's mistake. His parents had planned a military career for him, but just as the boy was about to undergo an operation for a completely different medical reason the parents and the doctor failed to understand each other. The latter, who was probably accustomed to carrying out orchidectomy, deliberately castrated the child. The father and mother could then only contemplate a career as a singer for the son whom they had destined for the army.

Even if Crescentini was eighteen years older than Velluti, the two men had much in common. In the first place they had been trained in Bologna, the former by Gibelli, the latter by Padre Mattei. The capital of Emilia remained the place where the training given to the castrati had been maintained best while the Neapolitan conservatoires were in a state of total collapse. Their subsequent careers had other things in common: both made their débuts at twenty, both enjoyed the same triumphs throughout Europe around the pole of attraction formed by La Scala in Milan, both retired at forty and both died in their eighties.

Crescentini's voice received so many admiring tributes that they cannot all be quoted. Even the Germans, although at this period they had turned towards other musical horizons, did not fail to recognise the singer's talent, comparing him to Marchesi or Pacchiarotti. The *Allgemeine musikalische Zeitung* of Leipzig praised him highly, while the philosopher Schopenhauer declared: 'His beautiful supernatural voice cannot be compared with that of any woman's voice: there cannot exist a finer and fuller timbre, and with that silver purity he acquires an indescribable power.'[7] Madame Vigée-Lebrun also saw Crescentini in Rome at the end of the eighteenth century, in the opera *Cesare*: 'His singing and his voice at this period had the same perfection; he was playing the role of a woman and was decked out in a large hoop-petticoat such as used to be worn at Versailles, which made us laugh a great deal. It should be added that at this time Crescentini possessed all the freshness of youth and acted with much expression.'[8]

Of all the singer's journeys abroad, including a stay of four years in London, the most interesting one for the historian is possibly that which took him to Paris, where he remained from 1806 to 1812. It was a curious paradox, in fact, to see this castrato at the end of his career experiencing one of his greatest successes in a country which had always been sceptical towards the castrati and under an Emperor who had been determined to eradicate emasculation in Europe. Strange also was the conduct of Napoleon, who after spending his life on battlefields only cared for 'sad and pretty melodies' and became ecstatic while listening to the pathos in the singing of 'his' favourite castrato.

While he was still only a general Napoleon had often had the opportunity to hear the castrati during his campaigns. On two occasions (Milan and Vienna) he was captivated by the voice of the man whom Europe named the 'Italian Orpheus'; as he did for Paër or Paisiello, Napoleon lost no time in inviting him to Paris, on the 'imperial' salary of 30,000 francs a year. Crescentini was then over forty and had been unable to escape the portliness and the heavy features of many castrati like himself, even if his talent as an actor and even his smallest gestures redeemed this unattractive figure: 'Movements full of grace and dignity,' wrote Mademoiselle Avrillon, 'a perfect understanding of the stage, controlled gestures totally in keeping with the dialogue, a face which reflected with the most astonishing accuracy all the nuances of passion; all these rare and valuable qualities endowed the singing of this artiste with a magic impossible to describe, unless one had heard him.'[9]

Napoleon had kept Crescentini and Giuseppina Grassini for his court theatre, situated in the Tuileries, reserved exclusively for the Imperial family, members of the court and guests of note. This select and elegant audience was not, however, made up of connoisseurs, far from it! Officers and members of the new aristocracy attended much more from duty than from pleasure and were somewhat bored as they listened to the smooth melodies sung by the voice of a castrato, to which they were not accustomed. 'The court yawned a good deal,' wrote an eyewitness, 'and moreover they were not allowed to applaud, which Madame Grassini found unfair and much too "likely to lead to mediocrity".'

In this scarcely stimulating context Crescentini at least had the satisfaction of pleasing the Emperor beyond all his hopes. In Paris, as in Milan, Vienna or Lisbon the singer carried in his baggage the score which had ensured his fame, Zingarelli's *Romeo e Giulietta*, in which he always included an aria allegedly of his own composition (but no doubt revised and corrected by Zingarelli), *Ombra adorata aspetta*; this aria began with a *messa di voce* which allowed the castrato to emit a sound of extraordinary purity on the opening syllable. Napoleon and Josephine listened to several performances of this work (or at least certain selected scenes) with unflagging pleasure. One evening Mademoiselle Avrillon observed the sovereign's attitude: 'From the box where I was, I could see perfectly with my lorgnette the face of His Majesty; while Crescentini was singing the famous *Ombra adorata aspetta* it was, without exaggeration, radiant with pleasure. The Emperor shifted on his seat, spoke frequently to the senior officers of the Empire who surrounded him, and seemingly wanted to make them share the admiration he felt.'[10] It was more than admiration, it was genuinely deep emotion: Crescentini was the only singer to bring tears to the eyes of Napoleon.

In 1812, after receiving the Cross of the Iron Crown, the singer explained to the sovereign that the climate of Paris was harmful to his health and that he wished to return to a country with more clement weather. In this way he retired from the stage and devoted himself to teaching, both at the Liceo Musicale in Bologna and the new Conservatorio di San Sebastiano in Naples, where he died in 1846. During a visit to this city in 1835 a Frenchwoman had the opportunity to approach him; she observed in particular the singer's melancholy and his nostalgia for a musical past that was lost for ever. 'This thin, elderly man, whose wrinkled face, white hair and stooping figure had struck the onlooker at once, was Crescentini! [...] The same Crescentini whose name, twenty years ago, was on everyone's lips, uttered along with hyperboles of praise! He approached, he spoke to you of his past fame, he spoke of his singing which had delighted Napoleon; his eyes were dull, his face thoughtful; he seemed to have left his soul and his voice behind in the time that no longer exists; and that wan face, those blank eyes, that life which was technically over but continued on its way dragging a corpse behind it, made you feel truly melancholy!'[11]

Giovanni Battista Velluti went a little farther along the path marked out by his predecessors before acquiring the 'privilege' of being the last castrato to appear on the operatic stage. The successes he obtained with audiences in Milan, London or St Petersburg had not, however, been so easily won. While his first appearances, right at the beginning of the nineteenth century, could still blend in with the late performances of the last great castrati, during his principal period of activity (1810–1830) he began to appear odd in a new musical landscape where the castrati had no place. Even the English public, formerly fascinated by Rauzzini or Rubinelli, had not heard any castrati for a quarter of a century; they regarded Velluti as a (splendid) curiosity, as the astonishing survivor of an art that had fallen into disuse.

Many composers had already stopped using the castrati. Gluck had entrusted his second version of the role of Orpheus to a tenor and Mozart, after several attempts, had clearly preferred women singers and light tenors. Much later Bellini was also to dissociate himself from Velluti, already regarding him as a contradiction in terms, vocally and physically. As for Rossini, he favoured the castrati, and wanted to offer Velluti the title role in his opera *Aureliano in Palmira*, in 1813. The singer, according to Stendhal, was then 'in the flower of his youth and talent, and one of the best-looking men of his century.'[12] Unfortunately the relations between the two men deteriorated rapidly. Velluti's talent and the legendary 'celestial sweetness' of his voice were not enough to make up for his ridiculous abuses in the ornamentation of arias: Rossini approved of virtuosity but above all he wanted recognition of his own score and did not want it sabotaged by the vocal acrobatics of a singer. A page in the history of music had been turned once and for all: the essentially virtuoso art of the eighteenth century, subject to the caprice of a singer, however talented, was no longer acceptable at the start of the nineteenth. Rossini, who had already begun to note down certain ornaments of his own, then decided to write them all out, from the first note to the last, so that each score would be totally respected. Even if some singers still continued for a few years to treat them as they chose, an important step had been taken and a definite limit set to the artiste's innate gift for 'improvisation'.

Rossini and Velluti were cool towards each other for a time, long enough for the composer to insist in future on women singers in his works, especially mezzo-sopranos, rather than castrati. But the quarrel did not last, since Rossini was more of a reformer than a revolutionary. His nostalgia for the eighteenth century was too strong for him to forget the castrati whom he had known with all they had brought to the art of singing. He not only saw Velluti again in Paris a few years later, and made a friend of him, but he never failed to remind his contemporaries of the predominant place that the castrati had won in the history of opera.

'It is impossible,' he confessed to Wagner in 1860, 'to imagine the delightful voices and the consummate virtuosity possessed through lack of something else and through a charitable compensation, by those bravest of the brave.'[13] The disappearance of the castrati made him add, 'This was the cause of the irreparable decline in the art of singing.' Three years later, when he composed his *Petite messe solennelle*, he demanded, on the score, 'twelve singers of three sexes, men, women and castrati'. It was obvious that his wish would not be granted, without calling on a few surviving castrati from the Papal Chapel, a solution that was quite improbable. Was this a further example of Rossini's customary humour or perhaps a kind of restrained nostalgia for that 'third' voice that was missing in 1863?

Despite the problems encountered by Velluti in Rossini's *Aureliano*—they had not hindered his triumph—it was in a now forgotten opera by Morlacchi, *Tibaldo e Isolina* (1822), that this singer was to reach the apex of his career. Stendhal, a fanatical lover of Italian music, who was deeply moved by the voices of the castrati, described the 'angelic sensations' produced in him by Velluti, as well as the disturbing reactions the voices aroused in a French spectator unaccustomed to them: 'This style may appear effeminate and fail to please at first, but every French music-lover of good faith will agree that this manner of singing is for him an unknown region, a foreign land of which the singing in Paris had given him no notion.'[14]

Stendhal's emotions were no longer shared by the general public: there was no universal approval for the singing of the last castrati, which was already in decline. However, a last possibility was to be offered to the singer by Meyerbeer, in his *Crociato in Egitto* (*The Crusader in Egypt*), first performed in 1824 at La Fenice in Venice and revived, again with Velluti, in Florence the same year, then in London in 1825, 1826 and 1828.

It was the 'nth' paradox in Velluti's career! Meyerbeer, the future creator of romantic historical 'grand opera'

(*Robert le Diable, Les Huguenots*...) wrote the role of Armando for the last man to preserve a vanished *vocalità*, a baroque universe already buried in people's memories! The composer, moreover, was far from acting as Scarlatti or Handel would have done; he did not use Velluti as a 'god' of song, indispensable for the success of his work and the approval of the public, but as an original 'phenomenon', allowing a different approach to the work; the composer, whose curiosity extended to everything, was trying out a vocal experiment which he knew would have no future.

In 1830 Velluti made his farewell to opera before appearing once more in concert performances the following year; he returned to his sumptuous villa on the banks of the Brenta, between Venice and Padua, and died thirty years later at the age of eighty. His departure from the stages of Italy was much more then the mere end to a career, it was the end of a world.

The Vatican and the last castrati

The disappearance of the castrati from opera did not mean a sudden end to emasculation nor to the use of castrati singers in churches and cathedrals. Many boys (no statistics can be established) still underwent the operation throughout the nineteenth century, especially in the Papal States which continued to receive castrati in their choir schools. It was not until 1870 and the end of the Church's sovereignty in temporal affairs that this practice was totally banned by the new regime. Shortly before that cases of castration could have been found more or less everywhere. Of the best known castrati from the end of the nineteenth century, Mustafà probably underwent the operation between 1835 and 1840, and Moreschi in about 1865. Some child singers just managed to escape emasculation: the great romantic tenor Gilbert Duprez tells us in his *Souvenirs* that his teachers were on the point of sending him for castration *en route* to the Sistine Chapel—only his father's categoric refusal saved him.

On all sides, in Italy as elsewhere, violent diatribes were uttered against a custom which had 'dishonoured', it was thought, the two previous centuries. It looked as though every intellectual, every contributor to every encyclopaedia, and even every music-lover, was trying to redeem his country for past errors. In future no anathema was too strong for the condemnation of this 'barbarous' custom which outraged 'morality, humanity and nature'. On the medical level the castrati were accused of all vices, all monstrosities: it was alleged that they had a greater fear of death, hated the human race, behaved in an imperious and despotic manner, possessed a morbid sensitivity, that their skin was rough and evil-smelling . . . ! In a century which tried hard to distinguish between the roles of men and women in opera, no singer wanted to evoke the voice and manners of the former castrati. In about 1845, in Paris, a tenor whose voice and appearance could recall those of the castrati demanded that the posters announcing each of his concerts should state that he 'had the honour to inform the public that he is the father of a family.'

The curiosity of the musicians and intellectuals in all countries was, however, awakened during the nineteenth century due to the few castrati who still survived, as happens in the case of all vanishing 'species'. People could satisfy this curiosity by going to one of the ceremonies in the Sistine Chapel where the famous papal choir sang every day. Despite the defects of some singers, which were noticed by contemporary observers, these services still produced a fervent atmosphere and a high-quality musical repertoire; the other Italian churches gave way to fashion and included in their Sunday masses overtures by Rossini and cavatinas by Bellini.

The whole of literary and musical Europe therefore went into that Holy of Holies to hear the famous choir in which the castrati had their place beside the tenors and basses. Reactions varied widely and became less and less enthusiastic as the end of the nineteenth century drew near. Berlioz was particularly astonished by the lack of general culture among the singers, for some of them had virtually never heard of Mozart. Mendelssohn, like many others, admired the tenor and bass voices but found the singing of the castrati often too strident. Spontini admired this choir for its skill in maintaining intact the great Gregorian or polyphonic tradition. Liszt too praised this bastion of tradition but deplored the many 'arrangements' which distorted the works of Carissimi, Allegri or Palestrina.

In 1839 Marie d'Agoult expressed a similar disappointment in a letter to Ferdinand Hiller: 'There is no point in telling you that the reputation of the Holy Week ceremonies is greatly exaggerated. You go there with admission tickets as you go to the theatre; you fight, you do battle with old English ladies; nothing could be less religious. The performance of the music is horribly bad. There are too few castrati and they sing out of tune with quavering voices; the cardinals are half asleep or absent-minded; nobody behaves as they should.'15

In fact the quality of the singing continued to decline and gave rise to unenthusiastic reports. In 1858 Bizet found the music particularly 'tedious' and the French historian Taine, six years later, deplored the 'bawling' of the Sistine Chapel singers.

However, 1878 saw the start of a great period, the last of all, when the castrato Domenico Mustafà was appointed director of the choir for life. Although he favoured his fellow castrati, he nevertheless permitted some children from the Schola Cantorum of San Salvatore and the Lutheran church of Santa Maria dell'Anima to sing in the choir. The work he carried out in the service of music was important but he perpetually came up against the ideas of Maestro Perosi who demanded the final exclusion of the castrati, preferring to rely on children and falsettos. Mustafà fought to the hilt to defend the rights of the castrati. This was much more than a stand on behalf of 'jobs', it was a symbolic struggle for the ideal represented by the very last church castrati. After their years of training, their total devotion to their choir schools, Mustafà believed they could not be compared to boys who sang for a time and without true vocation until their voices broke, when they gave up vocal work in music. As for Perosi, he worried about all the boys who were still being mutilated for the purpose of serving church music. He was to admit later that the struggle had cost him more than all the music he had composed. 'I pursued this policy for a serious moral reason,' he said, 'for as soon as I arrived in Rome I received so many requests from abnormal men who wished to enter the Chapel that I suspected this concealed a dishonourable motive, especially when I saw unhappy children. This fear alone gave me the energy to overcome the problem.'[16]

Perosi was so convincing that Pope Leo XIII granted his request: for the first time in three centuries he pronounced the decree banning for ever the use of castrati in church music. Mustafà, who had done all he could to dissuade the pontiff from this decision, realised he was defeated and abandoned his post to Perosi. The Pope's decision caused a great stir and a comment appeared shortly afterwards, not without humour, in *La Tribuna* on 28 December 1902: 'A decision *ex audientia sanctissima*, taken some months ago and kept secret until now, has just been transformed into a decree and will come into operation at once: as a result those singers who, let us say, are "imperfect" on the physical plane although ... complete as singers, are totally excluded from the Sistine Chapel. This constitutes a victory for Maestro Perosi who had suggested this reform ever since he entered the Sistine. [. . .] In any case, this recent decree means that the famous inscription which could be read barely a century ago outside a barber's shop in the Bianchi Vecchi, "Boys castrated here for the Papal Chapel", now becomes an ... archaeological memory.'

A photograph dating from 1898 can still show us the twenty-eight members of the Chapel choir, and in particular the seven last castrati who departed, one after the other, following the papal decree. The last one of all, Alessandro Moreschi, left as late as 1913, a year after the death of Mustafà, and died forgotten in 1922 at the age of 64. He had been one of the best singers in this Chapel and was known as 'the angel of Rome'. This is why he had been to Lyon, in France, and had also sung at the funerals of the Kings Victor-Emmanuel II and Humbert I of Italy. In 1902 and 1904, in the Vatican, he had made several recordings for the Gramophone Company of London. For a long time they remained collectors' items but they have been restored to us today on a single compact disc* which, as well as the voice of the singer, allows us to hear that of Pope Leo XIII. Despite very poor sound quality and the questionable vocal technique of this ageing singer, we still feel an emotional shock on hearing this evidence, which is unique in the world.

* 'Allessandro Moreschi. The Last Castrato', Pearl Opal CD9823.

Epilogue

The disappearance of the last castrati from the Sistine Chapel was of no real interest to the musical world of the early twentieth century, for it took place far too long after the golden age of the great 'sopranists'. The true 'death' of the castrati had occurred at the start of the nineteenth century, when opera had replaced the 'gods' by the 'divas', and romanticism had supplanted the last surviving traces of the baroque world. Since then (and until now) the general public had gradually forgotten the vanished world of the castrati, while Angus Heriot's book (*The Castrati in Opera*, London, 1956) probably came too soon.

We should be grateful to Dominique Fernandez for restoring to us for the first time, thanks to the magic of fiction (*Porporino ou les Mystères de Naples*, Grasset, 1974) and surely with more truth than reality itself, the musical world of eighteenth-century Naples and all the people who moved through it. The renaissance of baroque music, dance and particularly song has also made it possible to mention the castrati again, in the press, on radio or television, and to attempt a transposition to other voices, a source of many difficulties and disputes.

You may hear someone say, 'I heard a castrato the other day on television.' One thing must be made quite clear:

there are no more castrati now, for the obvious reason that there can be no castrati without castration and such an operation would not be tolerated today. There may be some pre-adolescent boys who have undergone castration before their voices broke, for essential medical reasons such as illness or accident, but these boys are unknown to the world of music. Who can say if one day, when certain taboos have been lifted, they will dare to make public their different condition and develop their voices in order to tackle the repertoire of the great *virtuosi* of the past?

Other contemporary singers, performing on television or on disc, may call themselves 'sopranists' since, due to some natural anomaly—such as a minimum level of testosterone—their voices did not break at puberty. These singers do not claim to be the 'Farinellis' of today, for they are not authentic castrati and above all they have not received a vocal training comparable in duration and difficulty with that of the young Neapolitan or Bolognese students of the past. Nevertheless they offer us a 'different' voice, a new experience, contributing to the rediscovery of the repertoire of the past and joining the voices of women, falsettos, counter-tenors and altos.

There is no agreement about how castrati can be replaced in our present-day baroque productions. Apart from the above-mentioned 'sopranists', the falsettos correspond to no tradition in Italian operatic music and their voices, however superb they are, cannot have the range and power of the castrato voices. On the other hand they can claim they are restoring more fully the ambiguity which created the fascination of the castrato, the 'feminised' voice in a masculine body. Women singers, even wearing men's costumes, cannot convey this disturbing quality, but the mellowness and power of their voices are better suited to scores written for castrati; we should not forget that a role like that of Handel's Rinaldo was sung alternately by castrati and women. The singer Nella Anfuso, whose voice has a remarkable range, claims to have added a *vocalità*, a voice character, taken directly from works on the art of song written during the sixteenth, seventeenth and eighteenth centuries. In 1994, Gérard Corbiau's film *Farinelli, Il Castrato* attempted to re-create the great range of Farinelli's voice by joining a recording of a soprano onto that of a counter-tenor. The two voices were then blended by computer to sound like one.

Where does the truth lie? Nobody can be certain of finding it, especially in relation to those *virtuosi* whose voices are lost to us. Truth is more likely to be found in the heart of each individual who will be fascinated and moved by one voice or one interpretation rather than another. The most important thing for us is surely to redis-cover one of the most fascinating myths in the history of music since that of Orpheus. This adventure lasted for three centuries, defying all the laws of morality and reason to achieve the impossible union of monster and angel.

Notes

Chapter 1: Castration
1 Ch. d'Ancillon, *Traité des eunuques*, p. 6.
2 Ch. de Brosses, *Lettres familières d'Italie*, vol.2, p. 318.

Chapter 2: Origins and Recruitment
1 Angelini Bontempi, *Historia Musica*, p. 111.
2 Ch. de Brosses, *op. cit.*, vol.2, p. 318.
3 J. Benjamin de Laborde, *Essai sur la musique ancienne et moderne* (1780), vol.3, p. 494.
4 Ch. Burney, *The Present State of Music in France and Italy*, 1771.
5 Quoted by A. G. Bragaglia, *Degli 'evirati cantori'*, 1959.
6 P. J. Grosley, *Observations sur l'Italie et sur les Italiens*, vol.3, p. 427.
7 Archives de San Pietro a Majella, *Conclusioni di Loreto*, vol.167.
8 Arch. S. P. XIII.7.18 (5).
9 Arch. S. P. XIII.7.18 (10).
10 *Ibid.*
11 Arch. S. P. XIII.7.18 (31).

Chapter 3: Training the Singers
1 Arch. S. P. *Conclusioni di Loreto*, vol.168.
2 Ch. Burney, *op. cit.*
3 S. Goudar, *Remarques sur la musique*, p. 20.
4 F. Raguenet, *Parallèle des Italiens et des Français*, pp. 88–89.
5 Comte d'Espinchal, *Journal d'émigration*, p. 106.

6 Ch. Burney, *op. cit.*

7 Espinchal, *op. cit.*, p. 106.

8 *Regole e Statuti dei Real Conservatorio della Pietà dei Turchini*, ch.7, art.12.

9 *Libro contabile dei Poveri di G. C.*, January 1673 to December 1678, f.61r.

10 *Ibid.* f.169r.

11 For all medical and phoniatric aspects of castration the reader will read with interest the thesis by Dr Philippe Defaye, *Les Castrats, aspects phoniatriques* (see Bibiography).

12 Arch. S. P. *Conclusioni di Loreto*, 23 September, 1763.

13 See numerous examples quoted in S. de Giacomo, *Il Conservatorio di Sant'Onofrio*, pp. 104–9.

14 Mme Vigée-Lebrun, *Souvenirs*, vol.1, p. 248.

15 P. F. Tosi, *Opinioni de'cantori antichi e moderni*. French edition of 1874, p. 86.

16 *Ibid.* p. 89.

17 *Ibid.* pp. 92–3.

Chapter 4: The Theatre in Italy

1 Abbé Coyer, *Voyages d'Italie et de Hollande*, vol.2, p. 207.

2 Ch. de Brosses, *op. cit.*, p. 344.

3 Abbé Coyer, *op. cit.*, vol.1, p. 326.

4 Ch. de Brosses, *op. cit.*, vol.1, p. 344.

5 J. de La Lande, *Voyage en Italie*, vol.1, p. 144.

6 J. de La Lande, *op. cit.*, vol.7, p. 48.

7 Abbé Coyer, *op. cit.*, Letter 30, pp. 196–9.

8 S. Goudar, *Relation du carnaval de Naples*, p. 10.

9 L. Tragiense, *De i Vizi e de i Difetti del Moderno Teatro*, p. 125.

10 Dufresny, quoted by Benjamin de Laborde, *op. cit.*, vol.1, p. 395.

11 Espinchal, *op. cit.*, p. 75.

12 C. Goldoni, *Mémoires*, p. 274.

13 Quoted in N. Bridgman, *La Musique à Venise*, p. 73.

14 L. Riccoboni, *Réflexions historiques et critiques . . .* p. 24.

15 G. Baretti, *Les Italiens . . .* (1773), p. 8.

16 Pöllnitz, *Lettres*, t.I, p. 411.

17 W. Beckford, *The Travel-Diaries*, vol.1, pp. 251–3.

18 Abbé Coyer, *op. cit.*, vol.1, p. 192.

19 Ch. Burney, *op. cit.*

20 Ch. de Brosses, *op. cit.*, vol.2, p. 313.
21 Espinchal, *op. cit.*, p. 85.
22 W. Beckford, *op. cit.*, pp. 251–2.
23 Abbé Coyer, *op. cit.*, vol.1, p. 244.

Chapter 5: The Road to Fame
 1 Angelini Bontempi, *op. cit.*, p. 111.
 2 Quoted in G. Monaldi, *Cantanti evirati celebri*, p. 94.
 3 Baron Grimm, *Correspondance*, vol.1, p. 53.
 4 W. Beckford, *op. cit.*, vol.1, p. 251.
 5 G. Sacchi, *Vita del Cav. Don Carlo Broschi*, p. 9.
 6 Quoted in F. Rogers, 'The Male Soprano', p. 417.
 7 J. Evelyn, *Diary*, vol.4, pp. 537 and 547.
 8 G. Sacchi, *op. cit.*, p. 11.
 9 L. Zacconi, *Prattica di musica*, p. 58.
10 F. Balatri, *Frutti del Mondo*, p. 256.
11 P. J. Grosley, *op. cit.*, vol.3, pp. 256–7.
12 P. F. Tosi, *op. cit.*
13 G. B. Mancini, *Riflessioni pratiche* . . . Vienna, 1774.
14 Ch. Burney, quoted in Blanchard et Candé, *Dieux et Divas de l'opéra*, p. 170.
15 G. Sacchi, *op. cit.*, p. 15.
16 F. Algarotti, *Saggio sopra l'opera in musica* (1755), quoted in *Enciclopedia dello Spettacolo*, see: *Coloratura*.
17 P. Brydone, *Viaggio in Sicilia*, Letter 36.
18 Maugars: *Réponse faite à un curieux sur le sentiment de la musique d'Italie*, p. 35.
19 J. de La Lande, *op. cit.*, 1769, p. 355.
20 Ch. Burney, *op. cit.*
21 Ch. de Brosses, *op. cit.*, Letter 51.
22 Abbé Labat, *Voyages en France et en Italie*, vol.2, p. 75.
23 P. J. Grosley, *op. cit.*, vol.3, pp. 61–2.
24 J. Addison, *Remarks on Several Parts of Italy*, 1705.
25 L. Tragiense, *op. cit.*, p. 96.
26 P. J. Grosley, *op. cit.*, vol.3, p. 256.
27 D. Confuorto, *Giornali di Napoli*, 1679–1699, vol.2, p. 245.
28 P. Metastasio, *Lettere*, 28 May, 1749.
29 L. Vanvitelli, Letter of 1 January, 1754.

30 Quoted in Bertolotti, *La Musica in Mantova*, p. 109.
31 S. Goudar, *Remarques sur la musique*, pp. 89–90.

Chapter 6: The Castrati and the Church
1 Quoted in Ph. Defaye. *Les Castrats*, p. 24.
2 Quoted in A. Milner, *The Musical Times*, March 1973.
3 J. de La Lande, *op. cit.*, vol.5, p. 437.
4 *Causa dei Cantori Pontifici*, p. 215.
5 Montesquieu, *Voyages*, p. 1147.
6 A. Adami, *Osservazioni* ... pp. 198–9.
7 *Avvisi di Roma*, 8 February 1668.
8 F. Raguenet, *op. cit.*, pp. 100–1.
9 Abbé Richard, *Description d'Italie*, vol.5, p. 184.
10 L. Tragiense, *op. cit.*
11 Espinchal, *op. cit.*, pp. 75–6.
12 Pöllnitz, *Letters*, quoted by G. Roberti, p. 707.
13 Bibl. di Palermo, C440, ms III, E3.

Chapter 7: The Castrati in Society
1 Mme Vigée-Lebrun, *op. cit.*
2 Quoted in G. Monaldi, *op. cit.*
3 P. Brydone, *op. cit.*, Letter xxxv.
4 Letter in the Conservatorio de Bologna, p. 143, Gd64, no.25.
5 Ch. d'Ancillon, *op. cit.*, pp. 159–60.
6 Quoted in G. Monaldi, *op, cit.*, p. 21.
7 Archenholz, quoted by Monaldi, *op. cit.*, pp. 20–1.
8 Mme du Boccage, *Lettres sur l'Italie*, 1774.
9 Montesquieu, *Voyages*, p. 1111.
10 H. Estienne, *Deux Dialogues du nouveau langage français italianisé*, Geneva, 1578.
11 Casanova, *Mémoires*, vol.2, ch.1.
12 Montesquieu, *op. cit.*, p. 1111.
13 P. Metastasio, Letter of 28 May, 1749.
14 P. Metastasio, Letter of 6 September, 1749.
15 P. Metastasio, Letter of 26 August, 1747.
16 *Ibidem.*
17 Quoted by Della Corte, *Satire e Grotteschi* ... p. 200.
18 Isaiah, Chapter 56, verses 3–5.
19 S. Rosa, *La Musica*, pp. 19–20 *et seq.*

20 Della Corte, *op. cit.*, p. 200.

21 B. Marcello, *Il teatro alla moda*, ch.3.

22 Della Corte, *op. cit.*

23 Pickering, *Reflections upon Theatrical Expression in Tragedy*, London, 1755.

Chapter 8: European Journeys

1 F. Balatri, *op. cit.*, pp. 69–71.

2 Quoted by F. Rogers, *The Musical Quarterly*, July, 1919.

3 S. Pepys, *Diaries*, 16 February, 1667.

4 J. Evelyn, *op. cit.*, vol.4, 30 January, 1687.

5 *Ibid.*, April, 1687.

6 Quoted by J. F. Labie, *G. F. Haendel*, p. 241.

7 *Ibid.*, p. 151.

8 Quoted in Della Corte, *op. cit.*, pp. 357–8.

9 J.-J. Rousseau, *Dictionnaire de musique*, see: Castrato.

10 S. Goudar, '*Avertissement*' (to *Remarques sur la musique*).

11 J. de La Lande, *op. cit.*, vol.5, pp. 437–8.

12 Saint-Evremond, *Lettres*, vol.2, pp. 49–50.

13 Baron Grimm, *Correspondance*, Letter concerning Omphale.

14 F. Raguenet, *op. cit.*, pp. 76–7.

15 J. Benjamin de Laborde, *op. cit.*, p. 508.

16 Quoted by Angus Heriot, *The Castrati in Opera.*, p. 56.

17 F. Balatri, *op. cit.*, pp. 196–7.

18 S. Goudar, *op. cit.*, Letter 3, p. 12.

19 *Ibid.*, p. 8.

20 *Ibid.*, Letter 5, p. 29.

21 *Ibid.*, p. 32.

22 P. Manzin, *Réponse à l'auteur des Observations* ... p. 74.

23 *Ibid.*, p. 29.

24 S. Goudar, *Avertissement*, *op. cit.*

Chapter 9: In the Evening of Life

1 Mme Vigée-Lebrun, *op. cit.*, vol.1, p. 248.

2 L. Vanvitelli, Letter of 23 January, 1762.

3 Stendhal, *Rome, Naples and Florence*, vol.3, p. 124.

4 Abbé Coyer, *op. cit.*, vol.1, pp. 96–7.

5 Quoted in the *Diccionario de Historia de España*, Alianza, 1979, vol.1, p. 594.

6 G. Sacchi, *op. cit.*, p. 43.

Chapter 10: The Twilight of the Angels

1 Voltaire, *Candide*, ch.25.
2 *Ibid.*, ch.12.
3 J.-J. Rousseau, *Dictionnaire de Musique*: see Castrato.
4 Stendhal, *Lives of Haydn, Mozart and Metastasio (Letter on the true state of music in Italy)*, p. 399.
5 G. B. Mancini, *Riflessione pratiche* ... pp. 45–5.
6 Barry O'Meara, *Napoléon en exil ou l'Echo de Sainte-Hélène*, 1822.
7 Quoted by Angus Heriot, *op. cit.*, p. 119.
8 Mme Vigée-Lebrun, *op. cit.*, vol.1, p. 171.
9 Mlle Avrillon, *Mémoires*, or C. Wairy, *Mémoires*, p. 345.
10 *Ibid.*
11 *Voyage d'une ignorante*, vol.2, p. 17, Paris, 1835.
12 Stendhal, *Life of Rossini*, vol.2, p. 128.
13 L. Rognoni, *G. Rossini (Rossini et Wagner)*, pp. 417–18.
14 Stendhal, *Life of Rossini*, *op. cit.*, vol.2, p. 30.
15 Letter from Marie d'Agoult to Ferdinand Hiller, 6 April, 1839, Cologne. Historischer Archiv, 1. Personen Verzeichnis, fol.890.
16 Quoted in A. de Angelis, *Domenico Mustafà*, p. 80.

Bibliography

Readers wishing to know more about the lives of each of the great castrati are referred to *Dieux et Divas de l'Opéra* (volume 1), by Roger Blanchard and Roland de Candé (Plon, Paris, 1986).

1 MEMOIRS, LETTERS, TRAVEL

Addison, J. *Remarks on Several Parts of Italy.* London, 1705.
Balatri, F. *Frutti del Mondo*, Naples: Sandron, 1924.
Beckford, W. *The Travel-Diaries of William Beckford of Fonthill.* Volume I (1781). Cambridge, MA: 1928.
Brosses, Charles de. *Lettres familières écrites d'Italie en 1739 et 1740.* Paris: Librairie académique, 1869 (2 vols.).
Brydone, P. *Viaggio in Sicilia e a Malta.* 1770, Milan: Longanesi, 1968.
Burney, C. *The Present State of Music in France and Italy.* London, 1771.
Casanova, G. *Mémoires.* Paris: La Sirène, 1924.
Coyer, G. F. *Voyages d'Italie et de Hollande*, Paris, 1775 (2 vols.).
Espinchal, Comte d'. *Journal d'émigration 1789–93.* Paris: Perrin, 1912.
Evelyn, J. *The Diary*, ed. E. S. De Beer. Oxford, The Clarendon Press, 1955.
Goldoni, C. *Mémoires.* Paris: Mercure de France, 1965.
Goudar, S. *Remarques sur la musique et la danse.* Venice: Palese, 1773.
Grimm, Baron de. *Correspondance littéraire, philosophique et critique.* 1753–1782. Paris, 1813.

Grosley, P. J. *Observations on Italy and on the Italians*, 1764 (4 vols.). London, 1770.

Grosley, P. J. *New Observations on Italy* (2 vols.), 1769.

La Lande, J. de. *Voyage en Italie*. Geneva: 1790 (7 vols.)

Metastasio, P. *Lettere disperse e inedite a cura di Giosué Carducci*. Bologna: Zanichelli, 1883.

Montesquieu. *Oeuvres complètes*. Paris: Nagel, 1950.

Pepys, S. *Diaries*, 1659–99, ed. R. C. Latham and W. Matthews. London: Bell, 1970–1983 (11 vols.).

Pöllnitz, Baron. *Lettres et Mémoires*. Amsterdam: Changuion, 1737 (5 vols.).

Saint-Evremond, Ch. de. *Lettres*. Paris: Marcel Didier, 1968 (2 vols.).

Saint-Non, Abbé dé. *Voyage pittoresque ou description des royaumes de Naples et de Sicile*. Paris: 1781–1785 (4 vols.).

Vigée-Lebrun, L. E. *Memoirs 1790–93*, trs. S. Evans. Camden Press, 1989.

2 ON THE CASTRATI

Adami da Bolsena. *Osservazioni per ben regolare il coro dei cantori della Capella Pontificia*. Rome, 1711.

Ancillon, Ch d'. *Traité des eunuques*, 1707.

Barbier, P. *Farinelli, le castrat des Lumières*. Paris: Grasset, 1994.

Blanchard, R. et Candé, R. de. *Dieux et Divas de l'Opéra*, vol.1. Paris: Plon, 1986.

Bouvier, R. *Farinelli, le Chanteur des rois*. Paris: Albin Michel, 1943.

Bragaglia, A. G. *Degli 'evirati cantori'*. Florence: Sansoni, 1959.

Caffi, Fr. *Storia della musica sacra nella già cappella di San Marco in Venezia dal 1318 al 1797*. New York: Olms, 1982.

Cecchini Pacchiarotti, G. *Cenni biografici intorno a G. Pacchiarotti*. Padua, 1844.

Celani, E. *I. Cantori della Cappella Pontificia nei secoli XVI–XVIII*. Turin: Bocca, 1909.

De Angelis, A. *Domenico Mustafà, la cappella sistina et la società musicale romana*. Bologna: Zanichelli, 1926.

Defaye, Ph. *Les Castrats, aspects phoniatriques*. Medical thesis, Limoges, 1983.

Haböck, F. *Die Kastraten und ihre Gesangkunst*. Stuttgart, 1927.

Heriot, A. *The Castrati in Opera*, London: Secker & Warburg, 1956.

Labanchi, A. G. *Gli eunuchi e le scuole di canto del secolo XVIII.* Naples: Tipografia Nuova, 1893.

Lodi caratteristiche del celebre cantore Signor Luigi Marchesi. Siena, 1781.

Malamani, V. *I virtuosi nel Settecento.* Naples: Giannini, 1901.

Mojon, B. *Dissertazione sugli effetti della castratura nel corpo umano.* Milan: Pirotta, 1822.

Monaldi, G. *Cantanti evirati celebri del teatro italiano.* Rome: Ansonia, 1920.

Parisi, R. *Un interprete di Cimarosa: Girolamo Crescentini.* Naples: Giannini, 1901.

Pleasants, H. *The Great Singers.* London: Gollancz, 1967.

Ricci, C. *Burney, Casanova e Farinelli in Bologna.* Milan: Ricordi, 1890.

Sacchi, G. *Vita del Cav. Don Carlo Broschi.* Venice: Caleti, 1784.

3 ARTICLES AND VARIOUS PUBLICATIONS

Biordi R. Gli evirati cantori. *Siena illustrata*, 1963.

Blondel, C. Les castrats. *Chronique musicale*, 15 September, 1875.

Bossa, R. Luigi Vanvitelli spettatore teatrale a Napoli. *Rivista italiana di musicologia*, 1976.

Causa dei Cantori Pontifici. Serie di scritti legali stampati dal Bernabo, 1761.

Celletti, R. Sopranisti e contraltisti. *Musica d'oggi.* Milan, June 1959.

Celletti, R. La vocalità al tempo del Tosi. *Nuova rivista musicale italiana*, November–December 1967.

Di Giacomo, S. I maestri e i musici del Tesoro di S. Gennaro (2 articles). *Rivista d'arte e di topografia napoletana*, 1920.

Duhamel, J. M. La grande vogue des castrats. *L'Histoire*, no.93, October, 1986.

Gaumy, C. Le chant des castrats. *Opéra international*, nos.76, 77, December 1984 and January 1985.

Milner, A. The sacred capons. *Musical Times*, March 1973.

Pagano, S. Una visita apostolica alla Cappella dei cantori pontifici al tempo di Urbano VIII (1630). *Rivista musicale italiana*, 1982.

Parolari, C. Gianbattista Velluti. *Rivista musicale italiana.* Turin, 1932.

Pozzi, R. Osservazioni su un libro contabile del Conservatorio dei Poveri di Gesù Cristo. *Atti del Convegno sul Seicento a Napoli.*

Prota Giurleo, U. Matteo Sassano detto Matteuccio. *Rivista italiana di musicologia*. Florence, 1966.

Rogers, F. The male soprano. *Musical Quarterly*, New York, July 1919.

Rouville, H. de Les castrats. *Opéra international*, no.101, March 1987.

4 ON THE MUSIC OF THE PERIOD, THE OPERA, VOCAL CHARACTER

a Works written in the seventeenth and eighteenth centuries

Algarotti, F. *Saggio sopra l'opera in musica*. s.l.1755.

Arteaga, S. *Le rivoluzioni del teatro musicale italiano*. Bologna, 1783 (2 vols.).

Baretti, G. *Les Italiens ou Moeurs et Coutumes d'Italie*. Paris: Costard, 1773.

Benigne de Bacilly. *L'Art de bien chanter*. Paris, 1668.

Benjamin de Laborde, J. *Essai sur la musique ancienne et moderne*. Paris, 1780 (4 vols.).

Bontempi, A., *Historia Musica*. Perugia, 1695.

Della Valle, P. Della musica dell'età nostra. In A. Solerti, *Le origini del melodramma*, pp. 148–79.

Eximeno, A. *Dissertazione del Progresso della Musica*. Naples: De Bonis, 1785.

Goudar, A. *Le Brigandage de la musique italienne*. 1777.

Lecerf de la Vieville. *Comparaison de la musique italienne et française*. Brussels, 1705.

Mancini, G. B. *Pensieri e riflessioni pratiche sopra il canto figurato*. Vienna, 1774.

Marcello, B. *Il teatro alla moda*. Venice, 1720. French edn. Paris: Fischbacher, 1890.

Maugars. *Réponse faite à un curieux sur le sentiment de la musique d'Italie* (1639). Paris: Claudin, 1865.

Raguenet, F. *Parallèle des Italiens et des Français en ce qui regarde la musique et les opéras*. New edn. Geneva: Minkoff, 1976.

Riccoboni, L. *Réflexions historiques et critiques sur les différents théâtres de l'Europe*. Paris: Guérin, 1738.

Rosa, S. *La Musica*. Amsterdam, 1770.

Sabbatini, N. *Pratica di fabricar scene e macchine ne'teatri (1638)*. Rome: Bestetti. 1955.

Tosi, P. F. *Opinions sur les chanteurs anciens et modernes ou Observations sur le chant figuré*. French edn. Paris, 1874.

Tragiense, L. *De i vizi e de i difetti del Moderno Teatro*. Rome: Pallade, 1753.

Zacconi, L. *Prattica di musica*. Venice, 1596.

b Works written in the nineteenth and twentieth centuries

Ademollo, A. *I primi fasti del teatro di via della Pergola in Firenze*. Milan: Ricordi, 1885.

Ademollo, A. *I teatri di Roma nel secolo XVII*. Rome: Pasqualucci, 1888.

Anthony, J. R. *La Musique en France à l'époque baroque*. Paris: Flammarion, 1981.

Beaussant, Ph. *Vous avez dit 'Baroque'?* Arles: Actes Sud, 1988.

Benoit, M. *Versailles et les musiciens du roi, 1661–1733*. Paris: Picard, 1971.

Bertolotti, A. *Musici alla corte dei Gonzaga: la musica in Mantova (XV–XVII sec.)* Milan: Ricordi, no date.

Bridgman, N. *La Musique à Venise*. Paris: PUF, Que sais-je? 2172.

Bottineau, Y. *L'Art de cour dans l'Espagne de Philippe V*. Paris: Féret, 1962.

Bouquet, M. Th. *Musique et musiciens à Turin de 1648 à 1775*. Memoria dell'accademia delle Scienze. Turin: 1968.

Bukofzer, M. *La Musique baroque*. Paris: Lattès, 1982.

Castil-Blaze. *L'Opéra italien de 1548 à 1856*. Paris: Castil-Blaze, 1856.

Celletti, R. *Histoire du Bel Canto*. French edn, Paris: Fayard, 1987.

Della Corte, A. *Satire e grotteschi di musiche e di musicisti d'ogni tempo*. Turin: Unione Tipografica, 1946.

Fabbri, M. *Alessandro Scarlatti e il Principe Ferdinando de'Medici*. Florence: Olschki, 1960.

Fage, A. de la. *Miscellanées musicales*. Paris: 1844.

Fassini, S. *Il melodramma italiano a Londra nella prima metà del Settecento*. Turin: Bocca, 1914.

Jarro-Piccini. *Storia aneddotica dei Teatro Fiorentini*. Florence: Bemporad, 1912.

Kirkpatrick, R. *Domenico Scarlatti*. Paris: Lattès, 1982.

Labie, J. F., *Georges Frédéric Haendel*. Paris: Laffont, 1980.

Machabey, A. *Le Bel Canto*. Paris: Larousse, 1948.

Massip, C. *La Vie des musiciens de Paris au temps de Mazarin*. Paris: Picard, 1976.

Molinari, C. *Le nozze degli dei: un saggio sul grande spettacolo italiano nel Seicento*. Rome: Bulroni, 1968.

Monaldi, G. *I teatri di Roma negli ultimi tre secoli*. Naples: Ricciardi, 1928.

Orloff, G. *Essai sur l'histoire de la musique en Italie*. Paris, 1822.

Pirro, A. *L'Italie au XVIIIe siècle*. Paris: Leroux, 1929.

Prod'homme, J. G. *Christoph Willibald Gluck*. Paris: Fayard, 1985.

Prunières, H. *Cavalli et l'opéra vénitien an XVIIe siècle*. Paris: Reider, 1931.

Ricci, C. *I teatri di Bologna nel secoli XVII–XVIIIe*. Bologna, 1888.

Ricci, C. *Vita barocca*. Rome: Modes, 1912.

Schrade, L. *Monteverdi*. Paris: Lattès, 1981.

Solerti, A. *Le origini del Melodramma, Testimonianze dei contemporanei*. Turin: Bocca, 1903.

Stendhal. *Rome, Naples and Florence*, trs. and ed. by Richard N. Coe, London, 1959.

Stendhal. *Life of Rossini*, trs. and ed. by Richard N. Coe, 2nd edn., London, 1970.

Stendhal. *Lives of Haydn, Mozart and Metastasio*, trs. and ed. by Richard N. Coe, London, 1970.

Striffling, L. *Esquisse d'une histoire du goût musical en France au XVIIIe siècle*. Paris: Delagrave, 1912.

5 ON NAPLES AND THE CONSERVATOIRES

Anconi, L. and Bossar. *Musica e cultura a Napoli dal XV al XIX secolo*. Florence: Olschki, 1983.

Biografia degli uomini illustri del Reame di Napoli, Naples: Gervasi, 1819.

Confuorto, D. *Giornali di Napoli*, vol.1, 1679–1691; vol.2, 1692–1699. Naples: Lubrano, 1931.

Croce, B. *I teatri di Napoli*. Archivio storico per le province napoletane, 1889, 1890, 1891.

De Filippis F. and Prota-Giurleo, U. *Il teatro di Corte del Palazzo Reale di Napoli*. Naples, 1952.

De Filippis, F. *Napoli teatrale. Dal teatro romano al San Carlo.* Milan: Curci, 1962.

Diario Napoletano dal 1700 al 1709 a cura di G. de Blasiis. Archivio storico per le province napoletane, 1885.

Di Giacomo, S. *Il conservatorio di Sant'Onofrio a Capuana e quello di Santa Maria della Pietà dei Turchini.* Naples: Sandron, 1924.

Di Giacomo, S. *Il conservatorio dei Poveri di Gesù Cristo e quello di Santa Maria di Loreto.* Naples: Sandron, 1928.

Dioguardi, G. *Un avventuriere nella Napoli del Settecento.* Palermo: Selleno, 1983.

Florimo, F. *La Scuola musicale di Napoli e i suoi Conservatori.* Naples: 1880 (3 vols.).

Goudar, S. *Relation historique des divertissements du carnaval de Naples.* Lucca, 1774.

Pannain, G. *La musica a Napoli dal '500 a tutto il '700.* Storia di Napoli, vol.3.

Pignoli, V. *Ricerche sul Conservatorio dei Poveri di Gesù Cristo di Napoli.* Thesis, University of Parma, 1969–1970.

Regole e statuti del Real Conservatorio della Pietà dei Turchini, 1746.

Robinson, M. F. *The Governor's minutes of the Conservatory Santa Maria di Loreto.* The Royal Music Association, Research Chronicle no.10.

Robinson, M. F. *Naples and Neapolitan Opera.* Oxford: Clarendon Press, 1972.

Stabilimenti per l'interno regolamento del Real Conservatorio di Musica di S. Sebastiano in Napoli. Naples, 1809.

Villarosa, Marchese di. *Memorie dei compositori di Musica del Regno di Napoli.* Naples: Stamperia Reale, 1840.

Vincenzi, M. *La Musica a Napoli.* Naples: Berisio, 1984.

6 ARCHIVES OF THE CONSERVATOIRES OF NAPLES AND THE SAN CARLO THEATRE

The archives of the Conservatorio dei Poveri di Gesù Cristo are held today in the Bishop's Palace, but have been inaccessible for a long time due to building work. The archives of the three other conservatoires are held in the library of the Conservatorio San Pietro at Majella. Refer to:

–The *Libri Maggiori* of the conservatoires (not classified).
–Series XIII.7.18 (1–216): manuscript documents and autograph letters.
–The four volumes of the *Conclusioni* of Santa Maria di Loreto.
–The *Album di Autografi* 4.3.7 (manuscript letters . . .).
The Neapolitan State Archives include the accounts (expenses and receipts) for the performances at the San Carlo between 1737 and 1753, and in particular the salaries of the singers. See *Dipendenze della Sommaria*. 1a Serie, fascicules 462 to 467.

7 DICTIONARIES AND ENCYCLOPAEDIAS

Biographie universelle des musiciens. F. J. Fetis. Paris: Firmin-Didot, 1870.
Dictionnaire historique. L. Moreri. Paris: 1732, vol.3, see: *Eunuques.*
Dictionnaire universel. A. Furetière. Paris: 1727, vol.2, see: *Eunuque.*
Dictionnaire de musique. J.-J. Rousseau. Oeuvres complètes, vol.12. Paris: 1819. See: *Castrato.*
Enciclopedia della Musica. Milan: Ricordi, 1963, vol.1. See: *Castrati.*
Enciclopedia dello Spettacolo. Rome, 1956. See: vol.4, *Evirato.*
Encyclopédie Catholicisme ed. G. Jacquemet. Paris: Letourzey et Ané, 1949. See: *Castration.*
New Grove's Dictionary of Music. London: Macmillan, 1980. See vol.3: *Castrato.*
Storia dell'Opera, 3 vols. Turin: UTET, 1977.

Index

Abbatini, Anton Maria, computer 131
Adami di Bolsena, Andrea, Sistine
    Chapel singer 129
Addison, Joseph, essayist 105
Adimari, Lodovico, writer 172
Agoult, Comtesse Marie d', writer 237
Agujari, Lucrezia, singer 85
Alexander VII, Pope 164
Alexander VIII, Pope 132
Algarotti, Francesco, theorist 99
Allegri, Gregorio, composer, Sistine
    Chapel castrato 3, 17, 128, 129, 223,
    237
Amadori, Giuseppe, composer and
    teacher 59
Amigoni, Giacomo, painter 207
Amorevoli, Angiolo, tenor 69, 114
Ancillon, Charles d', historian 11, 152
Anne of Austria, Queen of France 193
Annibali, Domenico, castrato 93, 182,
    183
Appiani, Giuseppe, known as
    'Appianino', castrato 85
Aprile, Giuseppe, castrato 21, 22, 87,
    101, 199, 219, 228
Arbuthnot, John, writer 184
Assoucy, Charles d', poet and musician
    26

Balani, castrato 12
Balatri, Filippo, castrato 30, 96, 119,
    175, 176–8, 186, 194, 211

Balsamon, Theodore, Byzantine
    canonist 7
Balzac, Honoré de, writer 155
Bannieri (or Bagniera), Antonio,
    castrato 24, 25, 192, 193
Barbara de Braganza, Queen of Spain
    204, 220
Barberini, Cardinal A., nephew of
    Pope Urban VIII 73
Baretti, Giuseppe, writer 76
Barnett, John, composer 221
Beckford, William, writer 77, 80, 90
Bellini, Vincenzo, composer 232, 236
Benjamin de Laborde, Jean, writer 193
Benedict XIII, Pope 109
Benedict XIV, Pope 124, 125, 225
Berlioz, Hector, composer 237
Bernacchi, Antonio, castrato 16, 60, 87,
    88, 138, 148, 150, 176, 182, 219
Bernardi, Francesco, see Senesino
Bernini, Gian Lorenzo, sculptor and
    architect 71, 131
Bertoldo (or Bertod), castrato 190
Bertoni, Ferdinand Giuseppe,
    composer and teacher 87, 128, 185,
    217
Bibiena, Ferdinando Galli and his sons
    Giuseppe and Antonio Galli,
    architects and scene-designers 71
Bizet, Georges, composer 237
Boccage, Mme du, writer 37, 153
Bonaparte, Joseph, King of Naples 227

Bonaparte, Napoléon, General and Consul 112, 216, 226

Bonavera, Giacomo, architect and designer of stage effects 205

Bononcini, Giovanni, composer 181, 183, 184

Bontempi (Giovanna Andrea Angelini), writer 20, 59, 90, 97

Bordoni, Faustina, singer 144, 148

Brivio, Francesco, singing teacher 57

Broschi, Carlo, see Farinelli

Broschi, Riccardo, composer 95, 114

Brosses, Charles de, writer 14, 24, 64, 79, 82, 104, 154, 201

Brydone, Patrick, writer 100, 144

Burney, Dr Charles, musicologist 10, 27, 28, 44, 48, 49, 64, 79, 102, 111, 184, 212, 220

Caffarelli (Gaetano Majorano), castrato 20, 22, 23, 24, 28, 53, 69, 74, 84, 86, 87, 88, 90, 91, 99, 110, 111, 112, 114, 115, 116, 118, 139, 150, 176, 179, 182, 194, 195–6, 198, 201, 205, 210, 213, 215

Calegari, castrato 127

Callas, Maria, singer 201

Canova, Antonio, sculptor 219

Caproli, composer 191

Carestini, Giovanni, see Cusanino

Casanova de Seingalt, Giacomo, adventurer and writer 36, 133, 153, 154–5, 190, 197, 217

Castellini, Teresa, singer 205

Catherine II, Tsarina of Russia 119, 178

Cavalli, Francesco, composer 3, 85, 127, 138, 165, 191

Cecchi, Domenico, see Cortona

Cesti, Marc'Antonio, composer 69, 129

Charles II, King of Spain 203, 207

Charles II of Bourbon, King of Naples and Sicily, later King of Spain 63, 207

Carlo III, Duke of Mantua 26, 117

Charles VI, Emperor of Austria 99

Charles Emmanuel II of Savoy, King of Piedmont 117, 163

Chiarini, Giuseppe, castrato 117, 138

Christina, Queen of Sweden 119, 120, 132, 163, 164, 165, 178

Cimarosa, Domenico, composer 103, 153, 219

Clement VIII, Pope 9, 19, 123, 124

Clement IX, Pope, poet and librettist 131, 164

Clement X, Pope 131

Clement XI, Pope 133

Clement XIV, Pope 125, 133

Cosimo de' Medici, Grand Duke of Tuscany 30, 151

Confuorto, Domenico, writer 108, 140

Consolino, castrato 139

Conti, Gioacchino, see Gizziello

Corelli, Arcangelo, composer 129, 164

Cortona (Domenico Cecchi), castrato 85, 117, 124, 142, 151, 163, 165

Cossa, castrato 22

Courcelle, Francesco, composer 205

Coyer, Abbé Gabriel-Francino, writer 62, 64, 69, 70, 78, 81, 217

Crescentini, Girolamo, castrato 99, 120, 121, 127, 138, 228, 229, 230–1

Cusanino (Giovanni Carestini), castrato 2, 84, 91, 93, 110, 116, 136, 138, 148, 176, 182

Cuzzoni, Francesca, singer 118, 144, 148, 151, 183, 184

Davies, Mary, singer 85

De Amicis, Anna Lucia, singer 144, 146–7

De Castris, Francesco, known as 'Checco', castrato 92

De Mezzo, Pietro, bass 127

De Nicolellis, Antonio, known as 'Cicillo', castrato 85

Del Pane, Damaso, castrato 131

Del Pane, Domenico, castrato 131

Del Prato, Vincenzo, castrato 116, 179

Diderot, Denis, writer and *philosophe* 174

Dufresny, Charles, playwright 73

Duparc, Elisabeth, singer 85

Duprez, Gilbert, tenor 235

Durante, Angelo, composer 46

Durante, Francesco, composer and chapel-master 40, 46, 47

Elisabeth Farnese, Queen of Spain 203, 205, 207
Espinchal, Comte d', writer, 48, 49, 75, 79, 81, 134
Estienne, Henry, writer 154
Evelyn, John, diarist 95, 180–1

Fabri, Annibale Pio, tenor 219
Fabris, Luca, castrato 93
Farinelli (Carlo Broschi), castrato 14, 17, 20, 21, 22, 53, 69, 84, 86, 88, 89, 92, 93, 94, 95, 97, 98, 99, 118, 120, 150, 151, 156–8, 163, 173, 175, 183, 185, 194, 195, 198, 199, 201–8, 209, 217, 218, 219, 224
Favalli, A. castrato 193
Fede, Francesco Maria, castrato 131, 164
Fedi, Giuseppe, castrato 59, 131
Feo, Francesco, composer, chapel-master 46, 51
Ferdinand III, Emperor of Austria 178
Ferdinand IV of Bourbon, King of Naples 197
Ferdinand VI of Bourbon, King of Spain 204, 207
Ferdinand de' Medici, Grand Duke of Tuscany 165
Ferri, Baldassare, castrato 14, 20, 86, 90, 96, 119, 120, 137, 163, 164, 175, 178, 211
Ferrini, castrato 134
Finazzi, Filippo, castrato 142
Folignati, Pietro Pablo, Sistine Chapel castrato 9, 10
Foscolo, Ugo, writer 219
Francesco II d' Este, Duke of Ferrari 165
Francis I, Duke of Lombardy-Venetia 227

Gabrielli, Caterina, singer 53, 119, 144–6
Galitzine, Count Peter, Russian Ambassador 30

Galliari, Bernardino and Fabrizio, painters and scene-designers 71
Galuppi, Baldassare, composer 85, 93, 109
Gaudiosi, Ottavio, castrato 127
George II, King of England 185
Giacomelli, Girolamo, composer 96
Gizzi, Domenico, composer and chapel-master 53, 84, 150, 225
Gizziello (Gioacchino Conti), castrato 22, 53, 84, 99, 182, 183, 198, 199, 205
Gluck, Christoph Willibald, composer 46, 85, 100, 103, 111, 179, 187, 220, 232
Goldoni, Carlo, writer 69, 75, 78, 170, 219
Goudar Ange, adventurer and economist 142, 196–7
Goudar, Sarah, adventuress and diarist 5, 45, 68, 70, 118, 187, 196–201
Gozzi, Carlo, writer 219
Grassini, Giuseppina, singer 121, 230, 231
Greco, Gaetano, composer and chapel-master 35, 46
Gregory XIV, Pope 123
Grimaldi, Nicolo, see Nicolino
Grimani-Calergi, Abbé, theatre director 26
Grimm, Baron Melchior de, writer 90, 190
Grisando, Giovanni, Sistine Chapel castrato 10
Grosley, Pierre-Jean, writer 30, 70, 97, 98, 105, 107
Grossi, Giovanni Francesco, see Siface
Guadagni, Gaetano, castrato 16, 87, 91, 99, 112, 128, 179, 182, 212, 216
Gualberto, Giovanni, castrato 116
Guarducci, Tommaso, castrato 60, 212, 216

Handel, Georg Frideric, composer 16, 46, 100, 151, 174, 179, 182, 183
Hasse, Johann Adolf, composer 85, 97, 103, 107, 144, 183, 205

Haydn, Joseph, composer 46
Hubert, or Antonio Uberti, known as
    'Porporino', castrato 53, 84

Inglirami, Tommaso, known as
    'Fedra', castrato 85
Innocent XI, Pope 20, 124, 131, 132
Innocent XII, Pope 132

Jean-Gaston de' Medici, Grand Duke
    of Tuscany 151
Jommelli, Nicolo, composer 103
Joseph II, Emperor of Austria 220

Labat, Abbé, writer 105
La Lande, Jean de, writer 10, 64, 66,
    67, 102, 125, 187
Lanti, Teresa, alias 'Bellino', singer
    154-5
Lecerf de la Viéville de Fresneuse, Jean,
    writer 192
Le Maure, Nicole, singer 190
Lenzi, Monsignor Lodovico 131
Leo, Leonardo, composer and chapel-
    master 46, 51
Leo XIII, Pope 126, 238, 239
Leonardo da Vinci, painter and
    scientist 89
Leonce, Bishop of Antioch 7
Leopold I, Emperor of Austria 178
Liszt, Franz, composer 237
Louis XIII, King of France 190
Louis XIV, King of France 24, 25, 165,
    186, 191, 192-3, 194, 203
Louis XV, King of France 160, 186,
    194, 195, 196, 206
Luchini, castrato 199
Lully, Jean-Baptiste, composer 174,
    186

Majorano, Gaetano, see Caffarelli
Malibran, Maria, singer 201, 221
Mancini, Giovanni Battista, castrato
    and theorist 60, 93, 98, 181, 216, 219,
    225
Manuel, Greek castrato 8
Manzin, Paolo, musician 198, 199

Manzuoli or Manzoli, Giovanni,
    castrato 84, 199
Marcello, Benedetto, composer 110,
    111, 170, 216
Marchesi, Luigi, castrato 14, 21, 25, 86,
    88, 90, 93, 97, 110, 111, 112, 127, 137,
    138, 176, 178, 210, 211, 228, 229
Marianini, castrato 14
Marie-Anne de Neubourg, Queen of
    Spain 203
Marie-Antoinette, Queen of France
    186, 194, 195
Maria-Carolina, Queen of Naples 64
Maria Theresa, Empress of Austria 120,
    178
Martini, Andrea, castrato 88
Mattei, Colomba, singer 205, 226
Matteuccio (Matteo Sassano), castrato
    14, 31, 32, 85, 86, 87, 88, 108, 119,
    120, 131, 148-9, 160-1, 165, 203,
    212, 216
Maugars, André, musician and violinist
    101, 192
Mazarin, Jules, cardinal and politician
    120, 165, 186
Mazzanti, castrato 101, 141
Mazzocchi, Virgilio, composer and
    chapel-master 59
Melani, Atto, castrato 22, 120, 165, 166,
    191, 221
Melani, Bartolomeo, castrato 22, 191
Melani, Domenico, castrato 22
Melani, Nicola, castrato 22
Melchiorri, castrato 85
Mendelssohn, Felix, composer 238
Merighi, Antonia, singer 138, 144
Metastasio (Pietro Trapassi), poet and
    librettist 88, 89, 91, 103, 107, 111,
    156-8, 178-9, 202
Meyerbeer, Giacomo, composer 46,
    234
Mingotti, Regina, singer 53, 205
Monanni, Angelo, known as
    'Manzoletto', castrato 84
Montagnana, bass 183, 205
Montesquieu, Charles de, writer 62,
    128, 154, 155

Monteverdi, Claudio, composer 62
Moreschi, Alessandro, Sistine Chapel
    castrato 89, 126, 235, 239
Morlacchi, Francesco, composer 234
Mozart, Wolfgang Amadeus, composer
    46, 99, 128, 142, 179, 190, 219, 220,
    232
Musi, Maria Maddalena, singer 143
Mustafà, Domenico, Sistine Chapel
    castrato 26, 126, 159, 235, 237, 239
Mysliveçek, Josef, composer 103

Napoleon I, Emperor of the French
    120, 227, 230–2
Nicolino (Nicolo Grimaldi), castrato
    16, 85, 86, 102, 120, 131, 182, 185
Nicolino, Mariano, castrato 114, 115
Nuñez, Fernan, historian 217

Origen, Greek Christian writer 7

Pacchiarotti, Gasparo, castrato 84, 87,
    90–1, 93, 99, 100, 113, 115, 127, 128,
    139, 146–7, 149, 185, 194, 195,
    201–11, 213, 214, 216, 217, 218, 219,
    228
Paisiello, Giovanni, composer 79, 81,
    230
Paita, Giovanni, castrato and chapel-
    master 57
Palestrina, Giovanni da, composer 128,
    237
Parini, Giuseppe, writer 163, 171
Pasini, Ferdinando, tenor 127
Pasqualini, Marc'Antonio, castrato 86,
    101, 165, 191
Pasta, Giuditta, singer 89
Paul IV, Pope 128
Peli, Francesco, chapel-master 57
Pepusch, John Christopher, composer
    181
Pepys, Samuel, diarist 180, 181
Pergolesi, Giovanni Battista, composer
    103
Peri, Jacopo, composer 62
Perosi, Lorenzo, Sistine Chapel choir
    master 126, 238, 239

Peruzzi, Anna Maria, singer 114, 141
Philip V of Bourbon, King of Spain
    100, 203, 204, 205
Philippe Égalité, (Philippe d'Orléans)
    185
Piccini, Nicolo, composer 70, 88, 187
Pierre-Valentin (known as 'Pierrotin',
    then as 'Valentino'), castrato 26, 27,
    117
Pistocchi, Francesco Antonio (known
    as 'Pistocchino'), castrato and singing
    teacher 16, 21, 59, 60, 85, 148, 211, 219
Pollnitz, Baron, writer 77, 134
Porpora, Nicolo, composer and
    chapel-master 40, 46, 47, 53, 54, 84,
    160, 183, 225
Provenzale, Francesco, composer and
    chapel-master 40, 46, 47, 86

Quadrini, castrato 22, 53

Raaff, Anton, tenor 60, 205, 219
Raguenet, Abbé François, writer and
    musicologist 48, 82, 134, 192
Rascarino, Francesco Maria, castrato
    117
Rauzzini, Venanzio, castrato 88, 91, 99,
    138, 179, 185, 210, 211, 212, 232
Redi, Francesco, chapel master 58
Reginella, Nicola, castrato 149
Riccoboni, Luigi, writer 76
Richard, Abbé, writer 134
Richelieu, Cardinal de, statesman 101,
    190
Rivani, Anton, known as 'Ciccolino',
    castrato 85, 163, 169
Rosa, Salvatore, poet and satirist 167,
    168
Rosini, Girolamo, Sistine Chapel
    castrato 9, 10
Rossi, Luigi, composer 93, 191
Rossini, Gioacchino, composer 190,
    219, 232, 233, 234, 236
Rouget de Lisle, Claude Joseph, army
    officer 216
Rousseau, Jean-Jacques, writer and
    philosphe 19, 187, 224

Rovetta, Giovanni, composer 69 ;
Rubinelli, Giovanni Maria, castrato 87,
    99, 127, 175, 210, 232

Sabbatini, N., architect and machinist
    72
Sacchi, Giovenale, writer 92, 95, 220
Sacchini, Antonio, composer 103, 216
Saint-Didier, writer 76, 135
Saint-Evremond, Charles de, writer
    187
Saint-Huberty, Antoinette, singer
    89
Saint-Non, Abbé de, writer 35
Salimbeni, Felice, castrato 2, 53, 136,
    155, 199, 211, 221
Santacatanea, Maria, singer 114
Santarelli, Antonio, surgeon 29
Sarti, Giuseppe, composer 97, 103, 113,
    176
Sartorio, Antonio, composer 69
Sassano, Matteo, see Matteuccio
Sayer, Robert, theologian and moralist
    122
Scarlatti, Alessandro, composer 3, 46,
    90, 91, 148, 149, 164, 165, 181, 183,
    235
Scarlatti, Domenico, composer 169,
    170, 207
Scribe, Eugène, writer and librettist 221
Sedoti, Filippo, castrato 22, 53
Sedoti, Giuseppe, castrato 22, 53, 160
Senesino (Francesco Bernardi), castrato
    85, 91, 109, 114, 118, 120, 151, 175,
    176, 182, 183, 185, 210
Siface (Giovanni Francesco Grossi)
    castrato 85, 88, 95, 116, 117, 129, 140,
    165, 168, 169, 175, 180, 194, 195, 221
Silvagni, writer 10
Simonelli, Matteo, castrato and
    composer 129
Sixtus V, Pope 8, 130
Sografi, Simone, writer and librettist
    170
Sorlisi, Bartolomeo di, castrato 142
Soto, Francesco, Sistine Chapel
    castrato 9

Spagnoletto, Giacomo, Sistine Chapel
    castrato 9
Sperduti, Angelina, singer 22
Spontini, Gaspare, composer 237
Stendhal (Henri Beyle), writer 138,
    208, 216, 225, 233, 234

Taine, Hippolyte, philosophe and
    historian 237
Tamburini, Tommaso, theologian and
    casuist 123
Tarquini, Vittoria, singer 144
Tenducci, Giusto Ferdinando, castrato
    99, 120, 142–3, 179, 185
Tesi, Vittoria, singer 69, 114, 143, 144,
    219
Torelli, Jacopo, architect and scene
    designer 191
Tosi, Pietro Francesco, castrato and
    theorist 59, 60–1, 97, 176, 211
Traetta, Tommaso, composer 103
Tragiense, Laurisio, scholar and writer
    71, 106, 134

Ubaldini, Anna Vittoria, actress 117
Uberti da Cesena, Grazioso, writer 166
Urban VIII, Pope 73
Urbani, Valentino, castrato 181

Vanini Boschi, Francesca, singer 181
Vanvitelli, Luigi, architect 84, 101, 114,
    214, 215
Velluti, Giovanni Battista castrato 109,
    227, 228, 232–5
Vigée-Lebrun, Louise Elisabeth,
    painter 58, 122, 128, 138, 210, 229
Vitali, Giovanni Battista, composer 62
Vittori, Loreto, castrato and composer
    10, 20, 101, 128, 137, 159–60, 163
Vivaldi, Antonio, composer 103
Voltaire (Françoise Marie Arouet de)
    writer and philosphe 224

Zacconi, Lodovico, theorist 95
Zeno, Apostolo, poet and librettist 69,
    103, 178
Zingarelli, Nicola, composer 231